Opportunities for Women in Higher Education

THEIR CURRENT PARTICIPATION,
PROSPECTS FOR THE FUTURE,
AND RECOMMENDATIONS FOR ACTION

A Report and Recommendations by
The Carnegie Commission on Higher Education
SEPTEMBER 1973

MCGRAW-HILL BOOK COMPANY
New York   St. Louis   San Francisco   Düsseldorf
London   Sydney   Toronto   Mexico   Panama
Johannesburg   Kuala Lumpur   Montreal
New Delhi   São Paulo   Singapore

Library of Congress Cataloging in Publication Data
Carnegie Commission on Higher Education.
Opportunities for women in higher education.
Bibliography: p.
1. Higher education of women—United States.
I. Title.
LC1756.C36   376'.8'0973   73-14726
ISBN 0-07-010102-7

Additional copies of this report may be ordered from McGraw-Hill
Book Company, Hightstown, New Jersey 08520.
The price is $4.95 a copy.

The second most fundamental revolution in the affairs of mankind on earth is now occurring. The first came when man settled down from hunting, fishing, herding and gathering to sedentary agriculture and village life. The second is now occurring as women, no longer so concentrated on and sheltered for their child-bearing and child-rearing functions, are demanding equality of treatment in all aspects of life, are demanding a new sense of purpose.

ANON.

Contents

Foreword

From its inception, the Carnegie Commission on Higher Education has emphasized the need to eliminate all barriers to equality of opportunity in higher education. We have recommended that federal aid to higher education be substantially increased and that emphasis be given to grants to low-income students. In our report *A Chance to Learn*, we recommended special policies particularly designed to increase equality of opportunity for minority groups in higher education.

Intensified pressure for equal opportunity for women in higher education developed a few years later than the pressure for equal opportunity for minority groups, and it soon became apparent that policies designed to improve opportunities for minority groups did not fully meet the special problems of women. In the present report we have tried to deal as comprehensively as possible with these special problems as they relate to education, tracing them from the early acculturation of girls, to the role of the schools, to higher education at the undergraduate and graduate stages, and then to the faculty level and general institutional employment practices. Changes are needed in attitudes and in policies at all these stages if women are to have equal opportunity to develop and fully utilize their mental capacities and abilities.

To the many persons who were consulted and gave us helpful suggestions, we want to express our appreciation. A particularly valuable contribution was made by Elizabeth Scott, chairman, Department of Statistics, University of California, Berkeley, who prepared early outlines and drafts of the report, and who is responsible for some of the special statistical analyses included in this report, especially in Appendix C. We also want to acknowledge the helpful suggestions of Roger W. Heyns, president of the American Council on Education.

The Commission is also indebted to a number of women active in the movement to improve opportunities for women in higher education who read and commented on an earlier draft of this report. They include: Beatrice M. Bain, associate director, Center for Continuing Education for Women, University of California, Berkeley; Carolyn Shaw Bell, Katharine Coman Professor of Economics, Wellesley College, and chairperson, Committee on the Status of Women in the Economics Profession; Mariam Chamberlin, program officer, Ford Foundation; K. Patricia Cross, research educator, Center for Research and Development in Higher Education, University of California, Berkeley, and senior research psychologist, Educational Testing Service; Marjorie S. Galenson, assistant professor, Department of Consumer Economics and Public Policy, New York State School of Human Ecology, Cornell University; Diana R. Gordon, consultant, Fund for the City of New York; Arlie Hochschild, assistant professor of sociology, University of California, Berkeley; Herma H. Kay, professor of law and chairperson, 1973–74, Academic Senate, University of California, Berkeley; Juanita M. Kreps, vice-president, and James B. Duke Professor of Economics, Duke University; Virginia Davis Nordin, chairperson, Commission for Women, University of Michigan; Alice S. Rossi, professor of sociology, Goucher College; and Bernice Sandler, executive associate and director, Project on the Status and Education of Women, Association of American Colleges.

We would also like to thank the members of our staff who contributed to the work on this report, and especially Dr. Margaret S. Gordon, who was assisted by Laura Kent and Jane McClosky.

Eric Ashby
The Master
Clare College
Cambridge, England

Ralph M. Besse
Partner
Squire, Sanders & Dempsey,
  Counsellors at Law

Joseph P. Cosand
Professor of Education and
  Director
Center for Higher Education
University of Michigan

William Friday
President
University of North Carolina

Opportunities
for Women
in Higher Education

1. Major Themes

1 A substantial proportion of the intellectual talent of women has been and is being lost to society as a result of cultural circumstances. Men are given comparatively more opportunities to use their mental capacities.

Women and men have equal intellectual abilities. This is demonstrated by their performances on test scores and in class grades.

The supply of superior intelligence is limited, and the demand for it in society is ever greater. The largest unused supply is found among women.

2 Historically, women in higher education have been and still often are disadvantaged as individuals compared to the level of their potential abilities:

In admission to college. They perform better in college than their test scores predict, and yet their test scores are often discounted as against those of males in the admissions process.

In acceptance into graduate school.

In acceptance into and promotion within faculties (and administrative staffs).

In salaries paid. We estimate that on the average, women faculty members receive about $1,500 to $2,000 less per year than do men in comparable situations (see Section 7). This adds up to about $150 to $200 million per year across the nation.

Chart 1 shows the percentages of women at several successive key points of advancement within the academic world. At each "gate" the percentage declines.

CHART 1 *Women as a percentage of persons at selected levels of advancement within the educational system, 1970*

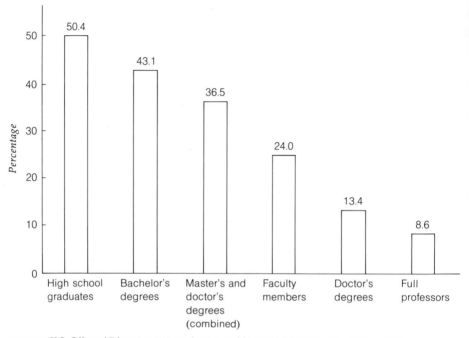

SOURCES: U.S. Office of Education (1971 and 1972); and National Education Association (1971).

3 We recognize that some of the failure of women to be given the same recognition as that accorded to men at the more advanced levels of academic life rests on "objective" grounds:

There is a frequent partial or even full loss of highly productive years of scholarship, often 5 to 10 years, for women who bear and rear children. The years involved are commonly years of high energy and fervent curiosity, and they can seldom be fully regained. These lost years can be particularly costly in the sciences and in other early-maturity fields, and in institutions that require published scholarship. Unfortunately, the years of high intellectual fertility in some fields and high childbearing fertility overlap in the same period of life. This fact of life, along with less mathematical training in high school, helps explain the lower present proportion of women in the sciences.

The market for academically trained persons wishing to enter college and university teaching and research is most active and most effective just after completion of graduate work. Once outside the standard market mechanisms of current referrals and recommendations, as is the case for women during a childbearing and child-rearing period, it is harder to get back in.

Women have less geographic mobility to the extent that they are tied to the locations of their husbands' employment.

The situation in the future may be quite different and more favorable to women in each of the above respects as more child-care facilities are provided, as child care is shared more by both parents, as market mechanisms are improved, and as the husband's position is less determinative of family location.

4 Other factors of particular importance that affect the situation of women in academic life are:

The roles for females presented to them in early life.

The comparatively greater absence of "role models" for women as they rise higher in academic life. Some and probably many college women clearly perform with greater distinction when they study under faculties that include women.

Prejudice and male monopolies.

5 The situation for women on college and university faculties has deteriorated over recent decades, beginning with the 1930s. The impact of the women's suffrage movement had faded out by then. The Great Depression put an emphasis upon the employment of men. The most rapidly expanding fields in the 1940s and 1950s were the "men's" fields of science, engineering, and business administration. The birthrate rose after World War II, interfering with the participation in higher education for many women. Domestic help became harder to obtain and more costly, so that more women stayed at home. The academic profession came to be better paid and attracted more men.

6 Concern for the situation of women in academic life has greatly intensified in the 1970s with a decline of the birthrate, a new concern for social justice—initially justice for members of minority groups—the rise of the women's movement, and the development of new attitudes about sexual roles.

7 We favor the removal of all improper barriers to the advance-

ment of women; an active search for their talents and active measures to develop their talents; and special consideration of their problems and for their contributions. We favor at the precollege level particularly:

More mathematical training for girls.

Counseling that is free of outmoded conceptions of male and female careers.

8   We favor at the level of college attendance:

• Greater concern for fairness in admissions at the undergraduate but particularly at the graduate level, with achievement and ability as the basic criteria.

• More efforts to increase the pool of women holders of the Ph.D., the doctor of arts degree, and other advanced degrees preparatory for research and teaching. We call particular attention to the opportunities inherent in the doctor of arts degree—it is more oriented toward teaching, and the difficulties that face some women in getting started in a research career do not apply to the same extent to teaching. This does not imply that research-oriented women should be discouraged from studying for the Ph.D. degree.

• More opportunities for women to return to college for advanced training after they have started their families.

9   We favor at the faculty level:

• Special efforts to recruit women into the pool from which appointees are selected.

• Special consideration, in making appointments, to the potential contributions of women to departmental and college excellence in their roles as models and as special sources of sensitivity to the problems and aspirations of women students.

• Policies that allow more part-time appointments, that provide for childbearing and child-rearing leaves, that reduce the severity of antinepotism rules, and other policies that will assist women to find a fuller place in the academic world.

10 We favor at the institutional level:

- Greater interest in the adequate provision of child-care facilities and policies of cooperation with groups seeking to provide child-care arrangements
- More efforts to place women on administrative staffs
- More women on governing boards

11 We support the general objectives of the "affirmative action" program for women that has been instituted by the federal government, while regretting the uncertainties and the occasional excesses in its application.

We equally support "affirmative action" programs for members of minority groups, for whom the barriers to access have been substantially greater than for women. Women are now found on faculties to something over one-half the extent of their participation in the general labor force; while the ratio for members of minority groups is about one-third. Measured this way, the problem is nearly twice as intense for the minorities. We particularly discussed this issue in our report entitled *A Chance to Learn* (1970a).

12 We favor the continuation of colleges for women. They provide an element of diversity among institutions of higher education and an additional option for women students. An unusual proportion of women leaders are graduates of these colleges. Women generally (1) speak up more in their classes, (2) hold more positions of leadership on campus, (3) choose to enter more frequently into such "male" fields as science, and (4) have more role models and mentors among women teachers and administrators. We oppose the homogenization of colleges in general, and of all special cultures within them.

13 We oppose:

- Any requirement that institutions employ specific numbers of women without regard to the availability of women possessing the skills required by specific departments.
- Suggestions that academic standards will necessarily be re-

duced by increasing the number of women faculty members. Academic standards in the long run, in fact, should be raised as faculty members are recruited from a larger pool of talent; in the short run, excellence, broadly defined, can also be increased by providing a better environment for all students and particularly for women.

14 How much can be accomplished by way of adding women to faculties? The answer: not a full reversal of past inequalities for quite some time. Expectations should not be overblown:

We start from a low base.

The pool of qualified women is restricted and it will take time to enlarge it—about 10 percent of all Ph.D.'s inside and outside academic life now are women.

The rate of new hires is decreasing. Few new hires will take place in the 1980s.

It will take until about the year 2000, under reasonable assumptions, before women are likely to be included in the national professoriate in approximately the same proportions as they are in the total labor force—this is a task for a generation of effort. The time it will take to accomplish a satisfactory level of absorption of women into faculties is lengthened by the concurrent need to absorb more members from minority and other underprivileged groups.

15 Particularly good use should be made of the remainder of the 1970s, since new hires are still being made in significant numbers. The 1980s will provide fewer opportunities for remedial action, since fewer new hires will take place. Thus the 1970s provide the best chance for improvement of the faculty status of women for some time ahead. No progress was made in the 1960s when it should have been made on a very major scale. Higher education is already at least 10 years too late in starting its efforts, first, to increase the pool of candidates and second, to add women into faculties from this pool.

The situation is not entirely unlike that of trying to add to the number of women railroad conductors. Providing equality of opportunity is tougher in a more static employment situation than in a more dynamic one.

16 Situations vary greatly, and this should be realized in developing expectations and in carrying out all policies:

Public community colleges and, to a less extent, public comprehensive colleges, have the most rapid expansion in enrollments ahead of them, and consequently they are in the best position to hire more women. Additionally, they make greater use of persons with the M.A. degree, where a larger pool of qualified women now exists and where the supply is much more readily expansible. It will take longer and be more difficult for research universities to increase their employment of women as faculty members because the supply of women with Ph.D.'s is now so low and because performance in some fields depends so heavily on the research contributions of scholars at an age when some women are otherwise engaged.

Fields vary. Some already have many women in the pool—like the humanities and the creative arts—and others do not.

Women vary. Black women and Jewish women are historically in better position to take advantage of current opportunities than are, for example, Spanish-speaking women, because more of the former have attended college in the past than have the latter.

Percentages of women in faculties, segment by segment, field by field, group by group, are informative and may even be useful across-the-board as guidelines for enforcement purposes, but they would make a cruel Procrustean bed if applied in specific situations without reference to the special characteristics of each individual situation.

We do not favor the application of simple rules to complex situations, and do not support conformist solutions to diverse circumstances—complex situations require complex rules and diverse circumstances deserve diverse solutions. Broad tests of performance, consequently, are more equitable and wise than are attempts at "fine-tuning" adjustments.

17 There are costs:

In money—particularly for salary equalization.

To majority male Ph.D.'s already in oversupply in some fields, and much more so in the humanities and the creative arts, where there is also a larger pool of qualified women than in the sciences and engineering.

To minority males seeking teaching positions. They must now compete with women as well as with majority males.

In the effort needed to change policies, to recruit women more actively, and in other ways.

In more federal influence over the campus; and in more central control at the campus level by presidents and deans over departments. Other forces, of course, operate in these same directions. To the extent that institutions assume the initiative, however, federal influence will be less necessary. And to the extent that departments take leadership on their own, central institutional control will be less required.

In potential frustration for women students if they overreact to current opportunities. Because of the time lag in training, women starting work for the Ph.D. now can expect to come out of the "pipeline" when new hires are approaching the zero point. They may come to share some of the frustrations of their male counterparts.

18 The gains potentially, however, are very great:

In greater fairness among individuals.

In enrichment of the educational world.

In greater talent for society.

In better care for and education of young children by more educated mothers.

In greater contributions to the quality of community life by more educated women.

Generally we should seek the maximum gains for women but at the minimum costs to academic institutions and to society.

19 Women should be given more freedom of choice—and more options—than they have had in the past, both for their own sake and for that of society. This can and should be done without loss of academic excellence, and without artificially contrived controls.

We should make possible the achievement of equality where situations are equal; but expect differences where situations are different. Women with free choice may, because of differing interests, make different choices from those of men, and their resultant patterns of action may not necessarily conform to those of men. Some women will lose productive years in the development of their competence. Differential patterns of activity are not evidence of discrimination if they are based on either free choice, or on different abilities to perform, or on a combination of both.

20 Revolutionary changes are underway in the development of greater occupational opportunities for women, in the nature of the family, in sexual roles, in child-rearing obligations, and in many other ways. No one can as yet know how they will all turn out. Thus the situation must be kept under continuing review. Few changes have ever taken place historically that potentially affect so fundamentally the lives of so many individuals. In the academic world, a necessary revolution is now underway in criteria for admissions and faculty promotions, in procedures, in personnel policies, and in attitudes of all faculty, staff, and students.

21 Substantial improvements are now taking place in the position of women within higher education. This momentum of improvement must be continued until loss of talent and unfair discrimination have been fully eliminated. It is equally important both to take effective action and not to expect too great results too soon.

2. The Scope of This Report

In the 1960s, the long struggle of women for equality in the United States entered a new phase. Not since the era of the suffrage movement that preceded the 1920 constitutional amendment granting women the right to vote has there been comparably vigorous activity on behalf of women's rights. The change has been closely associated with the broader civil rights movement, but the women's movement is concerned with a number of social issues that differ from specific concerns of the civil rights movement. Many types of women are involved, from older women who have long been active in the campaign for the Equal Rights Amendment to younger women, some of whom are radicals associated with the New Left and some of whom are not politically radical at all. Although there is a broad consensus within the movement on the need to eliminate discrimination on the basis of sex, there are intense controversies within the movement over issues and tactics.[1] In fact, there are many women's movements rather than just one, and if we occasionally refer to the "women's movement" in this report, it should be understood that we do not intend to imply that there is a single unified movement.

To the extent that black and other minority group women have participated in the women's movement, their participation has been "in limited numbers and primarily on an individual basis" (Hole & Levine, 1972, p. 149). To a large extent minority group women have perceived their problems as those of

---

[1]A particularly comprehensive and informative account of these controversies may be found in Hole and Levine (1972).

11

racism rather than of sexism.[2] In fact, a good many black, and also white, men and women argue that affirmative action programs should give low priority to white women. They perceive women's movement leaders as predominantly middle-class and do not regard white women as an especially oppressed group. On the other hand, some blacks argue that, because women are so much more numerous than minority group males, vigorous activity on the part of women against discrimination and toward affirmative action can be of great assistance also to minority groups. In addition, of course, the view that white women are not an oppressed group tends to ignore the abundant evidence of their relatively low status and low pay in most employment situations.

The women's movement is by no means confined to the United States. It is now an active force in most of the advanced industrial countries, and one writer on the international women's movement attributes its rise in the mid-1960s in large part to the pronounced increase in enrollment of women in higher education that was occurring in many of these countries. By and large, it is college-educated young women who tend to form the core of the movement (Mitchell, 1971). But it is thought that pronounced increases in labor force participation rates of women in many countries have also played a role.

This report will be concerned with only one aspect of the women's movement: equality of opportunity for participation of women in higher education. But this is an extremely important aspect of the movement, not just because higher education provides essential preparation for the more challenging and interesting jobs in the economy, but because women want an equal opportunity to benefit from the intellectual and cultural experience of higher education, whatever their future roles in life. In addition, relatively few women are in the higher ranks of university and college faculties. This suggests a lack of equal opportunity for women scholars and a loss of talent to society. It also means a lack of opportunity for undergraduate and graduate students, both male and female, to appreciate the fact that women are capable of distinguished performance in both teaching and research.

---

[2]For an illuminating discussion of the historical background of differences in attitudes of black and white women, see Lerner (1973).

Throughout the present century, women have been more likely to graduate from high school than men, but have been less likely to enter college. As we proceed from consideration of the undergraduate level to graduate and professional schools and to service on the faculties of institutions of higher education, we find relatively fewer women at each successive stage.

Our discussion will be concerned with women as students, faculty members, administrators, and nonfaculty academic employees. We shall not attempt to cover the problems of nonacademic women employees, because the policies needed in higher education to provide equality of opportunity in nonacademic employment do not markedly differ from those in other sectors of the economy. At the same time, we believe that affirmative action policies adopted by colleges and universities should apply to all employees, academic and nonacademic, as in fact those that have been adopted generally do. But it is in academic employment that institutions of higher education face problems that are frequently especially sensitive and that do not have precise parallels in other types of employment.

Before discussing the participation of women at the various stages of higher education, however, we need to consider the many roles of college-educated women—in their families, in their communities, and in the labor force. We need to have an understanding of the impact of higher education on women as adults before considering proposed policy changes in colleges and universities.

3. The Many Roles of College-Educated Women

Until the middle of the nineteenth century, opportunities for women to participate in higher education were almost, but not quite, nonexistent. Georgia Female College was chartered in 1836 and conferred its first degrees in 1840. Oberlin accepted women in its collegiate department in 1837 (and was also the first predominantly white college to enroll blacks).[1] But, according to Caroline Bird, the first coeds at Oberlin "were given a watered-down literary course and expected to serve the men students at table and remain silent in mixed classes" (Bird with Briller, 1972, p. 22). Several women's colleges were established in the following years, and two state universities (the University of Deseret—now the University of Utah—and the University of Iowa) began admitting women in the 1850s. But it was not until after the Civil War that the number of colleges and universities admitting women began to grow appreciably, and even then progress was slow. The determination of some unusually able young women who saw no reason why they should be barred from opportunities to develop their mental capacities, the sympathetic encouragement of a few male college or university presidents, and the growing need for college-educated teachers to serve the expanding public high schools appear to have been major factors encouraging the opening of college doors to women in the latter part of the nineteenth century.

In later sections we shall trace the growth of male and female enrollment in higher education during the present century. For the present, let us note that, by 1970, 43 percent of those receiv-

---

[1] For a more extensive discussion of the early history of higher education for women, see Newcomer (1959).

ing bachelor's degrees were women. And, although the propor- tion of women in the adult population who were college gradu- ates was considerably smaller (8.1 percent) than the corre- sponding proportion of men (14.6 percent), the difference was tending to narrow.[2]

Many factors have contributed to the weakening of prejudice against higher education for women. Perhaps the most impor- tant of these has been the general rise in the educational level of the population, for, as we shall see at a later point, the higher the educational level of parents, the more likely they are to en- courage higher education for their daughters as well as for their sons. But another contributing factor may well be the growing body of both impressionistic and statistical information on the impact of a college education on women as adults, to which we now turn.

THEIR LIFESTYLES AND ACTIVITIES In the last few decades, a vast literature has developed on the impact of college on students and its subsequent influence on college graduates as adults. Much of this literature fails to dif- ferentiate between the sexes or, especially as it relates to the economic impacts of education, is largely confined to men. To the extent that there have been special studies of female college graduates and holders of advanced degrees, they have tended to be concerned with their patterns of labor force participation and their ways of coping with the conflict between marital and career activities. But there are also beginning to be some studies that shed light on relationships between women's education and their roles as wives, mothers, and participants in communi- ty activities. The results of these studies suggest that the social benefits of higher education for women, perhaps even more than for men, include elements that cannot be quantified by conventional methods of measuring the social return to invest- ment in education.

Unlike the situation in the early decades of this century,

---

[2]The data are for the population aged 25 and older in March 1971 and are from U.S. Bureau of the Census (1971*a*).

women who graduate from college are just about as likely to marry as are women with less education, and the great majority of them do.[3] However, women with five or more years of college are considerably more likely to remain single than women with just four years of college—among women aged 35 to 44 and also among those aged 45 to 54, about 19 percent of those with five or more years of college were single in 1970 as against only about 8 percent of those with four years of college. The earliest census data available on marital status by educational attainment are for 1940 and do not distinguish between women with four years of college and those with some graduate education, but they do suggest that college graduates were considerably less likely to marry in earlier decades.[4]

But college-educated women tend to marry at a somewhat later age than women with less education, and this tendency to marry later largely explains why college-educated women have fewer children. Another factor is their greater tendency to use contraceptives (Michael, forthcoming). But these differences be-

---

[3]According to the 1970 census, 86.5 percent of women aged 35 to 44 who had completed four years of college were married, and this percentage differed very little from the corresponding percentages for women with lower levels of educational attainment. Among women with four years of college aged 45 to 54, 82 percent were married, and again the percentage was much like that for women with lower levels of education (U.S. Bureau of the Census, 1972b, Table 4). The slightly smaller percentage of married women among those aged 45 to 54 than among those aged 35 to 44 did not reflect a smaller propensity to marry in this slightly older cohort, but rather the fact that relatively more of them were widows, as would be expected.

[4]Among women aged 35 to 44 and also among those aged 45 to 54 who had completed four or more years of college in 1940, about 30 percent were single, as contrasted with proportions ranging from about 8 to 16 percent (and varying directly with educational attainment) for women who had completed grade school, high school, or some college (U.S. Bureau of the Census, 1945, Table 40).

Mabel Newcomer assembled data on Mount Holyoke and Vassar alumnae for the late nineteenth and early twentieth centuries. Among the Mount Holyoke graduates, about three-fourths of those who completed college before 1864 married, but the proportion fell to about 48 percent for the graduating classes of 1884 to 1893 and then rose to about 58 percent for those graduating from 1912 to 1921. Among Vassar alumnae, the trends were somewhat different. The proportion who married fell from about 62 percent for the classes of 1867 to 1871 to about 54 percent for those of 1872 to 1881 and then rose to 75 percent for those graduating from 1912 to 1921 (Newcomer, 1959, p. 212).

tween college graduates and women with lower levels of education are narrowing.[5]

A 1960 study indicated that college-educated respondents were considerably more likely (60 percent) to report their marriages as "very happy" than respondents with less education. Yet they were also somewhat more likely to report that they sometimes had marriage problems (Gurin, Veroff, & Feld, 1960, p. 105). This latter finding may suggest that college graduates are more frank about admitting the existence of marital problems.

College-educated women are more likely to participate in the labor force than women with less education, but are about as likely to withdraw from the labor force when they have young children. On the average, somewhat more than half of all women with four years of college, and about two-thirds of those with five or more years of college, were in the labor force in 1972. We shall consider their patterns of labor force participation in more detail later in this section.

In a study conducted for the Carnegie Commission by the National Bureau of Economic Research, it was found that college-educated women tend to spend relatively more time on child care than women with lower levels of education, but about the same amount of time on such activities as meal preparation (Leibowitz, forthcoming). This finding is based on an analysis of a study of the use of time in household work conducted at Cornell University. Leibowitz's results suggest that college-educated women tend to place a relatively high value on spending time with their children. This helps to explain the strong association that has been found in many studies between the performance of school children and such factors as the socioeconomic status of parents, mother's and father's education, and father's occupation. Some of those who have been

---

[5]Educational attainment of women appears to bear little relationship to marital stability. Among women aged 35 to 44, about 5 to 6 percent were divorced in 1970, regardless of educational attainment. Among those aged 45 to 54, the percentages were very similar.

However, the percentage was relatively low (about 4 percent) for those with just four years of college and relatively high (about 7 percent) for those with five or more years of college (U. S. Bureau of the Census, 1973*b*, Table 40).

active in research on human capital are beginning to point to this effect of mother's education on the development of children as one of the social benefits of higher education for women.[6] A great deal more research, however, is needed to illuminate all the relationships involved.

Other studies have shown that college-educated parents tend to take their child-rearing responsibilities seriously, but to worry about somewhat different aspects of child-rearing than parents with less education. For example, they are somewhat less likely than parents with lower levels of education to say that they "never feel inadequate" in dealing with the problems they have with their children. But, whereas less educated parents are more often concerned about problems of physical care and provision, college-educated parents are more likely to be concerned about parent-child affiliative relationships and problems of tolerance for the child's behavior (Withey, 1971, pp. 85–86). Of course, having higher incomes, college-educated parents are not as likely to have to worry about physical provision for their children.

More subtle, and less susceptible to statistical measurement, are the intellectual interests shared by college-educated spouses. To be sure, there have been studies of reading habits indicating that college graduates of both sexes are much more likely to read such periodicals as the *New York Times Magazine* and *Time* than less educated persons (ibid., p. 97). But we must rely on more impressionistic observations in noting shared interests in art, classical music, and literature, and the role that these shared interests probably play in leading college-educated spouses to report their marriages as "very happy." Because college-educated couples have a generally higher income than those with less education, their marriages may also be more rewarding because they are more often free from serious financial difficulties and can enjoy more material goods and leisure time.

More susceptible to statistical analysis are the roles of college-educated women in constructive community activity. Nu-

---

[6]For a group of papers bearing on this and related issues, see Schultz (1973).

merous studies have shown that participation in organizations is positively related to education. There are also clear indications of differences in the types of organizations in which highly educated and less educated persons participate.

A nationwide survey showed that extent of participation in volunteer activities varied directly with educational attainment for both men and women. Among women, the proportions reporting participation in volunteer activity during the preceding year varied from 9.5 percent for those with 8 years or less of schooling to 41.0 percent for those with 4 or more years of college. Rates of volunteer activity for men tended to be slightly lower (U.S. Manpower Administration, 1969, p. 29).

Particularly notable among women's organizations for its constructive legislative activity based on careful previous study of the issues is the League of Women Voters of the United States, and there is little question that most women who are active in the league are college graduates. Moreover, the league has been a training ground for a number of women who have gone on to active careers in politics. Similarly, in the black community, many of the leaders in the National Association for the Advancement of Colored People have been college-educated black men and women, a number of whom have also gone on to active political careers.[7]

College-educated women with children in school also tend to be very active in parent-teacher organizations and other groups concerned with the schools, although in these organizations they are probably somewhat less predominant than in the League of Women Voters. In the last decade or so, women, many of them college graduates, have also been among the leaders in organizations devoted to the preservation of the environment and to the protection of the consumer. They have long been active in charitable fund-raising activities and in organizations sponsoring artistic and musical activities.

The many community activities of college-educated women

---

[7]In some communities, whites have also been very active in the NAACP, but there is probably less tendency now than in earlier decades for whites to be chosen for positions of leadership, largely because more able black leadership is now available.

undoubtedly tend to make them more interesting and play a role in their college-educated spouses being "very happy." At times, also, both spouses are engaged in common community activities.

In discussing the lifestyles of college-educated women, we do not at all intend to undervalue the many accomplishments of women with fewer years of schooling, and we are far from suggesting that every woman should seek a college education. In earlier reports, we have called attention to the "reluctant attenders" of both sexes who are in college as a result of parental or social pressures and have made recommendations aimed at discouraging their enrollment.

LABOR FORCE PARTICIPATION   In the past, it has sometimes been argued that college education, and particularly graduate and professional education, for women is a poor social investment, because women who marry are relatively unlikely to participate in the labor force. Thus society gains little from investing in a woman's education. The argument has probably been used especially frequently in relation to medical education and to graduate education in the natural sciences, which are relatively costly and heavily subsidized. As we have suggested, however, the social benefits of college education for women are by no means confined to their productivity in the labor force, and in any case female college graduates and holders of advanced degrees tend to have relatively high rates of labor force participation among women.

In fact, labor force participation rates of women, and especially of married women, between the ages of 35 and 60 have increased dramatically since World War II, but the comparatively high labor force participation rates of college-educated women are less familiar (Chart 2). Except that there tends to be little difference between labor force participation rates of women who are high school graduates and those who have one to three years of college, the proportion of women in the labor force varies directly with educational attainment in all age groups.

Special studies have shown that women who have Ph.D. or M.D. degrees have exceedingly high rates of labor force participation. In a relatively recent survey of all women who received

CHART 2 *Percentage of women in the labor force, by age and education, March 1972*

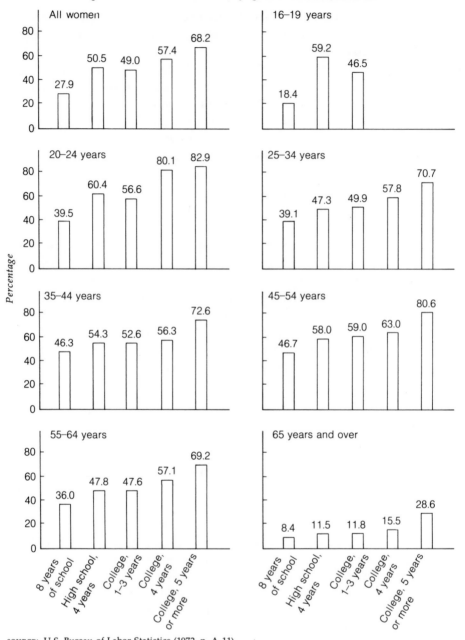

SOURCE: U.S. Bureau of Labor Statistics (1972, p. A-11).

the doctorate between three and nine years earlier, it was found that 96 percent of the unmarried women were working full time; 87 percent of the married women with no children were working full time and 4 percent were working part time; and, among married women with children, 59 percent were working full time and 25 percent part time (Simon, Clark, & Galway, 1967).[8]

A 1965 survey of medical school graduates of selected years from 1931 through 1956 showed that only 1.7 percent of the women graduates had not been in practice at any time since receiving the M.D. In 1964, 54 percent of these women worked 2,000 hours or more (that is, full time or more if we define a 40-hour week as full time). Another 37 percent worked on various part-time arrangements. Moreover, among the married women, it was only those who had had three or more children who had an appreciably lower rate of activity than single women. The study also indicated a trend toward earlier marriage among medical students and physicians in training programs—29 percent of the women physicians were married at the time of graduation from medical school, as compared with only 15 percent indicated by an earlier study which had surveyed 1929–1940 graduates (Powers, Parmelle, & Wiesenfelder, 1969).

There is other evidence suggesting a trend toward earlier marriage among women undertaking prolonged professional or graduate education. In the early decades of the century, there was still so much aversion to the idea of a married woman working that many women contemplating a professional career took it for granted that they would not marry. Sometimes these

---

[8]Another study conducted in 1965 and relating to labor force patterns of women who received the doctorate in 1957 or 1958 showed that 79 percent of these women had never interrupted their careers, and 18 percent reported career interruptions of 11 to 15 months. Having preschool children was the greatest deterrent to full-time work among a number of factors investigated, but having a husband who was highly educated and earned a high income was also something of a deterrent. This second study also showed that only 9 percent of the women were not in the labor force at the time of the survey (Astin, 1969, p. 57; and Folger, Astin, & Bayer, 1970, pp. 288–291).

women deferred marriage because their future spouses were also pursuing advanced or professional study, and a young man was not expected to marry until he was in a position to support his wife. These attitudes slowly changed over the decades, but perhaps most sharply during World War II when there was sympathetic understanding of couples who wished to marry before a young man was sent overseas, and in the immediate postwar years when the desire of returning veterans to marry before completing their education was encouraged by the GI Bill of Rights. In the particular case of medical students, more than half of the women who obtain M.D.'s have physician husbands (ibid., p. 482) and the increase in available student aid and in stipends for interns and residents has undoubtedly played an important role in facilitating earlier marriage. Clearly, increased availability of contraceptives has also been important in the gradual change in attitudes toward early marriage.

The data in Chart 2 suggest that college graduates and women with five or more years of college (especially the latter) are considerably more likely to be in the labor force in the age group when married women tend to have young children in the home, especially from 25 to 34 years, than are women with lower levels of educational attainment. More detailed data from the 1970 census, however, indicate that labor force participation rates of married women with children under six and with four years of college tend to be only slightly higher than those of comparable women with lower levels of educational attainment (Appendix A, Table A-1). But married women with small children and with five years or with six or more years of college have appreciably higher labor force participation rates than corresponding groups of women with less education. Nevertheless, regardless of educational attainment, married women with children under six tend to have decidedly lower labor force participation rates than women in other marital-status and presence-of-children categories.

In a study mentioned earlier, Leibowitz (forthcoming) concludes that the supply of married women in the labor market is positively correlated with educational attainment, except that between the ages 25 and 40 all married women supply nearly the same amount of labor to the market. Her analysis took account of variations in weeks worked but did not distinguish between women with only four years of college and those with five or more years of college.[9] Other data suggest, however, that women with five or more years of college, like women in other education groups, are relatively more likely to work on a part-time than a full-time basis when their children are young.

In line with the views of Mincer (1962) and Becker (1965), Leibowitz indicates that highly educated women are relatively more likely to be in the labor market because education raises productivity in the labor market more than the productivity of time spent in home production, so that the "cost" of not being in the labor market rises as the educational attainment of women increases. In Becker's model, households function much like small firms, in which decisions on the allocation of each household member's time between "market" production and home production are based on careful economic calculations of the relative benefits and costs involved. We believe that this view is illuminating, but too limited. Other studies have shown that professional workers tend to be considerably more satisfied with their jobs and much less likely to wish they were in other lines of work than persons holding relatively routine white-collar jobs or blue-collar jobs (Withey et al., 1971, Ch. 5; and Special Task Force to the Department of Health, Education and Welfare, 1973). We believe that highly educated women are frequently motivated to work, not just for the income they will receive, but because they find their work intrinsically interesting and rewarding. Along with educated men, they want to develop and utilize their mental capacities to the greatest possible extent, to avoid wasting their previous investment in education and training, and, if holders of advanced degrees, to secure, as men do, the rewards that come from high accomplishment. These include the personal satisfaction of achievement, as well as the more obvious rewards associated with acquiring a distinguished reputation.

There are other advantages to a professional career as well, when compared with the types of work often performed by less educated women. Professional women, like professional men, have opportunities to travel in connection with their work, and if they are on college faculties, to have sabbaticals. Relatively pleasant working conditions, flexible hours of work, and other

[9]The study was based on unpublished data from the 1/1000 sample of the 1960 census. Only women who were not enrolled in school, and who had been married only once and were living with their husbands were included.

factors also play a role in making the kinds of jobs held by highly educated women frequently considerably more appealing than those held by less educated women.

In addition, college-educated women tend to marry men with comparable levels of education, and attitudes of men toward the participation of their wives in the labor force tend to be less unfavorable among college graduates and holders of advanced degrees than among men with lower levels of education (Withey et al., 1971, p. 73). Studies in other countries have shown similar variations in attitudes toward labor force participation of wives. In working-class families, there is acute consciousness of the fact that married women historically have had to work because of economic necessity, often in unpleasant, uninteresting, poorly paid, and routine jobs. Thus, they have a sense of pride and achievement if the family is in an economic situation that releases the wife from such work. These attitudes are less likely to be found in professional families in which the wife's level of educational attainment qualifies her for relatively interesting and satisfying work.

Nonwhite women are considerably more likely to be in the labor force than white women, regardless of age, education, or family income level. This has been true historically in the United States and, broadly speaking, is largely attributable to the relatively low income levels of black families, which have tended to make work a matter of economic necessity for black women. Moreover, if we consider detailed 1970 census data on labor force participation rates of nonwhite women as compared with those of all women, we find that having children under six is much less likely to keep nonwhite women out of the labor force than it is for women in general (Appendix A, Table A-2). The relatively high labor force participation rates of college-educated nonwhite married women with children under six are particularly striking. The reasons for this difference have not been extensively studied, but it seems likely that attitudes of black families tend to be more favorable to a working mother even when her children are young.[10]

[10]The data in Appendix A, Table A-2, of course, relate to all nonwhite women, but black women make up more than 90 percent of the nonwhite female population and therefore dominate the data.

MALE AND FEMALE PROFESSIONS College-educated women and men are distributed very differently among the professions. In fact, it is not an exaggeration to say that, in the United States to a greater extent than in some other industrial countries, we have a pattern of male and female professions. Women are overwhelmingly predominant in nursing. They also comprise a substantial majority of elementary and secondary schoolteachers—more so at the elementary than at the secondary level. On the other hand, as is well known, there have tended to be relatively few women in such traditionally male professions as medicine, dentistry, law, the ministry, engineering, the natural sciences, business administration, and economics.

Detailed occupational data from the 1970 census, however, show very pronounced increases in the number of women employed in many of the traditionally male professions (Appendix A, Table A-3). They still represent a comparatively small proportion of the total in many of these professions, but the percentage increases were frequently substantial:

Women as a percentage of all employed persons, selected occupations, 1960 and 1970

	1960	1970
Accountants	16.5	26.2
Architects	2.1	3.6
Engineers	0.9	1.6
Lawyers and judges	3.5	4.9
Life and physical scientists	9.2	13.7
Dentists	2.1	3.4
Pharmacists	7.5	12.0
Physicians, including osteopaths	6.9	9.3
Teachers, college and university	23.9	28.6*
Engineering and science technicians	11.1	12.9
Radio operators	16.7	25.9
Designers	19.3	24.2

*Census data on "teachers, college and university," include graduate teaching assistants, whereas other data to be discussed later do not include this group. According to National Education Association data (1972), women accounted for 27 percent of faculty members, not including teaching assistants, in 1971–72.

It is true that an increase in women as a percentage of all workers in any given occupation would be expected because the female labor force increased much more rapidly than the male labor force. But in each of the occupations listed above, the percentage increase in the employment of women was much greater than the overall percentage increase in the female labor force.[11] The proportion of salaried managers who were women also rose from 13.9 percent in 1960 to 16.1 percent in 1970.

But there is a great deal of evidence that these 1960–1970 changes in employment patterns do not fully reflect the changes that have been occurring in recent years. The proportion of women among medical and law students has been rising rapidly in the last five years or so, as we shall see in Section 6, and this change was not yet reflected in employment data for 1970. The proportion of women among those awarded degrees in such fields as physics and mathematics increased during the 1960s. Data on career choices of entering freshman women between 1966 and 1972 show increases in the percentages of women aspiring to be businesswomen, lawyers, physicians or dentists, nurses, other professional health workers, and farmers or foresters (Appendix A, Table A-4).

Black freshman women have been breaking out of conventional career aspirations substantially more than white freshmen. Historically, the percentage of elementary and secondary school teachers among employed black female college graduates has been even higher than among all employed female college graduates, about half of whom have tended to be schoolteachers. But, strikingly, the percentage of entering black freshman women choosing teaching as a career was even smaller in 1971 than among white freshman women, and the percentages of black women choosing a number of traditionally male occupations was considerably higher, as the following data for selected career choices show (Bayer, 1972, p. 34; and Appendix A, Table A-4):

---

[11]In a few of these occupations the increase in the relative representation of women between 1960 and 1970 followed a decline in the preceding decade, but this was by no means the predominant pattern. However, among social scientists, the percentage of women declined in both decades, and in the 1960s there was also a decline in the proportion of personnel and labor relations workers who were women.

Percentage of black and nonblack freshman women mentioning selected career choices, fall 1971

	Black	Nonblack
Businesswoman	8.5%	4.1%
College teacher	1.7	0.5
Physician or dentist	3.3	1.9
Elementary or secondary school teacher	20.8	25.0
Engineer	0.5	0.2
Lawyer	3.3	1.3

Young black women are apparently aware of the affirmative action programs that appear to be creating a particularly favorable job market for black female college graduates in positions formerly largely closed to them.

The fact that the United States has relatively fewer women in certain traditionally male occupations than a number of Western European countries has frequently been pointed out, but the data in Appendix A, Table A-5, suggest that the situation is more mixed than has usually been indicated. It is chiefly in the fields of medicine and dentistry that women form a larger proportion of those employed in some of the Western European countries than in the United States. The reasons for this have not been extensively studied, but the shorter period of training typically required in Europe before an individual receives the M.D. or its equivalent is almost certainly a factor. As in other fields of study in these countries, an individual usually begins his specialized study in medicine at the time of entry into the university. There is not the same distinction between premedical and medical education as in this country. In Great Britain, for example, a medical student usually has three years of training in basic sciences at the university, followed by two years of clinical training in a hospital. The B.A. is awarded after the first three years and the first degree in medicine (M.B.) after the two years of hospital training.[12] In Sweden, medical education begins immediately upon graduation from secondary school and lasts five and one-half years before the M.D. is awarded.[13]

[12]See the discussion of requirements in British Council (1970, pp. 156–158).

[13]A recent *New York Times* story reported the case of a married Swedish woman who was expecting her third child and her M.D. degree at about the same time, but she had served as an airline stewardess and had also received a degree in economics before deciding on going into medicine (Altman, 1973, p. 82).

Another factor that may play a role in accounting for the greater relative representation of women in medicine in Western Europe is that "in Europe family continuity in careers is stressed, so that a daughter is more encouraged to enter her father's profession than in the United States" (Lopate, 1968, p. 30).

On the other hand, women comprise a larger proportion of college and university faculties in the United States than in a number of the Western European countries for which we have data, and a larger proportion of full professors than in Great Britain or West Germany. As we shall see in Section 7, however, relatively few women are in the higher ranks of the faculty in research-oriented universities in the United States.

Comparisons with Eastern Europe, of course, tell a very different story. The fact that women represent about three-fourths of the doctors in the Soviet Union, for example, is well known. In the U.S.S.R., however, medicine is a considerably less prestigious occupation, as compared with science or engineering, than in the United States.[14] Moreover, the top surgical posts tend to be held by men.

In all European countries, as in the United States, women in professional positions tend to be less well paid and to hold less responsible jobs. The fact that women are more likely than men to be part-time workers is partially responsible for their lower annual incomes in occupation after occupation in this country (*Economic Report of the President*, 1973, pp. 103–106), but it is by no means the only factor. Even if we compare starting salaries for male and female college graduates in such occupations as accounting or chemistry, we find that starting salaries of women are consistently below those of men.[15] However, the situation is changing. In the spring of 1973, the annual Endicott survey indicated for the first time, that women engineers about

---

[14]For a recent and illuminating comparative study, see Galenson (1973).

[15]See the chart in Carnegie Commission (1973a, p. 54). See also the discussion in Kreps (1971, Ch. 2). In July 1973, members of the President's Council of Economic Advisers testified before the Joint Economic Committee, U.S. Congress, that "what appeared to be pure discrimination" reduced the average earnings of women to 80 to 90 percent of what men earned for the same work (Shanahan, 1973).

to graduate from college were being offered a slightly higher salary than their male counterparts (Endicott, 1972, pp. 4 and 7). We shall present a much more extensive analysis of sex differentials in compensation on college and university faculties in Section 7.

Even more striking than recent evidence revealing rising proportions of women in traditionally male professions in the United States are the indications of changing attitudes toward the relative importance of marriage and careers. A women's college that has administered questionnaires each year since 1964 to the entering freshman class reported that 65 percent of the 1964 class said they would like to be a housewife with one or more children. Over the years, there has been a steady decline in the percentage choosing this lifestyle—the percentages subscribing to a future as housewife and mother in subsequent years are as follows: 65, 61, 60, 53, 52, 46, 31. Two other alternatives increased in popularity: the percentage wanting to be a married career woman with children doubled, going from 20 percent in 1964 to 40 percent in 1970, and the percentage that were uncertain increased from 13 to 22 percent (Cross, 1971, p. 147).

Data relating to 1972 Stanford women graduates are even more dramatic. A study released by the university's Committee on the Education and Employment of Women showed that fewer than 1 out of every 25 women expected to be a full-time housewife in five years. In a 1965 survey, 70 percent of Stanford women said they would not work at all when their children were under the age of 6, and only 45 percent intended to work full time when their children were over the age of 12. Among the 1972 graduates, only 3 percent of the women said they would stop working when their husbands had finished school and only 7 percent said they would stop working to rear children. In all, only 18.5 percent of the 1972 women graduates mentioned the role of wife and mother as part of their plans for the next five years.

Comparison of the results of the 1965 and 1972 surveys also shows a sharp rise in the proportion of women interested in the professions, and a precipitous decline in the proportion expecting to be schoolteachers. There was also a pronounced decline, among both men and women, in the proportion expecting to be college educators or scientists (Stanford University, 1972, p. 4):

Occupational plans of Stanford seniors, 1965 and 1972

	1965		1972	
	Men	*Women*	*Men*	*Women*
Total sample				
Number	460	208	111	122
Percent	100.0	100.0	100.0	100.0
Medicine, law, other professions	36.2	5.8	41.5	26.1
Elementary and secondary education	6.2	36.1	2.0	10.4
College educator, scientist	19.1	13.9	11.6	6.6
Business	17.1	4.4	6.8	5.1
"Women's jobs"— housewife, secretary, nurse	0.0	11.7	0.0	3.2
Government	2.8	3.3	3.2	1.2
Other, including don't know	18.7	24.5	34.3	46.8

Several other aspects of these results are worthy of special attention. The sharp decline in the proportion of men expecting a business career probably reflects the increasing tendency of college students to question the goals and practices of large-scale business. Finally, the rise in the percentages responding "other, including don't know" may reflect growing uncertainty of many college students about their own goals. A significant rise in the percentages of entering freshmen who are uncertain about career choices also shows up for both men and women in Appendix A, Table A-4.[16] Indeed, it is sometimes suggested that the women's movement itself may be a factor in creating uncertainties about career goals for both men and women. To be sure, more college-educated women are opting for professional careers, and relatively fewer expect only to be housewives, but the 1972 Stanford survey suggests that a sizable proportion have no definite plans at the time of graduation from

[16]See also the data relating to uncertainty about career goals in Carnegie Commission on Higher Education (1973a, Section 9).

college. The growth of uncertainty among men may also reflect to some extent the impact of the women's movement in making less clear the relative roles of the sexes in adult life.

Stanford women, perhaps along with other women in highly selective institutions, are probably in the vanguard with respect to changing attitudes, but there are indications that changes are occurring among college women in general. In the summer of 1971, the American Council on Education conducted a follow-up survey of students who had entered college in 1967. Slightly more than one-fourth of the female respondents indicated that their long-run career expectations were to be a housewife or not to work.[17] The other three-fourths expected to have some type of career (Bayer, Royer, & Webb, 1973, pp. 21–22).

There is little question that decisive changes in attitudes toward their future roles in society are occurring among college women. How lasting these changes are likely to be is not clear, but it seems probable that recent trends toward greatly increased aspirations of women to train for traditionally male professions will continue. Are colleges and universities pursuing policies that will encourage more women to pursue successful careers in these professions or are their policies inhibiting this development? What is the role of the acculturation and education of women before reaching the college stage? These are among the central questions with which this report will be concerned as we consider women at the point of entry to higher education, as undergraduates, as graduate and professional students, and as members of college and university faculties.

---

[17]In classifying the responses, long-run plans to be a student were grouped with plans to be a housewife, but it seems likely, especially for female respondents, that "long-run" plans must have involved being a housewife rather than a student.

4. Women Entering Higher Education

SEX DIFFERENCES IN ENROLLMENT RATES Throughout the present century, women have been more likely to graduate from high school and less likely to enter college than men in the same age group, but in recent years the differences have been narrowing (Chart 3). By 1970, women comprised only slightly more than one-half of the high school graduates (Chart 4) and about 45 percent of the college entrants (not shown).

For the early decades of the present century, data on the number of degree recipients by sex are more readily available than enrollment data. From 1900 to 1940, the annual proportion of college graduates consisting of women rose from less than one-fifth to more than two-fifths.[1] Then there was a sharp decline between 1940 and 1950, reflecting both the pronounced increase in the number of male veterans enrolled after World War II and the impact of early marriage in preventing young women from enrolling. By 1960, women had increased their relative representation among college graduates substantially but had not yet restored their ratio to its prewar levels. All through the 1950s, the median age of first marriage for women (about 20.3 years) remained relatively low, as did that for men (about 22.8 years). But, as we shall see at a later point, marriage tends to be less of a barrier to college enrollment for men than for women. Women were bearing children in large numbers, also, during the 1950s. Although the postwar peak in the crude birthrate (26.6 per 1,000 population) was reached in 1947, the rate remained quite high for the next 10 years and then began the steady descent that has characterized it since 1957. Cause

---

[1]The data in Chart 4 include bachelor's and first-professional degrees, because bachelor's degrees were not reported separately until very recently, but the number of first-professional degrees is very small relative to the number of bachelor's degrees, although this was less true around 1900.

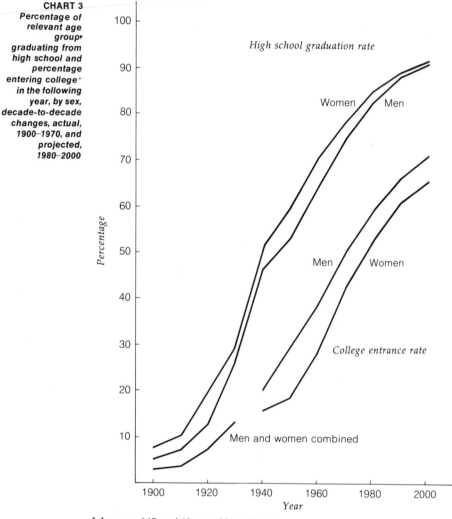

CHART 3
Percentage of relevant age group* graduating from high school and percentage entering college+ in the following year, by sex, decade-to-decade changes, actual, 1900–1970, and projected, 1980–2000

High school graduation rate

Women   Men

Men   Women

College entrance rate

Men and women combined

Year

* Average of 17- and 18-year old populations.
+ Includes only degree-credit enrollment.
SOURCES: Haggstrom (1971a and 1971b).

and effect are difficult to prove, but it seems highly likely that the failure of the relative representation of women among college graduates to return to its prewar level was associated with the pattern of early marriage and childbearing that characterized the first 15 years after the war. Returning veterans were acurately aware of the prolonged separation from female companionship and family living that they had experienced during the war, and they and their wives seemed intent on devoting

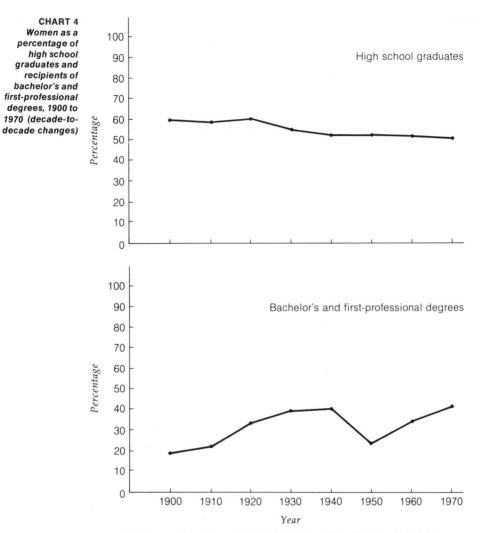

sources: U.S. Bureau of the Census (1960, Series H-223 to 233 and H-237 to 338); U.S. Bureau of the Census (1971*b*, Table 192); and Haggstrom (1971*a*).

themselves to enjoying mutual companionship and time spent with their children in the late 1940s and 1950s. Undoubtedly this factor also had something to do with the quiet and lack of political involvement that prevailed among college students in those years.

Then in the late 1950s things began to change. Along with the development of student activism, something else happened of significance to the subject of this report—the beginning of a steady decline in the birthrate. Whether the development of an effective birth control pill or a change in attitudes was primarily responsible is not entirely clear, but in any event the birthrate dropped steadily from 25.3 in 1957 to 15.6 in 1972 (U. S. Public Health Service, 1973, p. 1).[2] During the years from 1967 on, the birthrate was lower than at any time since birth statistics were first maintained in the United States, including the years of the Great Depression. And throughout most of the 1960s and early 1970s the absolute number of live births also declined. In addition, the median age of first marriage rose slowly after about 1960 for both men and women.

It seems probable that the rise in college enrollment rates of women during the 1960s was associated to some extent with the rise in the age of marriage and the decline in the birthrate, but again we cannot be certain which was cause and which effect. The rise in per capita income, the favorable job market for college graduates, the increased availability of student aid, and the spread of low-cost public colleges were also factors encouraging increased enrollment rates of both men and women in the 1960s. Toward the end of the decade, however, enrollment rates of white college-age men began to decline, except in older age groups, and the rate of increase of enrollment of white college-age women showed, in general, a tendency to slow down (Table 1). The virtual cessation of the draft, sharply rising costs of attending college, and the less favorable job market were all apparently playing a role in depressing enrollment rates of young white men, and the latter two factors were evidently influencing young women. Among blacks, however, enrollment rates continued to rise, more rapidly for men than for women, between 1969 and 1972.

For our purposes, the central problem is to explain the lower college enrollment rates of women than of men, even though the difference has been narrowing and may well continue to narrow in the future.

SOCIOECO-NOMIC STATUS For a variety of reasons, low socioeconomic status has tended to be more of a barrier to enrollment in college for women than for men. In 1957, even among women in the highest ability and the

---

[2]We refer here to the crude birthrate, the total number of live births per 1,000 population.

TABLE 1 *Percentage of persons aged 14 to 34 enrolled in degree-credit programs in college by age, race, and sex, October 1967, 1969, and 1972*

| | *Percentage enrolled* | | | | | |
| | *Men* | | | *Women* | | |
Race and age	*1967*	*1969*	*1972*	*1967*	*1969*	*1972*
White						
Total, 14 to 34 years	15.0	16.4	15.2	9.0	9.7	10.2
14 to 17	1.4	1.6	1.7	2.2	1.7	2.0
18 to 19	43.7	47.3	39.6	33.7	35.8	35.6
20 to 21	45.5	47.3	37.5	23.7	24.6	26.8
22 to 24	21.1	23.5	21.0	6.7	9.1	8.7
25 to 29	9.9	11.7	12.4	2.8	3.7	5.0
30 to 34	4.8	5.4	5.7	2.3	3.0	2.9
Black						
Total, 14 to 34 years	6.7	7.3	10.4	4.9	6.8	8.1
14 to 17	0.8	1.0	1.7	1.0	0.9	1.3
18 to 19	21.8	21.7	23.0	14.8	24.3	24.7
20 to 21	19.6	24.8	24.0	13.4	17.4	16.4
22 to 24	8.3	9.2	17.1	4.1	4.5	7.8
25 to 29	2.7	2.4	7.3	3.9	3.4	4.6
30 to 34	2.2	1.9	5.2	0.7	2.6	5.2

SOURCES: U.S. Bureau of the Census (1969, 1970; tables for 1972 provided in advance of publication).

highest socioeconomic status quartile, the proportion of high school graduates going on to college (76 percent) fell below that of comparable men by 15 percentage points. But for high ability women in the *lowest* socioeconomic status quartile, the percentage going on to college was 24 percentage points below that of the comparable group of men (Table 2). By 1967, women in the highest ability and highest socioeconomic quartile were on a par with men, with more than 90 percent of both sexes going on to college. For the most able women in the lowest socioeconomic quartile the percentage going on to college had risen sharply, although it was still below that for comparable men. Nevertheless, especially in the two lowest socioeconomic status quartiles, the general pattern was one of lower enrollment rates for women than for men of comparable ability.

TABLE 2 Percentage of high school graduates going to college the following year, by academic aptitude, socioeconomic background, and sex, 1957, 1961, and 1967

Socioeconomic quartile and ability quartile	Men			Women		
	1957	1961	1967	1957	1961	1967
1 (low) Socioeconomic quartile						
1 (low) Ability quartile	6	9	33	4	8	25
2 ↑	17	16	43	6	13	28
3 ↓	28	32	60	9	25	44
4 (high) Ability quartile	52	58	75	28	34	60
2 Socioeconomic quartile						
1 (low) Ability quartile	12	14	30	9	12	28
2 ↑	27	25	39	20	12	36
3 ↓	43	38	69	24	30	48
4 (high) Ability quartile	59	74	80	37	51	73
3 Socioeconomic quartile						
1 (low) Ability quartile	18	16	29	16	13	36
2 ↑	34	36	55	26	21	50
3 ↓	51	48	68	31	40	68
4 (high) Ability quartile	72	79	89	48	71	83
4 (high) Socioeconomic quartile						
1 (low) Ability quartile	39	34	57	33	26	37
2 ↑	61	45	61	44	37	67
3 ↓	73	72	79	67	65	77
4 (high) Ability quartile	91	90	92	76	85	93

SOURCE: Cross (1971, p. 7).

There is a good deal of evidence that parental attitudes are an important factor in explaining these differences. A recent study indicated that in blue-collar families, but not in white-collar families, males have first claim on family resources allotted for education.[3]

The less positive parental attitudes toward college-education of daughters in blue-collar families are related to levels of

[3]This finding was based on an analysis of the relationship between college attendance and family size, which showed that, in blue-collar families, as the number of brothers in a family increased, college attendance of their sisters declined precipitously (Adams & Meidam, 1968).

parental educational attainment. A recent report prepared for the U.S. Office of Education showed that the higher the educational level of the parents, the less likely they were to distinguish between the educational needs of sons and daughters.[4]

There is evidence, however, that black parental attitudes have traditionally been relatively more favorable to college education for daughters than for sons. In fact, it has been found that "the black female has historically been given more of an opportunity to advance educationally and occupationally than has the black male" (Coble, 1971, p. 16). There have tended to be relatively more nonwhite women than nonwhite men who were college graduates in the labor force. This pattern is likely to change in the future, because college enrollment rates of black men now exceed those of black women. But rates for blacks of both sexes have been increasing rapidly in recent years. In an analysis of the probable reasons for the relatively favorable attitudes of black parents toward college education for daughters, Bock (1971, pp. 124–125) developed the following hypothesis, which seems to be largely confirmed by employment data from the 1950 and 1960 decennial censuses:

> Negro females have a greater chance of entering professional occupations designated as open to women than Negro men have of entering professions open to men. In fact, it might also be hypothesized that Negro men have a greater chance of entering professional occupations open to women than they have of entering professions open to men.

As we noted in the previous section, black women have been even more heavily concentrated than white women in elementary and secondary school teaching. In recent decades, they have also been moving in substantial numbers into social work and professional nursing. The salaries black women could receive in these professions undoubtedly compared more favorably with the compensation that they could have received in routine white-collar or blue-collar occupations. On the other hand,

---

[4]For example, 73 percent of the mothers with a grade school education hoped for college for their sons, as compared with only 60 percent who had the same desire for their daughters. But among mothers who had attended college, 98 percent wanted their sons to go to college and 97 percent had the same desire for their daughters (Froomkin, 1970, p. 17).

the salaries of black men who went into teaching or social work were not much higher than those they could receive in many types of blue-collar jobs. And, until recently, opportunities for black men have been very poor in the more highly paid professional and managerial occupations. However, there is a good deal of evidence (e.g., Freeman, forthcoming) that black male college graduates are now successfully entering professional and managerial occupations formerly largely closed to them.

Another factor helping to explain the role of low socioeconomic status in inhibiting college attendance of women is early marriage and early childbearing. According to the demographer Kingsley Davis, "the poor marry somewhat earlier" and young women in low-income families tend to have more children than women in high-income brackets (Davis, 1965). He has also shown that illegitimacy occurs more frequently among the poor. Moreover, women tend to marry earlier than men, and marriage is a more important barrier to enrollment of women in higher education than it is for men, although it also seriously inhibits male enrollment (Table 3). In his book *Poor Kids*, Alvin Schorr (1966) has skillfully assembled data of various kinds showing how couples involved in very early marriage and childbearing are especially likely to experience persisting poverty in later years. Thus, young women in this group are likely, also, to encounter financial difficulty in enrolling in higher education at a later point in their lives.

Even so, it is exceedingly important to keep in mind that all the relationships we have been discussing are subject to change. With rising levels of parental education and real family income, the proportion of parents who are likely to be unenthusiastic about college education for their daughters is clearly declining. And sex differences in the relationship between marital status and college enrollment may be changing as more and more college-age young people are affected by a feeling that the burdens as well as the pleasures of child rearing should be shared more equally by parents than in the past.

ACCULTURATION Almost from the moment of birth, boys and girls are subject to a wide variety of cultural influences that tend to prepare them for differentiated roles in life. Little girls are typically given dolls or miniature cooking utensils for toys; boys are generally given trucks and electric trains and mechanical toys. School readers

TABLE 3 *Percentage of population aged 14 to 34, married, by age and sex, and percentage enrolled in college, by marital status, age, and sex, October 1971*

	Men			*Women*		
	Percentage married	*Percentage enrolled*		*Percentage married*	*Percentage enrolled*	
Age		*Nonmarried*	*Married*		*Nonmarried*	*Married*
14 to 34 years	42.6	19.0	10.5	49.5	15.4	3.7
14 to 15	0.3	0.1		0.8	*	
16 to 17	0.7	3.2	3.6	4.4	4.0	2.3
18 to 19	7.7	43.7	12.2	20.1	41.8	4.9
20 to 21	24.5	43.8	19.1	43.5	38.6	9.0
22 to 24	53.8	29.6	16.6	66.5	15.7	4.0
25 to 29	76.0	15.1	10.5	79.3	7.5	2.9
30 to 34	85.0	6.3	6.0	82.3	6.4	2.5

*Less than 0.05.

SOURCE: Computed from data in U.S. Bureau of the Census (1972*a*, p. 31).

show pictures of father going off to work and mother waving good-bye at the window, or of father playing baseball with his sons while mother bakes cookies. Girls play jump rope or tag on the school playground, while boys play ball. At about the seventh or eighth grade, boys take a course in manual training, while girls are taught cooking and sewing.

We are not suggesting that matters ought to be reversed, or that little girls should be forbidden to play with dolls, but rather that there ought to be more freedom of choice. Girls who show signs of a mechanical bent should be given an opportunity to play with mechanical toys and to enter the course on manual training. Boys should not be barred from courses on cooking and sewing if they are interested—in fact, some schools have changed their policies in this respect. And one of the objectives of the women's movement is to alter the exclusively house-wifely image of women in elementary readers and in books for children generally (Hole & Levine, 1972, pp. 333–337).

These changes will come slowly. Even if state and local boards of education show an inclination to sponsor more sex-ually balanced readers, it takes time to produce new books and get them adopted, as somewhat earlier efforts to portray blacks and other minority groups more frequently in school readers have indicated. An especially important need is for a change in the attitudes of teachers, but this, too, will probably come slowly. One factor that is exerting an important influence, however, is the rapid increase in the proportion of women who are successfully combining marriage and careers. These women are increasingly becoming the models observed by their children.

COUNSELING AND CAREER ASPIRATIONS Beginning at about the ninth grade, students are given vocational aptitude or interest tests, but in some cases these tests differ for the two sexes. In a widely used test, the Strong Vocational Interest Blank (S.V.I.B.), girls were not to be scored on certain traditionally male occupations, while boys were not to be scored on certain traditionally female occupations. Protesting against this practice, the American Personnel Guidance Association passed a resolution at its March 1972 meeting calling for the appointment of a committee authorized to negotiate with the S.V.I.B. publishers to revise their instruments so as to eliminate discrimination (see Appendix D for the text of the resolution). The test has since been revised and converted into a single form for both sexes.

Similar criticisms can be made of other vocational interest measures. In view of the rapid changes now occurring in women's vocational roles and the development of many new occupations under the influence of technological and social change, the problems in measuring vocational interest have tended to become more complex. In general, research on these problems as they pertain to women has been inadequate. Predictive accuracy of the tests is low, and most theorizing on the subject has been based on research on predominantly male samples.

Efforts are now being made to combine the most satisfactory items of men's and women's tests into a single test designed to be sexually neutral. At the same time, other efforts are directed toward constructing new tests for men and women separately but opening all vocations to both sexes.[5]

Many accusations have also been made that high school girls are discouraged by teachers and counselors from aspiring to

---

[5]For the results of some recent research on sexual differences in vocational choice, see Rose and Elton (1971) and Cole (1972).

traditionally male occupations. In fact, it is charged that girls are frequently told that work is likely to be subordinate to marriage and child rearing in their future lives, and that it would therefore be foolish to aspire to an occupation requiring long training. Another accusation frequently made is that high school boys are counseled to pursue mathematical studies longer than girls, on the grounds that advanced mathematical training is needed for many of the traditionally male professions, such as engineering.

Another complaint of women who are familiar with high school counseling is that girls from working-class homes are sometimes advised to pursue a vocational, rather than a college preparatory, curriculum, even when they have the ability to prepare for college.

These accusations are not easy to document, because much of the literature on counseling has failed to focus on sex differences.[6]

However, a doctoral thesis based on a study of counselors in Indiana public schools during the 1968–69 school year did tend to confirm the charges, but found significant differences in atti-

[6]An analysis of a random sample of applications for admission to the Berkeley campus of the University of California in the fall of 1972 showed striking differences between male and female applicants in the number of years of mathematics they had had in high school (Sells, 1973, p. 45).

Number of years of high school mathematics recorded in applications for admission as freshmen, Berkeley campus, by sex, 1972

	Men	*Women*
Total Number	42	39
Total Percentage	100%	100%
Two years	7	36
Three years	36	56
Four years	57	8

Responses of women to a questionnaire distributed to members of an upper-division social science class indicated a clear relationship between encouragement by parents, teachers, and peers and decisions to take more than the number of years of high school mathematics required for admission to the University of California (ibid., p. 46).

tudes between male and female counselors. Male counselors tended to associate college-bound girls with traditionally feminine occupations at the semiskilled level, whereas female counselors perceived the college-bound girls as interested in occupations requiring a college education. Indeed, "female counselors tended to expand the traditional image of female work roles and projected women's roles into careers presently occupied predominantly by men" (Friedersdorf, 1969, p. *x*).

In any case, women perform somewhat less well than men on college entrance mathematical aptitude tests, as we shall see at a later point, although their performance on verbal ability tests is superior. But girls who do continue mathematics in high school evidently tend to be those with superior mathematical ability, for there is a consistent tendency for girls to receive better high school grades than boys in mathematics as well as in other subjects (Cross, 1971, p. 138). Furthermore, when we consider the fields in which students major in college, we shall find that almost.as large a percentage of women as of men receive bachelor's degrees in mathematical sciences, although women are considerably less well represented than men among recipients of degrees in fields calling for the use of mathematics as a tool, such as the natural sciences, engineering, and economics.

In an earlier report, we have called attention to three major weaknesses of high school counseling: insufficient numbers of high school counselors, insufficient training for counselors, and lack of easily accessible and useful materials for informing students about curricular and career choices (Carnegie Commission, 1973*b*). The current ratio of students to counselors nationwide is 621 to 1 at the senior high school level and 654 to 1 at the junior high school level. Only 14 percent of the high schools meet the ratio of 250 to 300 students per counselor recommended by Conant in 1959 (Conant, 1959, p. 44).

A recent survey of high school seniors indicated that parents were far more frequently mentioned than counselors or teachers as the most important source of advice on future plans. This was more true in suburban middle-class schools than in urban working-class or semirural mixed schools, where parents also predominated but counselors and teachers were mentioned somewhat more frequently than in suburban schools (Armor, 1969, p. 122). Thus, reduced ratios of students to counselors might have relatively greater effect in schools with less affluent students, whose parents are presumably less well informed and less likely to encourage career aspirations calling for prolonged higher education. Some observers, however, think counseling tends to be poor and that increased counselor-student ratios would not have beneficial effects.

Whatever the relative importance of counseling, career aspirations of women high school graduates have not been very high. Results of a 1960 survey indicated that slightly more than one-fifth expected to train for teaching, and approximately another fifth wished to enter professions and other fields for which a college education would be necessary. But in this second group, the most popular choice was "health fields," for which two years of college would suffice in many cases. This left nearly three-fifths who mentioned office work, housewife, or other pursuits (Folger, Astin, & Bayer, 1970, p. 286).

There are indications that career aspirations of female high school graduates have been rising, although recent data are not precisely comparable with the 1960 data. A statewide survey of 1972 Indiana high school seniors indicated that more than half of the women expected to go on to more advanced education and also that more than half aspired to professional occupations (Purdue University, 1973, pp. 36, 70). Earlier we have noted the changes in career aspirations of college freshman women.

From the age of about 15, or perhaps earlier, every young woman becomes aware of the personal conflicts that must be resolved over the relative roles that marriage, motherhood, and career are likely to play in her future life. As she attempts to work out these conflicts, counselors can perhaps be most helpful in encouraging her to aspire to a career that is consistent with her abilities. If she responds that this is inappropriate because she hopes to marry, she needs to be informed that married women are increasingly returning to the labor force when they no longer have young children in the home and that this is likely to be even more true in the future. Thus her life as a whole is likely to be more rewarding if she aspires to an occupation that will challenge her abilities and interests. We are not suggesting that every woman who marries should definitely plan on returning to work. Surely our society would miss the immensely valuable volunteer activities of married women if this were to happen. But at the high school stage a young woman should keep her options open, and, as suggested earlier, she should be encouraged to continue the study of mathematics throughout high school in view of the growing number of occupations in which knowledge of mathematics is important.

Caroline Bird (with Briller, 1972, p. 132) links the rising demand for continuing education for mature women in the 1960s to the pattern of early marriage and immersion in child rearing of women in the late 1940s and 1950s, suggesting that many of these women who did not participate in or did not complete a college education at an earlier stage of their lives began to recognize a need for it later.

Counselors, teachers, and parents should also keep in mind that sex roles are clearly changing and may change more dramatically in the future. Effective contraceptives have long since begun to effect important changes. There is increasing pressure for parental leave for both fathers and mothers, and eventually employer policies may no longer be geared to the assumption that it will always be the married female employee rather than the married male employee who will take leave to care for a sick child. Already there are beginning to be some indications that young fathers are deliberately seeking part-time work to share child-rearing responsibilities more evenly with their wives. With rising real incomes, the combined part-time earnings of two parents will increasingly suffice to provide a reasonably adequate standard of living.

We have no way of knowing whether sex differences in occupational choice might eventually disappear under the influence of less sex-oriented attitudes on the part of students, parents, teachers, and counselors. Anthropologists have studied primitive cultures in which sex roles and family structure are very different from those to which we are accustomed, but they do not provide much basis for predicting what changes might occur in societies that have evolved very differently. Occupational analysts point out the tendency for women to be more inclined than men toward people-oriented occupations like nursing and social work and less inclined toward occupations calling for abstract thinking or mechanical knowledge. These differences may be entirely attributable to acculturation, but they may also be intimately associated with the biological differences between the two sexes. Yet it must be kept in mind that there is a great deal of overlapping in occupational interests between the sexes—differences are anything but clearcut. Only time and major changes in acculturation will tell us whether the differences will be greatly modified.

DISCRIMINATION IN ADMISSIONS? The proportion of students entering higher education who are women is now close to 50 percent, but the relative representation of women as undergraduates varies rather widely in various types of institutions. Discrimination against women is clearly much less widespread than in the past, but the choices of women may be more restricted than those of men because of discrimination on the part of some types of institutions.

Before considering variations in the representation of women in different types of institutions, however, we need to examine somewhat more carefully their relative performance on tests widely used in college admissions. Data for mean scores on tests administered by the American College Testing Program indicate, as we have noted earlier, that women do somewhat less well than men on mathematics tests (Table 4). They also do somewhat less well on natural sciences tests and slightly less well on social sciences tests. But they perform better than men on English tests, and their overall performance is only slightly below that of men.

However, women receive higher grades in college than men. On the basis of undergraduate responses to the Carnegie Commission Survey of Faculty and Student Opinion, 1969, with respect to their grade-point averages, percentages of women with averages of B or higher exceeded those of men, and percentages

TABLE 4
Mean ACT scores of college-bound students, 1966–67

Test	Male	Female	Difference
English	17.8	20.0	—2.2
Mathematics	20.1	17.8	2.3
Social studies	20.1	19.9	0.2
Natural sciences	21.4	19.4	2.0
Composite	20.0	19.4	0.6

SOURCE: Cross (1971, p. 136).

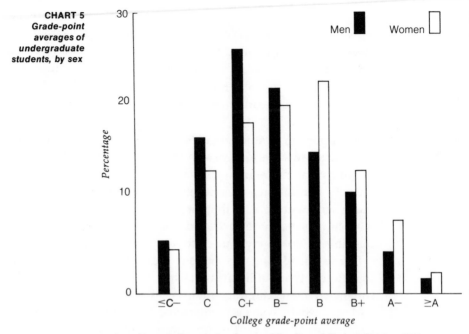

CHART 5
Grade-point averages of undergraduate students, by sex

Men ■ Women □

Percentage

College grade-point average

SOURCE: Carnegie Commission Survey of Faculty and Student Opinion, 1969.

of men with averages of B– or lower exceeded those of women (Chart 5). Data from other sources also indicate that women tend to receive higher grades than men in college. But a more significant finding in relation to admissions practices is that women receive higher grades than men in *relation* to both their ACT scores and their high school grade-point averages.[7] There is also evidence that the performance of men is more variable in relation to test scores, that is, less consistent with what test scores would predict.

It might be suspected that this tendency of women to receive higher grades is largely explained by their majoring in fields like the humanities and some of the so-called softer social sciences rather than in relatively rigorous fields requiring extensive use of mathematics, such as the sciences, engineering, economics, statistics, and mathematics itself. But this does not turn out to be the case. Women consistently receive higher grades than

[7]This finding is also based on an analysis of data from the 1969 Carnegie Commission survey. The survey was sponsored jointly by the Commission and the American Council on Education, which has also published a number of reports based on the data.

men in field after field, with a margin of between one-half of a grade point and a full grade point, depending on the field. Information from the Educational Testing Service also confirms the tendency of women to receive higher grades in college in relation to entering test scores.

Although women tend to score slightly less well than men on tests administered to college applicants, their high school grades, which are the best predictors of performance in college, tend to be considerably higher than those of men. Studies going back as far as 1929 have shown better grades for females from elementary school through college. The difference at the high school level is appreciable. Among 1960 Project Talent seniors, 51 percent of the girls and 39 percent of the boys reported high school averages of "mostly As and Bs" or above, and the 1969 SCOPE data indicated similar percentages (Cross, 1971, p. 137).[8]

Among the types of institutions in the Carnegie Commission classification,[9] women form relatively small proportions of undergraduates in private Research Universities I (the most research-oriented universities and in public Research Universities II (the moderately research-oriented universities. See Table 5). The explanation in the first case is clear. This group of private institutions includes a number of formerly all-male universities such as Harvard, Princeton, and Yale. Princeton and Yale have recently begun to admit women, but in relatively small numbers. Harvard and Radcliffe have long had a coordinate relationship, and Radcliffe undergraduates have been attending Harvard classes since the mid-1940s. As recently as the fall of 1971, the ratio of Harvard to Radcliffe undergraduates was 3.7 to 1, but reducing the ratio to 2.5 to 1 is now under consideration, and a further reduction will be possible if space for additional students can be found.

---

[8]Project Talent is a large-scale longitudinal study of about 440,000 students included in a scientifically selected sample of 1,353 secondary schools who took a battery of tests in March 1960. The study was conducted at the University of Pittsburgh (Flanagan & Cooley, 1966). SCOPE is a longitudinal study based on a large sample of high school graduates in four states, conducted at the Center for Research and Development on Higher Education, University of California, Berkeley.

[9]For a description of the criteria used in developing the classification and a list of institutions in each group, by state, see Carnegie Commission (forthcoming).

TABLE 5 *Women as a percentage of undergraduate students, graduate students, and faculty members, b* type and control of institution, 1969

Type of institution	Undergraduates		Graduates		Faculty	
	Public	Private	Public	Private	Public	Privat
Research universities I	41.7	27.4	27.4	23.5	12.9	10.9
Research universities II	30.5	44.2	22.6	17.2	12.8	13.2
Doctoral-granting universities I and II	44.2	39.1	22.9	22.1	13.1	19.9
Comprehensive universities and colleges I	54.4	43.5	33.8	34.0	24.8	16.1
Comprehensive universities and colleges II	63.2	57.4	29.6	58.3	23.5	29.6
Liberal arts colleges I	*	60.3	*	55.3	*	22.6
Liberal arts colleges II	53.3	59.0	*	20.2	19.5	33.2
Two-year colleges	41.2	41.5	*	*	23.5	40.1

*Percentages not reported because number of respondents was small or zero.
SOURCE: Carnegie Commission Survey of Faculty and Student Opinion, 1969.

Formerly all-male institutions have tended to make room fo women by increasing the size of the student body, rather tha by reducing the number of males. The main problem in thi process appears to be the provision of additional dormitory an classroom space. Both Princeton and Williams[10] found that the could admit women at a marginal educational cost per studen that was below their tuition and fee charges and very muc below their quite heavily subsidized average cost of education per student.[11] This was possible in part because women tende to choose fields of study that were not especially popular wit men, thus permitting the institution to take advantage of eco nomies of scale by utilizing faculty and other resources in thos fields more intensively.

Among other institutions classified in private Researc Universities I, Cornell and Stanford have been said over th years to pursue policies that held down the number of wome admitted, and the California Institute of Technology, with it

[10]Williams College is classified in the private Liberal Arts I group.
[11]See the discussion in Carnegie Commission (1972*b*, pp. 42–43).

heavy emphasis on the sciences, has always been a predominantly male institution.

As for public Research Universities II, the main explanation of the low ratio of women to men in this group seems to be that a number of these universities are land-grant institutions with a tradition of heavy emphasis on agriculture, engineering, and natural sciences. In general, however, ratios of women to men are higher in public than in private universities.

The ratio is also much higher in public than in private Comprehensive Universities and Colleges I. Here the explanation may well be chiefly that many of the public institutions in this group are former state teachers colleges that have recently broadened their programs by adding some predominantly male programs like business administration or engineering and some predominantly female programs like nursing. As teachers colleges, they probably attracted more women than men, and, by adding both traditionally male and traditionally female fields, have not changed their proportions of each sex a great deal. On the other hand, the private institutions in this group are somewhat less oriented to teacher training, and some of them are technological or engineering institutes that have attracted chiefly males. Even so, this may well be a group in which some institutions have deliberately held down the number of women admitted.

Ratios of women to men are especially high in Comprehensive Universities and Colleges II. Here the explanation undoubtedly is that these institutions are largely involved in teacher training. Ratios of women to men are also high in both groups of private liberal arts colleges. There are a number of single-sex institutions in these two groups, but, as we shall see in the next section, the number of all-male institutions has declined more sharply than the number of women's colleges. Another reason for the high ratio of women to men in liberal arts colleges is that many students in liberal arts colleges have traditionally trained to be teachers while majoring in liberal arts subjects.

Women form 41.5 percent of the students in private two-year colleges, some of which began as "finishing schools," and 41.2 percent of the students in public two-year colleges. Public two-year colleges have relatively more students from low-income families than any other group of institutions, and, as we have seen, women from low-income families are less likely to enter college than men in such families.[12]

Despite rapid increases in the enrollment of blacks and members of other minority groups since the mid-1960s, blacks represented slightly less than 9 percent and persons of Spanish origin just under 3 percent of all students enrolled in degree-credit programs in college in the fall of 1972, according to a preliminary report from the Census Bureau's *Current Population Survey* (U.S. Bureau of the Census, 1973a). Their proportions of the college-age population were about 12 percent and slightly more than 5 percent, respectively. Separate data were not provided on Japanese-American and Chinese-American students, but for some years they have been well represented in higher education.[13]

Because colleges and universities do not frequently make available data relating to the test scores and high school records of admitted and rejected students separately by sex, it is difficult to determine how widespread sexual discrimination in undergraduate admissions may be. Cross (1971, pp. 150–151) presents data derived from 1969 College Entrance Examination Board reports on one prestigious private four-year liberal arts college and on one state university. In the liberal arts college, lower percentages of female than of male applicants were accepted even among those who were in the top fifth of their high school classes, and the difference widened among those ranking lower in high school. On the basis of Scholastic Aptitude Test (SAT) scores, the ratios of admissions to applications were approximately the same for those with very high, 700–800, scores, but dropped off much more sharply for women than for men as SAT scores fell. The picture was very similar for the state university.

---

[12]These patterns of sex differences among institutions are generally consistent with those shown by American Council on Education data on entering college freshmen, including those for 1972, the most recent year available.

[13]Because enrollment rates of black women fall below those of black men by a smaller margin than is the case for white women in relation to white men (Table 1), black women represent a slightly larger percentage of female college enrollment than black men represent of male college enrollment. According to American Council on Education data on entering college freshmen, this was particularly true in predominantly white universities in 1971 (Bayer, 1972, p. 11).

Other evidence of discrimination in undergraduate admissions has been developed in special experiments, such as one conducted at the University of Wisconsin, in which bogus applications for admissions using fictitious names were submitted to 240 colleges. They found that a fictitious female applicant with high grades was as likely to be accepted as a male applicant with equally good grades, but male applicants with low ability were much more likely to be accepted than female applicants with the same low credentials ("Race, Sex Bias," 1970, p. 8).[14]

Under Title IX of the Education Amendments of 1972, sex discrimination is prohibited in the admission of students to institutions of higher education receiving federal financial assistance, but the provision does not apply to undergraduate education in private institutions. There is also an exception for undergraduate education in public institutions that have traditionally and continually from their establishment admitted students of only one sex.

The Commission believes that, in general, colleges and universities should use the same standards in admitting men and women. In fact, there is a case for using a lower cutoff point for women on high school grades and on test scores, because of the evidence that women receive higher grades in college even in *relation* to high school grades and test scores than do men. At the same time we have taken a strong position in favor of maintaining diversity in American higher education. In one of our earliest reports we emphasized the importance of strengthening the colleges founded for Negroes, and in the next section we shall discuss the unique contribution of women's colleges.[15] We recognize that there have been special considerations—especially, perhaps, reluctance to reduce the number of men admitted while not wishing to increase the overall size of the institution markedly—that have led formerly all-male institutions to

---

[14]Another factor that has been cited as restricting the relative number of women who can be admitted to coeducational institutions is the practice of requiring freshman women but not men to live in on-campus housing. These regulations can discriminate against women if campus dormitory space is limited in relation to the number of qualified applicants (Cross, 1972, p. 36).

[15]See Carnegie Commission (1971).

move slowly in increasing the number of women admitted. A similar problem confronts a coeducational institution like Stanford. However, we believe that decisions on this important matter may not best be made by all-male boards of trustees, and we have previously recommended adequate representation of women and members of minority groups on boards of trustees.[16]

The great majority of public institutions are now affected by the antidiscrimination provisions of the Educational Amendments of 1972 in admitting undergraduates, and we believe that decisions on the important matter of sexual balance among undergraduates in private institutions should be made on the basis of the most careful consideration. Their deliberations should give due weight to certain undesirable social and educational consequences of high male-female ratios. For example, some Harvard undergraduates give up any attempt to date "Cliffies" because the competition is so intense. And, if some coeds tend to be inhibited from active participation in class discussions—a matter we shall consider more fully in the next section—there is little question that this hesitancy will be intensified if women are a tiny minority in a class. The argument in favor of maintaining a high male-female ratio on the ground that male alumni are likely to give more heavily to their colleges than female alumnae does not find much support in the facts. Some of the leading women's colleges rank very high on such measures as endowment per student and annual average contributions by alumnae.

RECOMMEN-DATION
Recommendation 1: The first priority in the nation's commitment to equal educational opportunity for women should be placed on changing policies in pre-elementary, elementary, and secondary school programs that tend to deter women from aspiring to equality with men in their career goals. This will require vigorous pursuit of appropriate policies by state and local boards of education and implementation by school administrators, teachers, and counselors.

For example, high school counselors and teachers should en-

[16]See Carnegie Commission (1973c, p. 35).

courage women who aspire to professional careers to choose appropriate educational programs. They should also encourage them to pursue mathematical studies throughout high school, because of the increasing importance of mathematics as a background, not only in engineering and the natural sciences, but also in other fields, such as the social sciences and business administration.

Recommendation 2: There should be no discrimination on the basis of sex in the use of either high school grades or test scores as admissions criteria.

Recommendation 3: Efforts to eliminate sex bias from vocational interest questionnaires should be encouraged, as should research designed to achieve a more adequate understanding of similarities and differences in patterns of vocational choices among men and women.

Recommendation 4: Policies that prevent part-time study or that discriminate against admission of adults desirous of continuing their education should be liberalized to permit enrollment of qualified mature men and women whose education has been interrupted because of family responsibilities or for other reasons. High school or college records should not be ruled inapplicable as evidence of eligibility for admission simply because the records were acquired some years earlier.

Although relatively fewer women than men from low-income families attend college, entering women freshmen are slightly more likely than men to mention financing their education as a "major concern" or of "some concern" (American Council on Education, 1972, pp. 22 and 30). But there is no clearcut evidence of discrimination against women in the provision of scholarships or grants. Among the 1972 entering college freshmen, almost exactly the same percentages of men (21.6 percent) and of women (21.9 percent) mentioned scholarships and grants as major sources of support (ibid.). Given the somewhat higher income levels of women's parents, it is not surprising that relatively more of the women (60.4 percent) than of the men (47.8 percent) reported that parental or family aid or gifts were major sources of support.[17] A 1971 follow-up study of 1967 entering college freshmen indicated that a considerably larger percentage of men than of women had had income from employment (Appendix A, Table A-6), and opportunities for part-time employment frequently seem to be more favorable for men than for women in college communities. This factor, as well as a greater sense of dependence on parents, may help to explain why slightly more women than men express concern about financing their education.

As we have noted in earlier reports, the major existing federal loan program, the Insured Student Loan Program, is inadequate in many respects, not the least of which is the difficulty that repayment arrangements are likely to present to married women. The Carnegie Commission has recommended a National Student Loan Program, which differs in many respects from the Insured Student Loan Program. In contrast with the 10-year repayment period and the fixed annual schedule of repayments under the Insured Student Loan Program, the national program we have recommended calls for repayments based on income and a variable repayment period ranging from about 20 to 30 years. For borrowers filing a joint tax return, the appropriate rate of repayment for the combined debt of the husband and wife would be applied to their combined income. The initial repayment would not be due until two years after earning an undergraduate degree or one year after earning a graduate degree, and repayment could be deferred during any period in which the income of the borrower (or the combined income of husband and wife in the case of a borrower filing a joint tax return) falls below a certain minimum subsistence level.[18] Married women are likely to have young children, especially

[17]One of the most comprehensive studies of student sources of support ever conducted was recently published by the California State Scholarship and Loan Commission (1972). The results indicated that the percentages of men and women who were recipients of student aid were almost identical in each of the four groups of institutions surveyed—the University of California campuses, the California State University and Colleges, independent colleges, and community colleges—though the percentages receiving student aid were highest in the independent colleges with their relatively high student costs (about 39 percent) and lowest in the community colleges (about 6 percent).

[18]For other provisions, see Carnegie Commission on Higher Education (1970*d*, Section 3).

during the first 10 years after graduation. Thus, the longer repayment period and basing the amount of repayment on the combined income of husband and wife would make indebtedness far less burdensome for a married woman who leaves the labor force while she has young children.

We have also urged the full funding of the Basic Opportunity Grants program enacted under the Educational Amendments of 1972. This would encourage college enrollment for young people of both sexes from low-income families and would also widen their freedom of choice among institutions.

5. Women as Undergraduates

Thus far we have been considering the factors that determine whether women enter college and the types of institutions they attend. In the present section, we shall shift our attention to their experiences as undergraduates as compared with those of men.

Women have slightly higher dropout rates than men, but those who stay in college receive their bachelor's degrees more quickly. The 1971 follow-up study of 1967 entering college freshmen by the American Council on Education is especially illuminating on this range of questions. The proportion of women who had received a bachelor's degree by the summer of 1971 substantially exceeded that of men (Appendix A, Table A–7), but the percentage of women who had received an associate degree fell slightly below that of men.[1] Also indicative of the more rapid progress of women was the fact that considerably larger percentages of men expected to be attending college full time as undergraduates the following fall (Appendix A, Table A–8).

However, there are significant differences in dropout patterns of men and women. Women were somewhat more likely to report having dropped out permanently, and less likely to have dropped out temporarily than men in the 1971 study (Appendix A, Table A-9). These differences were doubtless related to the greater likelihood of women to report marriage (or, of

---

[1]This may have been related to the lower rate of enrollment of women than of men in two-year colleges. A similar 1970 follow-up study, on the other hand, indicated a slightly higher percentage of women than of men receiving associate degrees (Astin, 1972, p. 10). For additional information on retention rates, see Appendix B.

61

course, pregnancy) as a major reason for dropping out (Appendix A, Table A–10). On the other hand, the chief reason men were more likely to drop out temporarily was that they were much more likely to have spent time in military service.[2] However, it should be kept in mind that many dropouts of both sexes return to college at a later point, and that four years after entry is too short a time period for accurately measuring "permanent" dropout rates.

These follow-up surveys also provide additional evidence of the superior academic records of women. Men were much more likely to report having failed one or more courses (Appendix A, Table A-9). On the other hand, women were considerably more likely to report having graduated with honors and having been elected to a student honor society.

Contrary to a widely held impression that women's chances of becoming student leaders are poor except in women's colleges, the 1971 follow-up survey showed that the percentage of women who had been elected to a student office was higher than that of men, and that this relationship held consistently for two-year colleges, four-year colleges, and universities (Appendix A, Table A-9). Other data show, as we might expect, that the offices held by women are especially likely to be editor of the yearbook, a literary magazine, or the campus paper (but not on large campuses). They are highly unlikely to be student body president or class president in coeducational colleges, although their chances are better in small than in large institutions (Oltman, 1970, p. 10).

In view of the role played by marriage and childbearing in interrupting the progress of women in higher education, policy changes that make it possible for a student to earn a bachelor's degree in less than four years seem particularly desirable for women. The Commission has recommended several approaches to accelerating undergraduate education—encouraging entering students to take examinations that would provide credit for advanced standing, encouraging high school seniors to enroll in college on nearby campuses or to be enrolled as

[2]Another table based on the 1971 follow-up survey (not included in this report) showed that 10.3 percent of the men, as contrasted with 0.2 percent of the women, had been in military service during the preceding half year. On the other hand, 19.8 percent of the women reported that they had been housewives during the preceding half year.

freshmen in nearby colleges, and the adoption of a three-year B.A. program.[3] Experience in the three years since these recommendations were made suggests that the first and second of these approaches are gaining greater acceptance than the third. Although a number of institutions have studied the possibility of a three-year B.A., some have rejected it, and many of those that have adopted it require as many, or nearly as many, credit hours under a three-year program as they do under a four-year program.[4] On the other hand, there are examples of imaginative policy changes that have combined acceleration with other changes, such as year-round operation.[5] We continue to believe that an important argument for acceleration is the substantial degree of overlap between what is taught in the last two years of high school and what is taught in the first two years of college.

The Commission has also urged more flexible patterns of participation, including stopping out for a year or two between high school and college or, say, between the sophomore and junior years. However, we see potential disadvantages in stopping out for a woman, in view of the rapid rate at which the percentage of women who are married and have children increases with advancing age in the college-age years. Women are probably better off to complete their undergraduate education at as early an age as possible. Even so, the changes that are occurring in sex roles may ultimately mean that stopping out will be just as desirable for a woman as for a man.

CHOICES OF FIELDS　The fields women have traditionally chosen as majors in college are closely related to the types of professional jobs in which women have been represented in large proportions (Appendix

---

[3] For a further discussion of these recommendations, see Carnegie Commission (1970c).

[4] See the discussion in Carnegie Commission (1972a , Section 4). See also "Three-Year Degree Not Catching on as Anticipated" (1973).

[5] One of the most interesting and carefully developed examples is the recently adopted chemistry curriculum at Southern Methodist University, which includes (1) three-year B.S. and four-year master's degree programs, (2) an off-campus learning experience, (3) a multitrack system involving self-paced learning, (4) greater emphasis on applied science, e.g., environmental chemistry, and (5) a plan for the recruitment and education of greater numbers of minority-ethnic and women students.

A, Tables A-11 and A-12). To some degree their choices, especially their preferences for the humanities and arts, have also reflected the cultural interests of women who have expected to devote themselves to being spouses and mothers after college. In any event, women have been considerably more likely than men to major in the humanities and arts or in education. They have also been represented in larger proportions in such fields as home economics, library science, social work, and nursing. In the social sciences, they have tended to "shy away" from economics but to be relatively well represented in psychology and sociology. And they have been considerably less likely than men to major in the natural sciences, business administration, premedical or predental programs, or law. Not only have they preferred fields that lead to traditionally female professions, but they have also tended to avoid fields requiring extensive application of mathematical reasoning. As we noted in the previous section, however, the percentage of women receiving their bachelor's degrees in mathematics is only slightly below that for men.

To a very considerable extent, the changes in choices of fields that occurred between 1948 and 1970—as indicated by the distribution of bachelor's and first-professional degrees awarded—accentuated these patterns. The largest single change for women was an increase from about 24 to 36 percent in the proportion receiving degrees in education. This reflected the impact on the demand for teachers of the rapid increases in the number of children in school during the 1950s and the greater part of the 1960s, as the babies born in the high birthrate period of the late 1940s and early 1950s moved through the school system. The proportion of women receiving degrees in the humanities and arts also rose slightly, probably likewise reflecting to some extent the huge increase in the demand for schoolteachers, for many students preparing to teach major in these fields. The same factor may have been an influence in the increase in the proportion receiving degrees in the social sciences as well as the good job opportunities outside of teaching in some social sciences, e.g., clinical psychology.

In very recent years there have been signs of a reversal of these trends. For one thing, the market for schoolteachers has been steadily worsening for the last four years and may be expected to continue to be relatively unfavorable for the foreseeable future, because the children now entering elementary school were born in a period of steadily declining numbers of live births.[6] We referred in Section 3 to the decline in the percentage of entering women freshmen who expected to be schoolteachers and the shift to other fields, especially health professions (Appendix A, Table A-4).

Significant changes occurred in the relative representation of women receiving bachelor's degrees in a number of traditionally male fields in the latter half of the 1960s that do not show up in the 1948 and 1970 comparisons presented in Appendix A, Table A-12. These fields included agriculture (which was attracting both men and women in increased numbers because of the growing concern about environmental problems), computer science and systems analysis, physics, and mathematical sciences. There was also an increase throughout the 1950s and 1960s in the relative representation of women among those receiving degrees in health professions.

Especially dramatic indications of changing choices of fields appeared in the results of the Carnegie Commission's fall 1971 enrollment survey (Peterson, 1972). By the fall of 1971 it was very apparent that college students were aware of the changes that were occurring in the job market for college graduates, some of which were temporary, reflecting the impact of the 1970–71 recession, while others were of longer-run significance. Students were also influenced by concern about urban problems and the environment. The survey revealed, for both sexes combined, pronounced increases in enrollment in forestry (reflecting the growing concern with conservation), social work, nursing, and biological sciences, in that order, and declines occurring in engineering, education, ethnic studies, humanities, and physical sciences (again in order of the percentage decline). But women differed from men in that the percentage increases in their enrollment in architecture, agriculture, business, and urban studies/city planning were much more marked, and they enrolled in slightly increasing numbers in the physical sciences and engineering. "Conversely," the report on the survey commented, "there is one instance of dramatic movement of men into a women's field" (ibid., p. 15). This was a pronounced

[6]See the more extensive discussion of the changing job market in Carnegie Commission (1973a).

increase in the number of males enrolled in nursing. This shift was probably motivated partly by the favorable job market in nursing, as contrasted with a number of other occupations, and partly by the fact that men, as well as women, were beginning to be less influenced by former conceptions of appropriate male and female careers.

In Section 1, we pointed out that there were relatively fewer women at each successive stage of higher education (Chart 1). This is true, not only for higher education as a whole, but in virtually every field and in every type of institution. Chart 6 shows the decline in the percentage who were women at each stage in selected groups of fields in Research Universities I in 1969. The corresponding data for other types of institutions of higher education are presented in Appendix C, Table C-2. As undergraduates in Research Universities I, women comprised a majority of the students majoring in education, fine arts, and "new professions," which includes such fields as nursing, social work, home economics, and library science, as well as many fields in which the proportion of men students was undoubtedly higher than in these traditionally female fields.[7] Women formed a sizable minority of students enrolled in the humanities and social sciences, but relatively small proportions in such fields as the biological and physical sciences, business, and the medicine and law group. In all fields, including those in which women comprised a majority of the undergraduates, the declining representation of women at each successive stage, and the exceedingly small percentages of women at the full professor stage, are apparent.

The pattern was similar in other groups of institutions, but in Liberal Arts Colleges I—a group that includes the more selective women's colleges as well as men's colleges and coeducational colleges—relatively more women were in such fields as the physical and biological sciences among undergraduates as well as among faculty members. (Relatively few of these colleges have graduate education programs.) There were also relatively more women in these fields at all stages in Comprehensive Universities and Colleges than in universities, but the percentages of women in these fields were smaller than in Lib-

---

[7]For a classification of the fields included in each group of fields, see Appendix C, Table C-1.

CHART 6 *Women as a percentage of persons at successive levels of higher education, by field, Research Universities I*

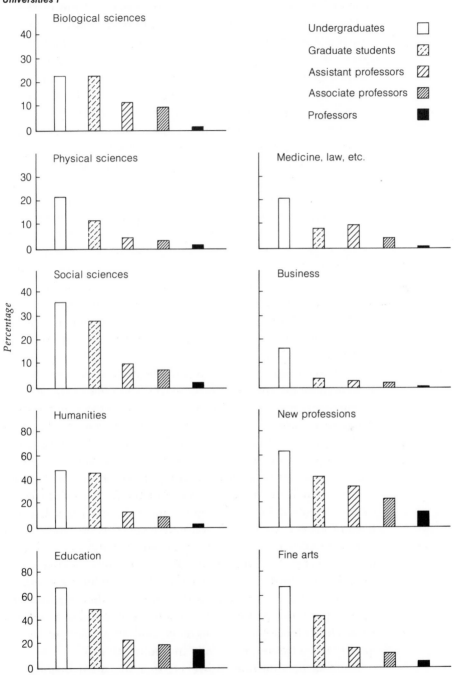

SOURCE: Carnegie Commission Survey of Faculty and Student Opinion, 1969.

eral Arts Colleges I. Another way of putting this point is that fields tended to be especially sex-differentiated in universities. The pattern of few women in traditionally male fields, especially in the higher ranks of the faculty, appears to have its origins, at least to some degree, in the relative reluctance of women to major in these fields in universities. But it may also be to some extent a chicken and egg proposition—undergraduate women may be discouraged from entering these fields because the sex composition of their faculties suggests that women have little chance of success in them.

There also remains the possibility that faculty members in leading research universities, who tend not only to be overwhelmingly male but also to have prestigious reputations, are more likely to discourage women from entering their fields than are faculty members in comprehensive colleges and liberal arts colleges. There is some evidence that this tendency is not confined to traditionally male fields. At Stanford, the 1972 report of the Committee on the Education and Employment of Women in the University includes a number of quotations from women students indicating that this type of discouragement has occurred at that university (see the excerpts from the report in Appendix D).

Women are being affected to a much greater extent, relatively, than men by the steady worsening in the job market for schoolteachers that has occurred during the last four years and may be expected to continue in the coming years. As we noted in Section 3, about one-half of all employed women college graduates have been in the field of elementary and secondary schoolteaching in recent decades. The comparable proportion for men is about 10 percent. Both men and women have been shifting out of education majors as undergraduates in recent years, but this has not yet occurred at the graduate level. The shift away from undergraduate majors in education will eventually result in a decidedly shrinking supply of college graduates seeking teaching jobs, but the demand side of the job market for teachers may turn out to be more favorable than some predictions have indicated if increased funds are forthcoming for child-care centers, early child development programs, and improvement in the quality of education, especially in ghetto schools.

There is no question, however, that the great majority of women who graduate will have to seek jobs in fields other than teaching, and a major question for the remainder of the 1970s is whether there will be enough job opportunities in other occupations to offset the decline in demand for teachers. Nursing and allied health occupations have been promising fields for women, but there are indications that long-time shortages of nurses, except for those with advanced or specialized training, are beginning to disappear in most urban areas. Shortages of allied health workers may also begin to disappear as increasing numbers of students flow into the health fields. Social work has had chronic shortages in recent decades, but the job market in this field is currently depressed, largely as a result of cutbacks in state and federal funds for programs employing social workers. Thus, college-educated women will have to seek employment in professional and managerial positions that have tended to be regarded as male occupations. We have noted signs of progress in the ratio of women to men employed in a number of these occupations, but the movement is just beginning. It will need maximum encouragement from both institutions of higher education and employers.[8]

Especially important in colleges and universities are policies aimed at encouraging women to enter fields of study that have been regarded as traditionally male. Our data suggest a special need for such changes in policies in this respect in leading research universities. But women should also be encouraged, within the humanities, to study languages like Russian and Japanese, rather than English or French. In addition, we have found a current demand for bilingual teachers who know Spanish and English. It is particularly important for colleges and universities to adjust their resources to changing student choices of fields in the next few years while enrollment continues to grow, for it will be much more difficult to achieve flexibility in this respect as enrollment levels off in the late 1970s and early 1980s.

An interesting effort is under way at the College of Engineering, University of California, Berkeley, to attract more women to choose undergraduate majors in engineering. Currently, only 2 percent of Berkeley's engineering students are women, but this exceeds the national average of 1 percent. The campaign to

---

[8]Colleges and universities that have been extensively engaged in training teachers will face especially difficult adjustments. For recommendations relating to these adjustments, see Carnegie Commission (1973*a*, Section 5).

entice more women into the field includes a special recruitin;
brochure, a counseling program, and visits by both students an•
faculty—male and female—to high schools and communit•
colleges in the area ("Women Sought by Engineering," 1973)
The effort is motivated in part by the current predictions of
coming shortage of engineers resulting from the sharp drop i•
enrollment in engineering that followed the appearance o•
unemployment among engineers in the late 1960s.[9] Similar pro
grams had been started earlier at the Los Angeles campus of th•
University of California and at Stanford.

Emphatically, however, we are not suggesting that womer
should be encouraged to enter traditionally male fields solel•
for job market reasons. We believe that women should have th•
opportunity to develop their mental capacities and utilize thei
abilities in whatever field of study is of greatest interest to them•

WOMEN'S COLLEGES   Women's colleges have played a unique role in the develop
ment of higher education for women. Many of them were es
tablished in the middle and latter part of the nineteenth centu·
ry, when many private colleges and universities, and som•
public institutions, were exclusively male. Over the decades•
however, the proportion of institutions that were exclusivel•
male declined sharply, the proportion of those for womer
declined more slowly, and coeducational institutions came t•
be overwhelmingly predominant in higher education (Table 6)
According to a study recently published by the Educationa•
Testing Service, about half of the women's colleges existing ir
1960 became coeducational or went out of business betweer
1960 and 1972. Moreover, in 1960 three out of every fiv•
women's colleges were Catholic, and they were the women's in·
stitutions most affected by developments of the last decade. B•
1972 their numbers had dropped from 185 to 73, chiefly as •
result of a shift to coeducational status ("Number of Women'•
Colleges Down," 1973). The total number of women's college•
was down to 146, and they enrolled less than 10 percent of al•
female students.

Not only has the number of women's colleges declined, bu•
the proportion of men on their faculties and in their administra
tive ranks has steadily increased. This has come about, at leas•

___

[9]For additional discussion of changes in demand and supply in engineering, se•
Carnegie Commission (1973a, pp. 119–127).

		Sex status			
Year	*Number of institutions*	*Total (percent)*	*Men only*	*Women only*	*Coeducational*
1870	582	100	59	12	29
1890	1,082	100	37	20	43
1910	1,083	100	27	15	58
1930	1,322	100	15	16	69
1960	2,028	100	12	13	76
1970	2,573	100	6	8	86

TABLE 6 Institutions of higher education, by sex status, selected years, 1870 to 1970

SOURCES: Newcomer (1959, p. 37); and U.S. Office of Education (1972, p. 86).

in part, because of the increasing proportion of women scholars who are married and who are not available to teach in women's colleges because they prefer jobs in areas where their husbands are employed. In the 1960s, the trend of increasing numbers of male staff was also probably encouraged by enrollment of male students in courses on women's college campuses under various types of exchange relationships with neighboring male or coeducational institutions. These arrangements doubtless made the women's colleges more attractive to male teachers.

In the last few years, however, there have been signs of resistance to these trends, at least among some of the more highly selective women's colleges, and the women's movement clearly has played a role in stimulating this growing resistance. Recently, Mount Holyoke, Smith, and Wellesley have all made carefully considered decisions to remain single-sex institutions. "While the conditions that historically justified the founding of women's colleges have clearly changed to some extent," the Mount Holyoke Trustees Committee on Coeducation concluded in the fall of 1971, "they remain in the less tangible but still potent areas of attitude, feeling, spirit" (Bird, 1972, p. 65). The Smith report commented that "at the present time, when the status and roles of women in American society are being reexamined with a view to their improvement, an important option that should remain open to women is attendance at a college of the highest caliber in which women are unquestionably firstclass citizens" (ibid.).

In announcing Wellesley's decision to remain a women's college, President Barbara Newell said:

The research we have clearly demonstrates that women's colleges produce a disproportionate number of women leaders and women in responsible positions in society; it does demonstrate that the higher proportion of women on the faculty the higher the motivation for women students (Kovach, 1973).

Various studies have shown that women who attend women's colleges have academic records superior to those of their coeducational sisters, on the basis of such measures as persistence, proportion going on to graduate education, and proportion receiving Ph.D.'s.[10] In their study of the vocational and educational interests of college students, Astin and Panos (1969, p 144) concluded:

> Both men and women are more likely to drop out of college if they atten a coeducational institution. . . . The largest single environmental effec observed among the noncoeducational institutions occurs in the men colleges (technological institutions excepted) which tend to stee students out of potential careers in engineering and physical scienc and careers in law. Women's colleges do not show many pronounce effects on the various student outcomes, except for a slight tendency t channel students out of education and teaching and into the natur sciences. Colleges for men and colleges for women both have a sligl tendency to stimulate the student's interest in majoring in arts an humanities and in attending graduate school. . . .

In an analysis of bachelor's degrees awarded in 1969, we found that about 13 percent of those graduating from the Seven Siste colleges,[11] as compared with about 7 percent of all women receiving bachelor's degrees that year, were awarded degrees in the natural sciences and mathematics.[12]

Clearly, these differences cannot be attributed solely to the impact of women's colleges on their students. To some extent they result from the characteristics of women who enroll in

---

[10] Information supplied by Alexander W. Astin on the basis of unpublished dat from studies conducted by the American Council on Education.

[11] Barnard, Bryn Mawr, Mount Holyoke, Radcliffe, Smith, Vassar, and Wellesley

[12] The difference was largest in physical sciences and smallest in mathematical sci ences. Comparisons between the seven women's colleges and all undergraduat programs are complicated by the fact that nearly half of all the bachelor' degrees awarded were in education and "other" (chiefly professional pro grams), whereas in the seven women's colleges only 4.1 percent of the degree awarded were in these categories. On the other hand, more than half of th

women's colleges. The most selective women's colleges, for example, have long had exceptionally able students. Yet there are reasons for believing that the experience of attending a women's college is partially responsible. In women's colleges, female students are not reluctant to participate actively in class discussion for fear of losing their feminine appeal in the eyes of male students. They have far greater opportunity to gain experience in leadership roles in campus organizations and activities than women in coeducational institutions, where the top leadership positions nearly always go to men.

In a recent analysis of random samples of women from each of three editions of *Who's Who of American Women,* Tidball (1973) found that the number of women achievers per 1,000 women enrolled was about twice as high among graduates of women's colleges as among graduates of coeducational institutions. (Ratios of achievers to women enrolled were computed for each of the five decades in which the women graduated from 1910 to 1960.) She also found evidence that the larger proportion of achievers among graduates of women's colleges was related to the larger proportion of women on the faculties of those institutions.[13] In addition, there was a high negative correlation between the ratio of men to women among undergraduates in coeducational institutions and the ratio of women achievers among their graduates.

---

degrees awarded in the women's colleges were in arts and humanities, compared with 28 percent of all bachelor's degrees awarded to women, and the proportion of degrees in the social sciences was considerably higher in the women's colleges than among all degrees awarded to women. As we have suggested earlier, in liberal arts colleges men and women preparing for teaching tend to major in liberal arts subjects rather than in education. Even so, the data do suggest that women are less inhibited from majoring in the natural sciences and mathematics in women's colleges.

In a comparison of degrees awarded in 1956, Newcomer (1959, p. 95) found that substantially larger proportions of degrees in the physical sciences and mathematics were awarded to women in women's colleges than in state universities.

[13]That is, when the number of achievers per 1,000 women faculty members was computed for both the graduates of women's colleges and the graduates of coeducational institutions, there was no significant difference between the two ratios.

In a similar analysis of data from such sources as *American Men of Science* and the *Dictionary of American Biography,* Newcomer (1959, p. 195) showed that women's colleges over the relevant period accounted for 16 percent of all women students enrolled and 34 percent of all women scholars.

These accomplishments of the graduates of women's colleges are worthy of emphasis, not only as they bear on decisions on women's colleges to continue or abandon their single-sex status, but also—and far more significantly in terms of potential influence—as they suggest how changes in policies and faculty attitudes in coeducational institutions could affect the accomplishments of their women students.

A basic need is for women to overcome their feelings of hesitancy about entering traditionally male fields and participating actively in class discussion in coeducational institutions, but this change will come slowly and will probably depend more on changes in early acculturation than on what happens in higher education. Some observers believe that the women's movement is making matters more difficult for shy women. Typically it is their more aggressive sisters who are actively pushing for change, and shy women tend to draw away from participation in aggressive activities. Equally basic is the need for administrators, faculty members, and counselors to adopt positive and encouraging attitudes toward aspirations of qualified women to develop their capacities and, when they wish, to major in traditionally male fields. As a transitional measure, until women are better prepared psychologically to compete with men in the classroom, there is a case for experimentation with special sections for women in large introductory courses.[14]

An emerging problem for women's colleges is the absence from their curricula of such traditionally male professional subjects as business administration and engineering, in which their students would like to major. Whether students should be encouraged to major in business administration at the undergraduate stage is questionable, however.[15] On the other hand, certain courses like accounting may usefully be taken by undergraduate economics majors. We believe that women's colleges would be well advised to enter into arrangements, wherever

[14]Recently, 10 women at Harvard successfully insisted on the organization of a separate section of the introductory physics course for them ("Women Physicists," 1972).

[15]Two influential studies of higher education in business conducted in the late 1950s concluded that it was preferable for students preparing for a business career to gain a broad liberal arts background at the undergraduate stage, with some emphasis on economics and other social sciences, and to postpone specialization in business until the graduate education stage (Gordon & Howell, 1959; and Pierson, 1959).

possible, with neighboring male or coeducational institutions to enable their students to enroll in accounting courses or to undertake an engineering program rather than attempting to develop their own programs in these fields. The cost per student is high in a field like engineering, particularly when the number of students is small, because there are appreciable economies of scale.

Another quite different realm in which women frequently have greater opportunities in women's colleges is competitive sports. In coeducational institutions, women are now seeking and sometimes aggressively demanding, opportunities to participate in athletic training and to participate in some of the competitive sports formerly regarded as male preserves.[16]

WOMEN'S STUDIES One of the most decisive effects of the women's movement in higher education has been the growth of women's studies. Five or six years ago they were almost unknown. In the last few years, their growth has been so rapid that last year's statistics are out of date. The most recent report we have been able to obtain indicates that, in the fall of 1972, there were about 1,300 courses relating to women in some 800 to 1,000 colleges and universities.[17] Most of these were single courses, but Robinson (1973, p. 1) reports that there were 32 campus women's studies programs in December 1972, defining women's studies programs as a women's studies major or an organizational unit responsible for women's studies. A list of the campuses offering these programs is included in Appendix D. Only two of the programs offered a bachelor's degree, and three schools offered master's programs in women's studies. The programs tend to be interdisciplinary.

Only a small minority of women's courses appear to be concerned with the women's movement as such. Most of them are oriented to a particular discipline and focus on the role of women in the concerns of that discipline: for example, women in history, women in literature, the psychology of women, women in the economy, and women's legal rights. The majority

---

[16] In *The Lonely Crowd*, Riesman (1969, pp. 81–82) called attention to the importance of "antagonistic cooperation" and the role of competitive sports in encouraging this trait.

[17] Information provided by KNOW, a publishing firm specializing in feminist publications in Pittsburgh, Pennsylvania.

of the courses are at the undergraduate level, and the great ma
jority are taught by women, but some are taught by men. Th
students who enroll are predominantly women, but in mo
cases men are permitted to enroll and do enroll in relativel
small numbers.

As in ethnic studies, controversial policy issues are involve
Some of the more activist promoters of these courses and pro
grams, for example, would like to exclude men both as teache
and as students. Others are pressing for the establishment c
separate departments of women's studies. And there has bee
some controversy over whether the courses should have
primarily academic orientation or should be involved with th
women's movement in an activist manner. For the most par
these more activist and aggressive ideas have not gained dom
nance, but it is likely to be the more activist women who are ir
volved in promoting and teaching the courses. The rapi
growth of women's courses and study programs clearly ir
dicates their popularity with women students. Whether intere
will eventually show signs of waning, as seems to have hap
pened in the case of ethnic studies, is purely speculative a
present.

We believe that there is a case for women's studies, but fc
the most part as a transitional phenomenon. Historical researc
has paid little attention to the role of women, except as it ha
concerned itself with a Mary Queen of Scots or a Cleopatra. Th
concentrated attention to developing more adequate informa
tion on changing roles of women in society will not only giv
both men and women a better understanding of their contribu
tions over the centuries, but will also move the study of histor
more effectively toward a goal that many historians have lon
desired—greater relative emphasis on social and economic his
tory, as opposed to the traditional heavy concentration on poli
ical history and wars.

In the field of psychology there are serious complaints of th
inaccuracy of Freudian concepts in relation to women an
charges that, in any case, they may have been more relevant t
late nineteenth century Viennese society than to contemporar
living.

. . . as I read on through the feminist critique. . . and, more decisiv
than that, went back to Freud's own writings, the evidence of his rad

cal bias against women and the existence of that bias in the very tex-
ture of psychoanalysis came to seem indisputable. . . .The astonishing
thing, which had only rarely been pointed out until the feminists
began waving their arms at it, is that Freud's entire theory of sexuality
is built from a masculine model. In psychoanalysis, maleness is the
norm and femaleness an incomplete or, even worse, deficient aspect of
it (Gilman, 1971, pp. 10–11).[18]

Another accusation in the field of psychology is that, until
recently, nearly all the research on achievement motivation was
based on studies of men. Matina Horner, now president of
Radcliffe, turned her attention to research on sex differences in
achievement motivation, with results that are highly significant
to the major themes of this report:

A bright woman is caught in a double bind. In testing and other
achievement-oriented situations she worries not only about failure,
but also about success. If she fails, she is not living up to her own
standards of performance; if she succeeds she is not living up to socie-
tal expectations about the female role. Men in our society do not experience this kind of ambivalence. . . .

If a woman sets out to do well . . . she bumps into a number of obstacles. She learns that it really isn't ladylike to be too intellectual. She
is warned that men will treat her with distrustful tolerance at best, and
outright prejudice at worst, if she pursues a career (Horner, 1971, pp.
254 and 259).

We shall return to this problem of ambivalent motivation in
Section 7.

In law schools, there is pressure to include courses on
women's rights under the law, or on the differential treatment
of the two sexes under the law, or on the changes that would be
brought about by final ratification of the Equal Rights Amendment, now in some doubt.[19] As for women in the economy,
Ginzberg and others have effectively shown that the concept
that "women's place is in the home" developed among the
middle classes in the nineteenth century and was not an accu-

---

[18] Quoted in Robinson (1973, p. 5).

[19] The Amendment has been ratified by about 30 states but needs 38 for final
adoption. Although opposition has developed in some states and has been instrumental in defeating ratification in several of them, this has tended to be by a
very narrow margin.

rate reflection of the roles of women regardless of class in earlier centuries (Ginzberg and associates, 1966).

It is apparent that courses relating to women are likely to enrich the curriculum in many needed ways and eventually result in the discarding of outmoded and stereotyped ideas about the relative roles of the two sexes in many disciplines. Ultimately we would expect that these changes would be reflected in many parts of the curriculum and would not be dependent on the existence of special women's study programs. Indeed, in addition to the growth of courses on women, there has been an encouraging tendency in recent years—undoubtedly also influenced by the women's movement—for women's roles to be given more attention in courses on such phenomena as labor force participation. Extensive research on labor force participation in the last decade or so has yielded much information on sex differences in patterns of labor force participation. In fact, there is much to be said for the view that a major emphasis should be placed on introducing material on sex roles in courses in such fields as the social sciences and the humanities.

For the present, we believe that women's courses and women's study programs are serving an important purpose. However, we think that women's courses should be presented within relevant existing departments and that women's undergraduate study programs should take the form of interdisciplinary group majors or elective group course selections under the auspices of existing departments. The same general principles should apply in relation to graduate courses. We do not believe that separate departments on women's studies should be formed, partly because the ultimate goal should be the incorporation of adequate attention to women in the regular curricula of relevant departments and partly because the formation of separate departments of women's studies could more readily lead to second-class status for these programs.[20]

[20]Results of a questionnaire addressed to faculty members involved in women's studies or in academic reform throughout the country for a summer project at the University of Pennsylvania were mixed on this question. Those who were opposed to a separate department believed that it was of greater advantage to the faculty member to keep in touch with his or her discipline. They also feared that establishment of a separate department might create a "woman's ghetto," which would be considered inferior by other departments. Others thought only a separate department would legitimize women's studies (*Penn Women's Studies Planners*, 1972, p. iii).

An interesting aspect of women's studies is that in varying degrees "teachers of women's studies reject the traditional pattern of authority where the teacher. . . is the primary source of wisdom, the lecture is regarded as the most effective teaching medium, and the student is expected to digest facts to be reproduced on final examinations" (Sicherman, 1972, p. 88). Rather, the approach is one of a shared learning experience, with the student as an active participant. One reason is that the subject matter is novel, and the teachers have to recognize frankly that they are learners rather than experts.

RECOMMEN-DATIONS

Recommendation 5: Not only should colleges and universities take immediate steps to strengthen occupational counseling programs generally in this era of a changing job market for college graduates,[21] but they should also take special steps to strengthen career counseling programs for women. Counselors should be trained to discard outmoded concepts of male and female careers and to encourage women in their abilities and aspirations.

Recommendation 6: Colleges and universities have a responsibility to develop policies specifically designed to bring about changes in the attitudes of administrators and faculty members, where these have been antagonistic to enrollment of women in traditionally male fields.

Recommendation 7: Because of the evidence that many women enter college with inadequate mathematical training, special provision should be made to ensure that women desiring to major in fields calling for extensive use of mathematics are encouraged to make up this deficiency in order to enter the fields of their choice.

Recommendation 8: Opportunities for women to participate in competitive sports should be strongly encouraged.

Recommendation 9: The movement to introduce courses on women and interdisciplinary women's study programs should be encouraged by institutions of higher education, at least on a

[21]See the recommendations in Carnegie Commission (1973a).

transitional basis, but these courses and programs should be organized within existing disciplines and not under separate departments of women's studies.

6. Women in Graduate and Professional Schools

WHERE ARE
THEY
ENROLLED? Women form a somewhat smaller proportion of graduate than of undergraduate students, but enrollment rates of women in graduate programs have been rising rapidly. In 1970, women accounted for 46 percent of all prebaccalaureate students and 37 percent of graduate resident students. But they represented less than 10 percent of students in first-professional degree programs (e.g., in law schools and medical schools).[1]

In general, ratios of women to men tend to be higher in public than in private institutions. The Carnegie Commission Survey of Faculty and Student Opinion, 1969, showed that only in Comprehensive Universities and Colleges II (predominantly teachers colleges) did women form an appreciably larger percentage of graduate students in private than in public institutions (Table 5). The data also show that women tend to form a larger proportion of graduate students in both groups of Comprehensive Universities and Colleges than in any of the groups of universities. There are very few graduate students in liberal arts colleges, and thus our data on these groups of institutions are not especially reliable.

A major factor in explaining the lower proportion of women in graduate than in undergraduate education is that, as women reach the age group in which students tend to enter graduate school, 22 to 24, the proportion who are married increases, as does the proportion who have children (Table 3).

---

[1]Computed from data in U.S. Office of Education (1971, p. 159). "Unclassified" and undergraduate extension students are included among prebaccalaureate students; graduate resident students include all graduate students except those enrolled in extension programs.

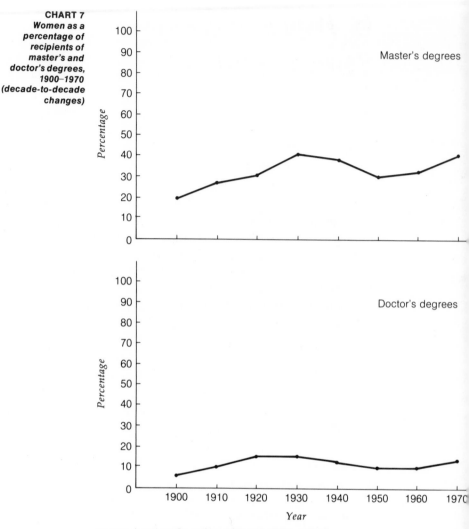

CHART 7
Women as a percentage of recipients of master's and doctor's degrees, 1900–1970 (decade-to-decade changes)

SOURCE: American Council on Education (1973, p. 1771).

During the early decades of the present century, the proportion of advanced degrees awarded to women increased very substantially—from about 20 percent of the master's degrees in 1900 to 40 percent in 1930, and from 6 percent of the doctor's degrees in 1900 to 15 percent in 1930. After that there was a sharp decline in the percentage of degrees at each of these levels awarded to women until 1950, followed by a reversal of the trend in the last two decades (Chart 7). The impact of the Great Depression undoubtedly was a major factor in explaining the decline during the 1930s, while the trend toward earlier marriage and a higher birthrate was a major factor in the 1940s, as it was at the undergraduate level. By 1970, women once more represented about as large a proportion of those receiving master's degrees as they had in 1930, but this was not quite true in the case of doctor's degrees. Data for 1971 are not yet available for master's degrees, but between 1970 and 1971, women again increased their proportion of doctor's degrees awarded—from 13.3 to 14.4 percent (National Research Council, 1972).

These trends must be viewed in the light of a rapid increase in the number of degrees awarded at all levels to both sexes over the decades (Chart 8).

MARITAL STATUS AND AGE The differences in marital status and age of male and female graduate students shed a good deal of light on the problems of women in participating in graduate education. The Carnegie Commission Survey of Faculty and Student Opinion, 1969, provided extensive data on these and other characteristics of graduate students. An American Council on Education report (Creager, 1971) made available the basic statistical data, which have since been subjected to additional analysis by Saul Feldman (1972) and Elizabeth Scott (Appendix C).

Women in graduate school were more likely to be single (41 percent) than men (31 percent), reflecting the problems married women encounter in attending graduate school, especially if they have children.[2] Regardless of marital status, women were more likely to be enrolled on a part-time basis than men, but the proportion of married women who were enrolled part time was especially high, and the proportion of divorced and separated women enrolled part time was also relatively high. Married men, also, were considerably more likely to be enrolled part time than single men.

Although the median age of both male and female graduate students was between 26 and 27, they differed markedly in age distribution. The most striking and significant difference was that relatively large proportions of both the married and divorced women were aged 35 and older. In fact, about one-fourth of the female graduate students were married, divorced,

[2] The percentages cited here are based on tabulations prepared by Elizabeth Scott and may differ slightly from those reported by Creager or Feldman.

CHART 8 *Number of master's and doctor's degree recipients, by sex, 1900–1970 (decade-to-decade changes)*

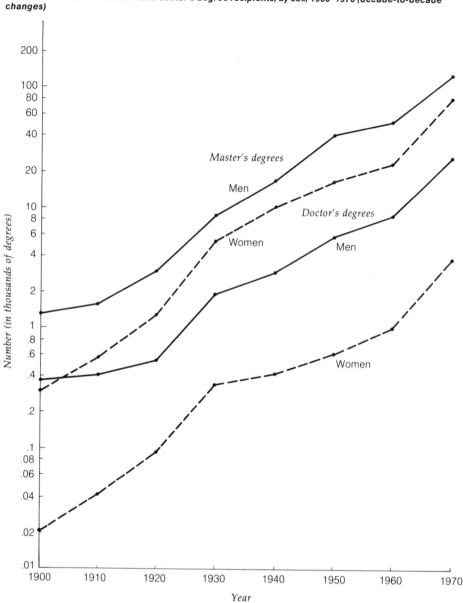

SOURCE: American Council on Education (1973, p. 1771).

or separated women aged 35 and older. These are women who are especially likely to be returning to graduate work after some years out of the labor force, and they are also especially likely to be enrolled in graduate schools within commuting distance. At a later point, we shall find that this factor has an influence on the types of institutions in which women graduate students enroll.

Of special interest are data indicating that more than one-half of the married women graduate students, as contrasted with only about one-fourth of the married men, had spouses who attended graduate school or had attained a graduate degree. This suggests that women who are married to graduate students or to men who have attained a graduate degree are especially likely to seek graduate education. In a good many cases, these women are undoubtedly married either to current graduate students or to faculty members in the institution in which they are studying. Probably in many cases the wives of the male graduate students were not enrolled either because they had small children or because they were working for their "Ph.T.'s" (putting hubby through). Although we shall be looking more closely at relative sources of financial support for male and female graduate students at a later point, it is of interest to note at this stage that 15.5 percent of the male graduate students and 30.4 percent of the female graduate students reported that "spouse's job" was their main source of financial support in the current year. This means that about 24 percent of the married men and 57 percent of the married women were depending primarily on spouse's earnings.[3]

A considerably larger proportion of women than of men are enrolled in master's programs in graduate school. At the time of the Carnegie Commission survey, one-third of the men, but only about one-sixth of the women, were working for doctor's degrees. However, a good many of the graduate students of both sexes expected to go on for a doctor's degree after completing the work for the master's degree. In response to a question about the highest degree they "expected," the distribution of

[3]We have included in these computations the very small numbers of women who were separated from a former spouse, but not those who were divorced or widowed, along with those currently married (see Creager, 1971, p. 20).

responses was quite different. Among the men, 64 percent expected a doctor's degree, 11 percent a first-professional degree, and 22 percent a master's degree. For women, the highest degree expected was the doctor's for 46 percent, a first-professional degree for 6 percent, and a master's degree for 43 percent.[4]

THEIR
FIELDS

An important factor in explaining these differences is that a very large proportion of women in graduate school are enrolled in fields like education, library science, and social welfare, in which relatively few students go on for a doctor's degree. In 1970 no less than 53 percent of the master's degrees awarded to women were in the field of education (Appendix A, Table A-12). Another 13 percent were in "other social sciences" (chiefly social welfare) and in library science. The sizable proportion (about 17 percent) in arts and humanities probably included a good many women who were planning to go into secondary education and did not expect to go on for doctor's degrees. Also significant in this connection is that a large proportion of both men and women working for master's degrees in education are teachers who are studying on a part-time basis.

At the master's level, however, more decisively than at the bachelor's level, there has been a recent substantial increase in the number of women receiving degrees in certain traditionally male fields. The increase has been large enough to result in an upward trend in the proportion of master's degrees awarded to women in agriculture, the biological sciences, engineering, chemistry, physics, health sciences, and the mathematical sciences (Chart 9). The percentage of degrees awarded to women is still very small in some of these fields, especially in engineering, but the changes have been appreciable.

Differences in the proportions of doctor's degrees awarded to women, as compared with men, in the various fields are not as extreme as at the master's level. One reason is that, in the fields in which women are heavily represented at the master's level, relatively more men than women go on for the doctorate. In other words, there is a sharp decline in the relative representation of women between the master's and doctor's levels. But

[4]The percentages cited here are those reported by Creager.

CHART 9 *Women as a percentage of persons receiving master's degrees in selected fields, 1950–1970*

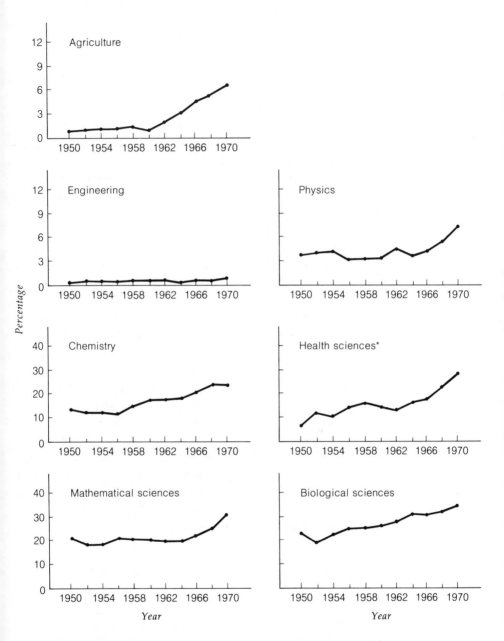

*Includes all health professions other than dentistry, medicine, nursing, physical therapy, and dental hygiene.

SOURCE: U. S. Office of Education data, adapted by D. L. Adkins.

another reason is that women who go on for the doctorate tend to be exceptionally able, as we shall see, and quite capable of competing in any field, including the traditionally male fields. For example, 20.9 percent of the doctor's degrees awarded to women in 1970 were in the natural sciences (including mathematics and computer science), as compared with only 7.2 percent of the bachelor's degrees and 5.6 percent of the master's degrees (Appendix A, Table A-12). The proportion of women receiving doctor's degrees in the social sciences was also somewhat higher than the percentages receiving degrees at either the master's or bachelor's levels.

As at the master's level, the increase in the number of women receiving doctorates in certain traditionally male fields in recent years has been sizable enough to result in a rise in the proportion of degrees awarded to women. The fields in which this has occurred are much the same as those in which women have been gaining in their share of master's degrees. However, women were much better represented among doctoral recipients in mathematics and considerably better represented in other physical sciences, life sciences, economics and statistics, and social sciences in 1920–1924 than in 1969–1971 (Chart 10). Even in engineering, the percentage of degrees awarded to women in 1920–1924, though very small, was larger than in any more recent period. These data tend to be consistent with a great deal of other evidence suggesting that women were less inhibited from entering traditionally male fields in the 1920s than they have been in recent decades. The fact that relatively more of them did their undergraduate work in women's colleges and the lingering impact of the suffrage movement were probably influential. But it must also be kept in mind that the total number of doctor's degrees in 1920–1924 was very small compared with more recent years.

RETENTION
RATES
There is evidence that women are more likely to drop out of graduate school than are men, even after taking account of differences in field of study. The most illuminating data we have been able to obtain on attrition among graduate students are based on a secondary analysis conducted by the Graduate Assembly's Committee on the Status of Women, University of California, Berkeley, on the basis of data originally developed

CHART 10 *Women as a percentage of persons receiving Ph.D. degrees in selected fields, 1920 to 1971*

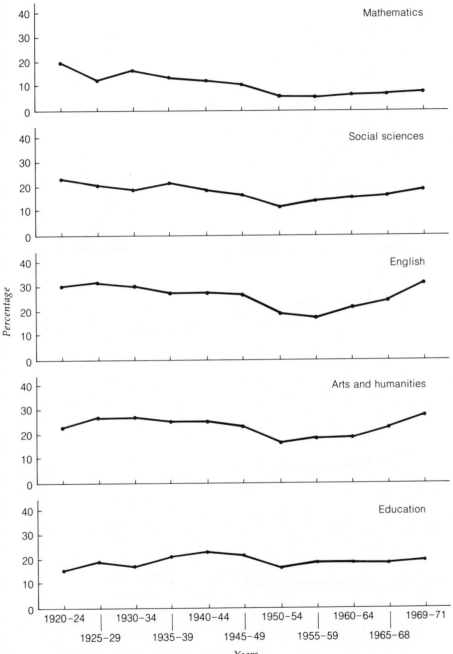

CHART 10 *Women as a percentage of persons receiving Ph.D. degrees in selected fields, 1920 to 1971* *(continued)*

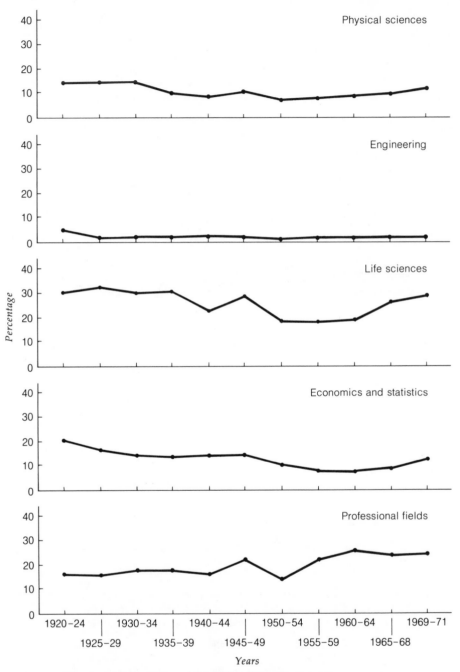

SOURCES: Harmon and Soldz (1963); and U.S. Office of Education (annual).

by Mooney in 1966. These data relate to Woodrow Wilson fellows who entered graduate school from 1958 to 1963. Because Woodrow Wilson fellows are a highly selective group, we would expect attrition rates to be relatively low among them. Yet, at the time of the study, 44 percent of the men and 64 percent of the women had not obtained doctorates and were no longer enrolled, that is, were defined as dropouts for purposes of the study (Appendix A, Tables A-13 to A-16). Among both men and women, dropout rates were highest in the humanities, intermediate in the social sciences, and lowest in the natural sciences, but the differences by field were much wider for men than for women. The very lowest dropout rate was found among men with excellent graduate ratings in the natural sciences. Having no support in the second year of graduate work made a greater difference for women than for men, as did having children. (Among men, the effect of having children was not statistically significant.) Even among the students who were rated "excellent" by their professors, and who presumably would have qualified for second-year support, dropout rates were considerably higher for women than for men. One suspects that many of these women dropped out because of marriage and childbearing, but the relevant data on this point are not available.

Although probably less true of Woodrow Wilson fellows than of female graduate students in general, an important explanation of the high attrition rate of women is that many do not intend to go beyond the master's degree, especially in such fields as education, social work, and library science. As is well known, there are wide differences by field in the average length of time spent in obtaining the doctorate, varying from relatively few years in the physical sciences to many years in foreign languages. Education tends to take longer than any other field, but this is partially because many graduate students in education are teachers studying on a part-time basis.

Relevant to this question is evidence from the Graduate Center at City University of New York, where the only degree now granted is the Ph.D. Among students admitted between 1962 and 1970, women formed nearly as large a percentage of those who had received the Ph.D. by 1972 as they did of the students admitted (Rees, 1973), but no adjustments were made for differences by field.

RELATIVE
ABILITY

Most of the available evidence suggests that women who enter graduate school are relatively able and that women who receive the doctorate are more able, on the average, than men who receive the doctorate. We have noted that women receive higher grades in college than men. Among the graduate students in the Carnegie Commission Survey of Faculty and Student Opinion, 1969, about 24 percent of the women, as compared with 17 percent of the men, reported an undergraduate grade-point average of A. On the other hand, only 11 percent of the women, as contrasted with 22 percent of the men, reported undergraduate averages of C or less.[5]

On Graduate Record Examination (GRE) scores, however, the record is more mixed and resembles that on college admission tests. In the period from 1969 to 1972, mean GRE scores of women on verbal ability tests were 503, as compared with 493 for men, but on quantitative ability tests, the averages were 468 and 545 for women and men, respectively (Educational Testing Service, 1972, p. 16). The fact that far fewer women, relatively, major in fields requiring extensive use of mathematics as undergraduates must be kept in mind in interpreting these differences.

In a frequently quoted study, Harmon (1963) obtained high school records of a large sample of men and women who were awarded Ph.D.'s in the years from 1959 to 1962. The results showed superior performance for the women not only in terms of high school rank but also in terms of intelligence test scores. An especially interesting aspect of these results was that the difference between male and female test scores in physical science was larger than the average for all fields. This suggests that women who have the motivation and persistence to attain a Ph.D. in physical science are exceptionally able.

IS THERE
DISCRIMI-
NATION?

To what extent is there discrimination against women in graduate education? Some of those who have done research on the status of women in higher education tend to believe that discrimination is a more serious problem at the graduate than at the undergraduate level, but it is difficult to document.

---

[5] These percentages are from tabulations prepared by Elizabeth Scott and differ slightly from those given by Creager (1971).

Whereas undergraduates tend to be selected by the institution's admissions office in most instances, departments and schools typically screen and select applicants for graduate programs. Candidates must meet the institution's general qualifications (such as a minimum grade-point average in undergraduate work), but departmental committees typically go through the applications and make the decisions in the awarding of fellowships, teaching assistantships, and research assistantships. It seems likely that attitudes toward male versus female applicants vary from department to department within the same institution.

In her study of graduate education, Ann Heiss interviewed presidents, chancellors, and faculty members in 10 leading graduate schools. Her conclusions on the subject of sex discrimination are of considerable interest:

Not excluding academic qualifications, sex is probably the most discriminatory factor applied in the decision whether to admit an applicant to graduate school. It is almost a foregone conclusion that among American institutions women have greater difficulty being admitted to doctoral study and, if admitted, will have greater difficulty being accepted than will men. Department chairmen and faculty members frankly state that their main reason for ruling against women is "the probability that they will marry." Some continue to use this possibility as the rationale for withholding fellowships, awards, placement, and other recognition from women who are allowed to register for graduate work. . . .

In the interviews for this study several department chairmen volunteered the information that women are purposely screened out as Ph.D. prospects and as faculty members. For example, the chairman of a department of biochemistry mentioned that the men on his faculty had a pact in which they agreed "not even to look at applications from women. . . ." In another interview the chairman of a psychology department worried about "what would happen to the department next year" as a result of admitting seven female students in a class of twenty-five. The imponderable effect of the military draft on male students had impelled the department to cover the available slots (Heiss, 1970, pp. 93–95).

Even though the Heiss study was completed only a few years ago, it is doubtful that any department chairman would express himself in such terms today, especially to a woman interviewer.

The climate has changed, and graduate and professional schools are now subject, as we have seen, to the provisions prohibiting discrimination on the basis of sex in the Educational Amendments of 1972. Furthermore, in the years from about 1969 on, women's groups were organized on many campuses and, among other things, compiled data on admission to graduate and professional schools.

Perhaps because they were compiled after pressures to remove discriminatory practices had already had some effect, recent data on graduate admissions for several large research universities show a pattern that is somewhat variable, but by no means always unfavorable to women. For example, the Report of the Task Force on Women, Stanford University, on admissions in the fall of 1971 showed that percentages of women applicants admitted tended to be considerably higher than corresponding percentages of men in professional schools and in humanities, but were slightly lower in physical sciences and social sciences (Stanford University, 1972, p. 311). Somewhat similar data for the Berkeley and Los Angeles campuses of the University of California, though not pertaining to the same year, suggest more favorable treatment of women applicants at UCLA than at Berkeley (Pearce et al., 1972).

Comparisons of ratios of admittees to applicants do not, of course, provide conclusive evidence one way or another about possible discrimination, because the data do not tell us anything about the comparative qualifications of the applicants. Even so, given the overall superior undergraduate records of women, it seems unlikely that women who apply to prestigious graduate schools such as the three mentioned above are not at least as well qualified as men who apply.

In political science, able women do very well in obtaining admission to high quality graduate schools. Data compiled by the American Political Science Association show that women applicants to graduate school were as successful as male applicants of comparable ability in gaining admission to distinguished institutions (American Political Science Association, 1971, p. 26).

On access to graduate fellowships, the evidence is mixed. A study conducted by the Association of American Colleges showed that the percentages of female applicants who received fellowships were equal to or higher than those of male applicants in most fellowship programs, but that women represented less than 25 percent of the applicants in many of the programs. The fact that relatively few women enter such fields as the "hard" sciences and educational administration, in which many of the fellowships are offered, was cited as a reason for the small percentage of women among applicants, but the study also provided some indications that women were the victims of lack of encouragement. Much information about fellowships, it was pointed out, tends to be handled informally through the so-called old boy system of recruitment (Fields, 1972, pp. 1–2).

The Carnegie Commission Survey of Faculty and Student Opinion, 1969, showed that a slightly larger percentage of male than of female graduate students (17.7 versus 15.0 percent) currently had some income from a fellowship, while a slightly larger percentage of men (31.1 percent versus 30.0 percent) also had teaching or research assistantships.[6] In a more intensive analysis of primary sources of support by field, we found much wider differences. In physics, for example, three-fifths of the men, as contrasted with about one-third of the women, received their primary support either from a fellowship or an assistantship. On the other hand, more than half of the women, as compared with only about one-sixth of the men, indicated that a spouse's job was the primary source of support. The contrasts between sources of support for men and women in the humanities were less pronounced but showed a similar pattern.

A recent analysis of holders of pre- and postdoctoral fellowships awarded by the National Institutes of Health indicated that highly qualified scholars tended to have access to the same types of schools regardless of sex. But women did appear to be somewhat more concentrated in universities located in large urban centers.[7] This suggests that married women were more limited in their choice of institutions, because they had to enroll in one of those that were within commuting distance. Analysis of student migration data also indicates a consistent tendency

[6] These percentages are those reported by Creager (1971).

[7] For example, 10 percent of the female recipients, as compared with only 4 percent of the men, were enrolled in New York City alone. However, Alice Rossi has called our attention to data in reports prepared by the American Council on Education indicating that male doctoral candidates are more likely than female candidates to express a preference for future location in relatively small cities.

for women graduate students to be enrolled in institutions within their state of residence in larger proportions than male students (Solmon, 1973).

Even though graduate and professional schools are likely to be more evenhanded in admitting men and women in the future under both legal and social pressures, it may be a long time before women escape the psychological consequences of negative attitudes on the part of some faculty members. In an intensive analysis of the data on graduate students from the Carnegie Commission Survey, Holmstrom and Holmstrom (1973) found that perception of the faculty as having negative attitudes toward women not only contributed to the emotional stress felt by at least one in three women but also decreased their commitment to stay in graduate school. They concluded that some of these problems could be eased by increasing the proportion of women on the faculty, especially in the senior ranks.

Substantial proportions of graduate students responding to the Commission's survey expressed agreement with the statement that "professors in my department don't really take female graduate students seriously" (Chart 11).[8] In most fields and in both groups of universities represented in the chart, the percentage of women exceeded the percentage of men agreeing with the statement. This is not surprising. Somewhat more surprising is the fact that in Research Universities I, percentages of both women and men agreeing with the statement were considerably higher in humanities and in the social sciences than in the more traditionally male biological and physical sciences. In other universities, the percentage was especially high for women in the social sciences and was also relatively high for women in biological and physical sciences.

We also sought to explore the attitudes of faculty members on this issue, asking them to indicate the extent of their agreement or disagreement with the following statement: "The female graduate students in my department are not as dedicated as the males"[9] (Chart 12). Percentages of male faculty members agree-

[8]Four responses were possible: strongly agree, agree with reservations, disagree with reservations, or strongly disagree. Percentages in Chart 11 include those who strongly agreed and who agreed with reservations.

[9]Possible responses were the same as in the case of the preceding question, and again the percentages on the chart include those who strongly agreed and agreed with reservations.

CHART 11
Percentage of graduate students agreeing with the statement "professors in my department don't really take female graduate students seriously," by sex and field of study, 1969

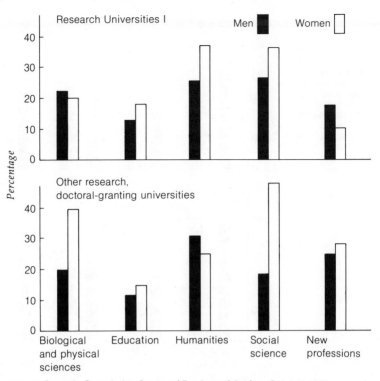

SOURCE: Carnegie Commission Survey of Faculty and Student Opinion, 1969.

ing with the statement consistently exceeded the percentages of female faculty members agreeing, as we might expect. Moreover, it is not surprising to find that the percentages of men agreeing with the statement were considerably higher in the biological and physical sciences than in other fields. What is somewhat surprising about the results is that percentages of female faculty members agreeing with the statement varied by field in much the same manner as the corresponding percentages of male faculty members.

Probably the most important factor tending to discriminate against women in admission to graduate study is a variety of rules and informal policies discouraging admission of students who wish to study on a part-time basis. Faced with a choice between a married woman planning to study part time and a student who plans full-time graduate work, a department is highly likely to favor the full-time student. He or she will complete the work for the degree much more rapidly, will be more likely to obtain a teaching position in a prestigious college

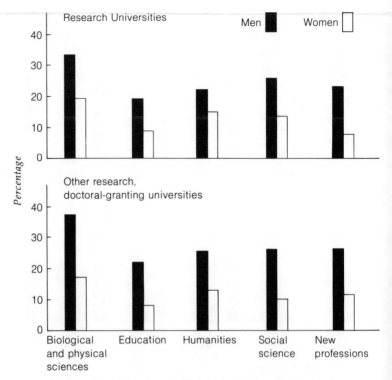

CHART 12 Percentage of faculty members agreeing with the statement "the female graduate students in my department are not as dedicated as the males," by sex and field of study, 1969

SOURCE: Carnegie Commission Survey of Faculty and Student Opinion, 1969.

or university, and will be considered more likely to gain a reputation through subsequent publications that will redound to the graduate department in which the student received his or her training. This type of consideration is likely to discriminate especially against the older married woman hoping to return to graduate work after her children are in school. If it played a role ten years ago, it is far more likely to play a role today, when departments in prestigious universities are faced in a good many instances with administrative ceilings on the number of graduate students they can admit. They also tend to have considerably less fellowship money to distribute. If it would have been easier a decade ago to add women to the faculty, as we shall point out in the next section, it would also have been considerably easier to accommodate more married women studying on a part-time basis in graduate school, for a somewhat different set of reasons.

Although attitudes unfavorable to mature married women are rather common, it would be a great mistake to imply that they are universal. Some faculty members, perhaps especially in certain of the social sciences, seek out and welcome mature married women to their classes because they bring so much life experience and dedication to their work and raise the level of class discussion.

As for admissions policies in graduate and professional schools, we would urge against any simple formula, such as accepting the same percentage of female as of male applicants. Such a formula not only ignores the possibility of differences in the relative qualifications of male and female applicants, but also could encourage women to submit applications to numerous schools, thus building up the proportion of female applicants at many schools. What is needed, rather, is a general administrative stance of encouragement of opportunities for women, regardless of field, as well as requirements that departments and schools actively recruit women and maintain detailed records that will indicate the reasons for acceptance or rejection of all applicants of both sexes, as well as the reasons for decisions on the awarding of fellowships and assistantships.[10]

Some faculty members point out a special need for a change in attitudes in mathematics departments, perhaps particularly in research-oriented universities. A tendency in these mathematics departments is to encourage only those students who are of such superior mathematical ability as to be capable of original contributions as doctoral candidates. The needs of other students—both graduate and undergraduate—who require mathematics as a tool for study in the natural or social sciences are regarded either unsympathetically or with contempt. Again, however, it is important to recognize that there are exceptions, including dedicated faculty members in mathematics or statistics departments who have been actively engaged in programs especially oriented toward the needs of women and minority groups.

LAW SCHOOLS AND MEDICAL SCHOOLS
Any attempt to cover all types of professional schools would be beyond the scope of the present report. However, the fields of law and medicine are of particular interest. Traditionally, they have been important and prestigious professional fields for men, whereas there have been relatively few women lawyers or

[10]For a similar view, see Chalmers (1972).

00123

physicians. Moreover, in recent years women as well as men have been applying for admission to law schools and medical schools in record numbers. For both sexes, the poor job market for Ph.D.'s has been a factor in inducing shifts away from Ph.D. programs to these two professional fields, and the growing desire of young people to prepare themselves for professions that deal directly with important social problems has also clearly been an important influence. But the greatly accelerated influx of women into both law schools and medical schools is undoubtedly a reflection, as well, of the impact of the women's movement on the aspirations of young women.

In recent decades, women have represented only 3 to 4 percent of all lawyers in the United States, and surveys of their status in the law have indicated that, as in many other spheres of employment, they have occupied less prestigious and lower paid positions than men (Epstein, 1971*b*, and White, 1971). However, civil rights pressure is affecting the hiring practices of law firms, and many of them are now actively recruiting women. It is also opening up legal jobs for women in government and industry.

In 1961, only 3.6 percent of the students enrolled in law schools approved by the American Bar Association were women—a percentage that was almost exactly equal to the proportion of lawyers who were women according to the 1970 census. The proportion of women students crept slowly upward to 4.6 percent by 1967, but after that the situation changed much more rapidly. By 1972, 12.0 percent of students enrolled in approved schools were women, and in some schools women represented a much larger proportion of the students (American Bar Association, 1973; Task Force, 1973; and Trebilcock, 1972). Of the relatively small number of students enrolled in unapproved schools in 1972, 13.4 percent were women.

Despite the more favorable climate for women entering the law, it is clear that discrimination in employment has not disappeared and that women law students frequently encounter negative attitudes on the part of faculty members in law schools. In a number of law schools, female students have organized, in large part to urge their schools to bar discriminatory firms from using the school's placement facilities and in other ways to combat discrimination against women in employment. In the fall of 1971, women students at the University of Illinois School of Law staged a walkout from class in protest against the school's alleged reluctance to send a questionnaire to law firms about their hiring practices toward women and minorities (Trebilcock, 1972).

Women have been almost entirely absent from the ranks of law school professors. Data compiled from the Association of American Law Schools Directory for 1968–1970 showed that only 28, or 1.6 percent, of the faculty members in 38 leading law schools were women, and only 7 of these 28 women were full professors (*Special Subcommittee on Education,* 1970, Part 1, p. 591). However, between 1970 and 1972, the proportion of those listed in the directory (for all law schools) who were women rose from 3.1 to 5.6 percent.[11] The directory lists librarians and certain administrators, as well as faculty members, but it seems probable that the relative representation of women on law school faculties rose somewhat over the two-year period.

Rising law school enrollments and burgeoning applications for admission, along with rising ratios of women and minority-group students, has led a good many members of the legal profession to express concern about the probability of a serious oversupply of lawyers. Fanning these fears was the unfavorable job market for lawyers that developed during the 1970–71 recession. However, as we pointed out in an earlier report, the rise in law school enrollments from 1965 to 1971 was very much in line with the lower of two projections that had been developed by the Commission on Human Resources and Advanced Education in the late 1960s.[12] It is the number of applications, rather than the number of enrollments, that has been rising spectacularly, and law schools have been rather cautious in increasing the number of student places available. In fact, in 1972, total freshman enrollment in law schools was reported to be down 3 percent from the previous year, and the decrease was attributed to admission cutbacks that were forced on the schools as a result of movement into the upper classes of the two large entrant classes of the preceding two years.

A task force of the American Bar Association examined the

[11]Data for 1970 from Association of American Law Schools (1970); data for 1972 provided by Association of American Law Schools.

[12]Carnegie Commission (1973*a*, p. 100) and Folger, Astin, and Bayer (1970, p. 80).

changing demand and supply situation in the field of law with considerable care in 1972 and stated in the concluding section of its report that it "has not been convinced that there will be more lawyers than can be utilized to fill the total requirements of society for the skills and knowledge with which lawyers are equipped" (Task Force, 1973, p. 51). This is very similar to the conclusion reached by the Carnegie Commission in its analysis of the changing situation in the field of law. The task force also expressed its concern that "the relative shortage of supply of legal education at the present time may act to diminish opportunities for providing legal education to members of minority groups" (ibid., p. 53). As we indicated in a previous report,

We agree with the staff report of the Commission on Human Resources and Advanced Education that the American Association of Law Schools (AALS), the American Bar Association, state planning agencies, and individual colleges and universities should devote major attention to strengthening the weaker law schools, which, in any case, appear to be absorbing much of the current increase in enrollment (Carnegie Commission, 1973a, p. 108).

Women seeking to enter the field of medicine face obstacles far more difficult than those facing would-be women lawyers, because of the prolonged length of medical education. The long hours of service required of interns and residents in hospitals have created special difficulties for married women, although these conditions have become somewhat less arduous in recent years. The years of internship and residency required in many medical specialties mean that a total of some 12 to 14 years of study beyond high school is often needed. This means that an individual is 30 or more years of age, on the average, before being fully prepared to practice in a medical specialty, and specialization has, of course, been increasingly the prevailing trend. For women who marry while in medical school (and many do), childbearing must either be postponed until this long period of training is completed or it must interrupt that training.

Thus the recent trend toward acceleration of medical education is likely to be especially advantageous for women, and may well be one of the factors responsible for the pronounced increase in women as a percentage of entering medical students in the last few years.

As we have seen in Section 3, women have represented a considerably smaller proportion of physicians in the United States than in many other industrial countries, but women are now moving into the field of medicine in rapidly increasing numbers. The relative representation of women among physicians in the United States rose from 6.9 percent in 1960 to 9.3 percent in 1970. Moreover, there has been a rapid increase in the relative representation of women among medical school entrants in recent years—from about 9.3 percent in 1967 to 16.8 percent in 1972 ("Women Students," 1973, p. 188). This occurred during a period of a rapid increase in the number of medical school entrants. The increase in the *number* of women entrants during this same period was from 934 to 2,284, or 345 percent.

In his enormously influential 1910 report on medical education, Abraham Flexner had some things to say about opportunities for women to enter medical schools. Based on his data on the number of women applying to, accepted at, and graduating from medical schools in the first decade of the present century, Flexner suggested that opportunities for women to enter medical school were plentiful, but that they were showing less interest in doing so than formerly:

Medical education is now, in the United States and Canada, open to women upon practically the same terms as men. If all institutions do not receive women, so many do, that no woman desiring an education in medicine is under any disability in finding a school to which she may gain admittance. ... Now that women are freely admitted to the medical profession, it is clear that they show a decreasing inclination to enter it (quoted in Lopate, 1968, p. 16).

During the 1960s, data on applications and admissions indicated that about the same proportion of female as of male applicants were admitted to medical schools. Yet more qualitative evidence, as well as anecdotal evidence based on comments of women seeking medical training, has indicated over the years that medical school admissions officers and faculty members in medical schools often had an unfavorable attitude toward medical education for women. On the basis of a mailed questionnaire and personal interview survey conducted over a seven-year period in the 1960s, Kaplan concluded that, although all medical schools officially admitted both sexes, many were unwilling to admit women, particularly those with children (*Special Subcommittee on Education,* 1970, pp. 559–562). In other testimony before the Special Subcommittee on Education of the House Committee on Education and Labor, 17 medical schools that had been most demonstrably discriminating against women were named, while 4 medical schools were reported to include statements that were adverse to the admission of women in recent editions of the annual summary of Medical School Admissions Requirements, published by the Association of American Medical Colleges (AAMC) (ibid., pp. 520–523). Now, of course, the 1972 legislation against sex discrimination in admissions to graduate and professional schools applies to medical school admissions.[13] Among other effects, it will certainly put a stop to statements adverse to the admission of women in the AAMC publication.

Consistently with ACT and other college test scores, and also with scores on the Graduate Record Examination, women tend to have higher scores than men on the verbal aptitude portion of the Medical College Admission Test, but slightly lower scores on the quantitative ability portion (Weinberg & Rooney, 1973, p. 246). A survey of major measures of academic performance of men and women in medical school revealed that, although women's performance in the early years was slightly but consistently lower than that of men, overall academic performance was equal by the senior year (ibid., p. 240).

A particularly interesting aspect of the status of women in medical education is that nearly half of all women interns and more than half of all women residents in United States hospitals in 1971 were foreign medical graduates ("Annual Report on Medical Education," 1972, pp. 1012–1013). We have discussed the role of foreign medical graduates in United States medicine in an earlier report.[14] Some foreign medical graduates come to this country primarily for further training, but there is a good

[13]Discrimination in medical schools, dental schools, and other schools providing training in health professions was actually banned earlier, under the Comprehensive Health Manpower Training Act of 1971 and the Nurse Training Act of 1971.

[14]Carnegie Commission (1970*b*).

deal of evidence indicating that a major reason for the influx of foreign medical graduates has been a shortage of United States medical graduates. The evidence on utilization of foreign women medical graduates in internships and residencies suggests that there is a demand for women in these positions that cannot be fully met by United States women graduates.

Although women form a relatively small proportion of full-time faculty members in medical schools (7.3 percent in 1971), they are not as rare a phenomenon in medical schools as in law or engineering schools (ibid., pp. 974 and 1014). However, efforts to increase the number of women on medical school faculties will be an important part of the effort to create an environment more stimulating to female and also to male medical students.

At present, the most serious problem facing medical schools in their current efforts to increase the number of student places and also to encourage the enrollment of women and minority-group members is the uncertain status of federal financial support. The Comprehensive Health Manpower Training Act of 1971 adopted well-designed provisions for the support of medical and dental education,[15] but funding in fiscal year 1973 amounted to only about 65 percent of authorized amounts, and the Administration budget for fiscal year 1974 reduced the amounts substantially below fiscal 1973 levels. In May 1973, the AAMC reported, on the basis of a questionnaire sent to medical schools, that the fiscal 1974 budget would "require the schools to release almost a tenth of their faculty members, reduce the size of the freshman classes, and kill or cut back curriculum innovation, research investigations, and special programs" ("Budget Would Require Major Cutbacks," 1973, p. 1).

The Commission has previously stated its view that the current shortage of physicians is not likely to be overcome until the latter part of the 1970s, if then. The encouraging progress of recent years in expanding medical school capacity, and opening doors to more women and members of minority groups, will receive a serious setback unless adequate funds are appropriated, not only for institutional support of medical schools, but also for student aid.

---

[15] The provisions were highly consistent with previous recommendations of the Carnegie Commission (1970*b*).

Recommendation 10: There should be no discrimination on the basis of sex or marital status in admitting students to graduate and professional schools.

Recommendation 11: Departments and schools should be required to maintain complete records on all applicants for admission to graduate and professional education and to make these records available to administrative officers on request. They should also be required to maintain records indicating that, in any programs designed to recruit able graduate students, equal efforts have been made to recruit women as well as men, for example, through letters or circulars addressed to departments in women's colleges as well as to those in male and coeducational institutions.

Recommendation 12: Rules and policies that discriminate against the part-time graduate or professional student should allow for exceptions to accommodate men or women whose family circumstances require them to study on a part-time basis. Any limitation on the total number of graduate or professional students admitted by departments or schools and by the institution as a whole should be applied on a full-time-equivalent rather than on a head-count basis.

Recommendation 13: Policies requiring students to obtain advanced degrees within a certain number of years should allow for a limited extension of the period for those graduate students whose family circumstances require them to study on a part-time basis.

Recommendation 14: There should be no discrimination on the basis of sex or marital status in appointing teaching or research assistants or in awarding fellowships. Furthermore, part-time graduate and professional students should not be barred from eligibility for fellowships.[16] In addition, there should be no antinepotism rules in connection with these appointments or awards.

---

[16] In most cases, the amount of the fellowship would be expected to reflect the part-time status of the student.

Recommendation 15: A woman desiring to enter graduate or professional school after some years away from higher education, and generally meeting departmental standards for admission (e.g., in her undergraduate grade-point average), should be given an opportunity to make up for her inability to meet any special requirements, such as specific mathematical requirements. Under no circumstances should she be denied admission because her undergraduate education occurred some years earlier.

A good example of the problem involved here can be found in the field of economics, in which mathematical requirements tend to be much more extensive and difficult than they were a few decades ago.

Recommendation 16: Positive attitudes on the part of faculty members toward the serious pursuit of graduate study and research by women are greatly needed. College and university administrations should assume responsibility for adoption of policies that will encourage positive, rather than negative, attitudes of faculty members in all fields.

7. Women as Faculty Members and Academic Administrators

WHERE ARE
THEY?
The relatively small number of women faculty members, especially in the higher ranks of the more prestigious institutions, has received major emphasis among academic women concerned with the status of women in higher education. This has also been the main focus of complaints filed with the U.S. Department of Health, Education and Welfare, and of investigations by HEW. Recently, complaints have also been filed by students, but, as we shall see in the following section, a legal basis for filing complaints existed earlier for faculty members than for students.

As we have seen, women represent about 46 percent of all undergraduates and about 37 percent of graduate students in higher education, but, according to the most recent data available, they represented only 27 percent of college faculty members in 1971–72 (National Education Association, 1972).[1] However, there is a tendency for ratios of women to men to be much smaller in universities, and especially in highly research-oriented universities, than in other types of institutions (Table 5). The largest percentage of women faculty in public institutions occurs in Comprehensive Universities and Colleges I, although in the corresponding private institutions the percentage is one of the smallest. The percentages are higher in Liberal Arts Colleges II than in Liberal Arts Colleges I, in part because Catholic women's colleges and predominantly black colleges, both of which have comparatively large proportions of women on their faculties, are mostly in the former group. National Education Association data for 1971–72, shown in Appendix A,

[1]Unlike the census data cited in Section 3, these data do not include graduate teaching assistants.

109

Table A-17, indicate a larger relative representation of women in public two-year colleges (31 percent) than do the Carnegie Commission 1969 data.[2]

Even more striking is that, during the decade of the most explosive growth in the history of higher education—the 1960s—women lost ground as a percentage of members of regular faculty ranks in four-year institutions, especially at the associate professor level, and gained ground only at the instructor level (Table 7). Other data for 1971–72 indicate that women represented about the same proportion of lecturers as of instructors in that year.[3]

Instructors are junior faculty members who may or may not be in line for advancement to positions on the regular or "ladder" faculty (assistant professor to full professor). They are usually graduate students who are employed in these positions on a temporary basis while completing their doctor's theses. Many universities have policies against advancing their own graduate students to regular faculty positions, on the grounds that a faculty drawn from the ranks of its own students is likely to become too "ingrown, " that is, indoctrinated with the particular approaches and emphases of influential senior faculty members in any given department. In general, we support such policies, but we recognize that they have tended to operate to the disadvantage of married women, who are unable to take advantage of opportunities at distant institutions unless their husbands can make the same geographical move.

Women also make up a sizable proportion of lecturers, and there have been accusations in many institutions that an important type of discrimination is the tendency to keep women in this "nonladder" and nontenure status. In some cases, married women are limited to this status because of antinepotism rules, in some cases because they lack the Ph.D., and in many cases because they wish to work only part time, and departmental or institutional policies discourage appointing part-time faculty members to regular or "ladder" positions. As Bernard (1964, p.

---

[2] Among respondents in the Carnegie Commission survey, faculty members in two-year colleges were somewhat undersampled.

[3] Furthermore, Bayer (1973) reports that the 1972–73 ACE survey of teaching faculty showed that any change in the percentage of women faculty since the 1968–69 survey has been "not so much an increase as a redistribution with the proportions decreasing at two-year and four-year colleges and increasing slightly at universities."

TABLE 7 Women as a percentage of faculty members in four-year colleges and universities	*Faculty rank*	*1959–60*	*1965–66*	*1971–72*
	All ranks	19.1	18.4	19.0
	Professor	9.9	8.7	8.6
	Associate professor	17.5	15.1	14.6
	Assistant professor	21.7	19.4	20.7
	Instructor	29.3	32.5	39.4

SOURCE: National Education Association (1972, p. 13).

100) points out, the availability of qualified married women has made it possible for colleges and universities to use their services as lecturers when and as needed, without having to make a long-term commitment, and many married women are quite content to provide their services in this manner, either because they do not want to go through the arduous program of completing the work for a Ph.D. or because they prefer to work part time. On the other hand, there are many women lecturers who have the doctorate and who deeply resent retention in this "second class" status, which, among other things, usually prevents their membership in the academic senate, and their right to vote on policy issues.

The Ad Hoc Committee on the Status of Women at Oberlin recommended that the position of lecturer be abolished. That recommendation, as well as virtually all the recommendations made by the committee, was adopted in the spring of 1973. One of the committee's reasons for believing that the position of lecturer should be abolished was that in a good many cases married women had been eligible only for lecturer positions because of the impact of the former antinepotism rule, which had been abolished in 1970. The committee commented that the antinepotism rule had "strengthened associations between part-time teaching and marginal status" (see Appendix D).

The salary comparisons in Appendix A, Table A-17, show that median salary differences between men and women tend to be greatest in large public and private universities and lowest in public two-year colleges. At a later point, we shall present a more intensive analysis of salary differences.

Perhaps the most surprising aspect of the status of women as faculty members, however, is the evidence that both the relative representation and status of women have deteriorated over the last 50 years. Chart 13 portrays what has happened to the rela tive representation of women in aggregative terms, while Tabl 7 shows in greater detail what happened in the 1960s.

This decline in the relative representation and status o women on college and university faculties is partly, but by n means wholly, explained by certain long-term trends to whicl we have called attention in earlier sections—changes in mar riage and birthrates, the decline in the relative importance o women's colleges, and the long-term trend toward greater sex differentiation of the fields in which men and women receivec the doctorate (only recently beginning to be reversed). Ther are also indications that the decline has been encouraged by the greatly increased emphasis on research, especially in th sciences, in the 1950s and 1960s. This trend was especially im portant, of course, in the universities that had long been leader in the development of graduate education and research, but it influence clearly trickled down to less prestigious universitie and four-year colleges, which showed an increasing tendency to regard the Harvards and Berkeleys as their models and t recruit faculty members with a record of research and publica tion or at least the potential for such a record in the future. Al this militated against women, and especially married women whose problems in achieving a record of research accomplish ment at a relatively early age we shall examine more intensively in Section 8.[4]

Partly reflecting this historical experience, women in 196! were represented in larger proportions among older faculty members and among the very young than among those aged 2 to 50. There were comparatively few women in the 31 to 40 ag bracket, when married women are likely to be out of the labo force while their children are young. The relatively large repre sentation of women among those aged 25 or less does not neces sarily suggest the "wave of the future," because women in thi age group are likely to be advanced graduate students who ar serving as temporary instructors.[5]

A far larger proportion of women than of men on colleg faculties were single. This reflects, as we found also in the cas

[4] For a more extensive discussion of factors underlying these historical trend see Bernard (1964) and Newcomer (1959).

[5] The data are from the Carnegie Commission survey, as analyzed by Fulto (1973).

CHART 13 *Proportion of total faculty who were women, 1869–1959 (decade-to-decade changes)*

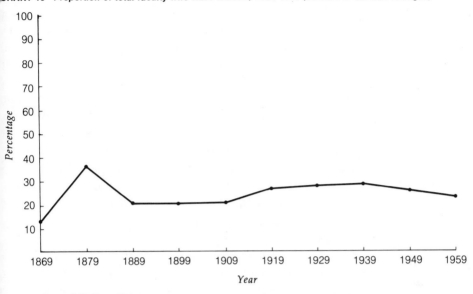

SOURCE: Bernard (1964, p. 39).

of graduate students, the greater difficulties facing married women in serving as faculty members. That younger women were much more likely to be married than older women is not surprising in view of the historical trends in marriage rates and the average age of marriage on which we have commented in earlier sections.

Not only were there relatively fewer women in highly selective research universities, as we noted in Section 5, but this was especially true in the higher ranks and in traditionally male fields (Chart 6 and Appendix C, Table C-2). For example, in these prestigious institutions, only 1 percent or fewer of the full professors were women in physical sciences and business; 2 percent were women in biological sciences and medicine-law; 3 percent were women in social sciences and humanities; and 6 percent in fine arts. Proportions were considerably higher in education (15 percent) and in the new professions (12 percent).

A factor in the lower status of women on college and university faculties is the smaller percentage of women who have doctor's degrees. The Carnegie Commission Survey of Faculty and Student Opinion, 1969, showed that about 83 percent of the male faculty members and 47 percent of the female faculty members in Research Universities I had doctor's degrees.

In other groups of universities smaller percentages of eithe sex had these advanced degrees. Sex differences in this respec were somewhat less pronounced in Liberal Arts Colleges I tha in either universities or comprehensive universities and col leges. In two-year colleges, of course, relatively few facult members of either sex held the doctorate.

Women were also considerably less likely to have tenure tha men. This was, of course, related to their comparatively wea representation in the ranks that usually have tenure (associat and full professors). In addition, men tended to have tenure at considerably earlier age than women. In part, this was ex plained by the fact that men are more heavily represented i such fields as the natural sciences, in which creativity tends t peak at an early age and which are highly competitive, so tha promotion tends to take place early.

The Carnegie Commission Survey of Faculty and Studen Opinion, 1969, yielded some interesting results in relation t religious and racial characteristics of faculty members. Jews o both sexes were represented on faculties in somewhat large proportions than would be expected on the basis of their repre sentation in the population as a whole, whereas the reverse wa decidedly true of Catholics (Appendix A, Table A-18). Howev er, Jewish men were found in relatively larger proportions tha Jewish women on the faculties of private institutions, and es pecially in research-oriented private universities. Catholi women represented a considerably larger proportion of a women on faculties, especially in private institutions, than wa true for Catholic men among male faculty members, but thi was in large part explained by their predominance as facult members of Catholic women's colleges.

Although blacks of both sexes were represented on facultie in much smaller proportions than in the population as a whole black women formed a considerably larger percentage of a women faculty members than did black men of male facult members (Appendix A, Table A-19). Black women facult members were especially likely to be found in liberal art colleges, however, and this undoubtedly represented in larg part their predominance in black liberal arts colleges.

One of the most significant manifestations of the women' movement among professional women has been the formatio of a committee on the status of women in just about every pro fessional field of any importance. Like so many other manifestations of the women's movement, this is a development of the last four or five years. A recent compilation listed more than 50 such committees or caucuses (Sells, 1973). One of the first activities of many of these groups was to survey college and university faculties in the particular discipline to develop more adequate information on the status of women within that discipline. The results have in some cases revealed a more complete absence of women in the more prestigious departments in various fields than our data on Research Universities I would suggest. For example, one of the first reports of this type was presented by Professor Alice Rossi at the 1969 meeting of the American Sociological Association. The survey found, among other things, that there were no women among the 44 full professors in five leading sociology departments—Berkeley, Chicago, Columbia, Harvard, and Michigan (Rossi, 1970). A survey conducted by the Committee on the Status of Women in the Economics Profession found that only about 6 percent of all faculty members in economics in a large sample of four-year colleges and universities were women. This proportion was not out of line with the proportion of doctoral degrees in economics awarded to women in recent years. But the survey also showed that there were no women among the regular faculty members in 18 of the 43 leading economics departments and that only 14 women in the other departments held tenured positions (Bell, 1973, pp. 509–510).

THEIR RELATIVE
SALARIES

The general pattern of lower salaries of women faculty members is revealed in Appendix A, Table A-17.[6] But it requires a complex analysis of appropriate data to determine whether these salary differences suggest discrimination against women or are explained by relatively objective factors, such as the smaller percentage of women faculty members who have Ph.D.'s. Such studies have been carried out by Astin and Bayer (1972) and by Elizabeth Scott, in both cases on the basis of the 1969 Carnegie Commission survey. Astin and Bayer used a linear regression equation with 32 predictor variables, includ-

[6]Detailed data on average salaries of men and women by rank and type of institution have also recently been made available by the U.S. Office of Education, but the general pattern is similar to that shown by the NEA data in Appendix A, Table A-17.

ing rank and various background and achievement characteristics, and found an average residual salary difference of $1,04(
in favor of men after controlling for all the variables.

Elizabeth Scott's analysis, conducted for the Carnegie Commission, was designed to explore more fully whether sex differences in salaries were greater in some types of institutions
and in some fields than in others. Her results confirm and extend the conclusions of Astin and Bayer. They are discussed at
some length in Appendix C and will be summarized only
briefly here.

Scott's results indicate that, after controlling for all the predictor variables included in her equations, the actual average salary of male faculty members exceeded the average that would
have been predicted on the basis of the female equation by
nearly $2,300 (Table 8). Conversely, the actual average salary of
female faculty members was about $1,400 lower than the
average that would have been predicted on the basis of the male
equation. The two amounts differ because (1) the coefficients in
the prediction equation for men are not the same as those for
women and (2) some men, but almost no women, have excep
tionally high actual salaries. When faculty members were clas
sified by type of institution, these residual salary differences
were largest in Research Universities I. They were more moder
ate in other types of institutions and smallest in comprehensive
universities and colleges.

TABLE 8 *Differences between actual average salaries of male and female faculty members and average salaries predicted on the basis of the equation for the opposite sex, by type of institution, 1969*

Institutional type	Number of men*	Average difference for men	Number of women	Average difference for women
Research Universities I	3,760	+$2,729	2,649	−$2,009
Research Universities II and other Doctoral-Granting Universities I and II	3,151	+ 2,303	2,551	− 1,015
Comprehensive Universities and Colleges	985	+ 1,066	1,066	− 358
Liberal Arts Colleges I	605	+ 1,635	714	− 1,025
Liberal Arts Colleges II and two-year colleges	831	+ 1,886	1,342	− 2,002
TOTAL	9,332	+$2,264	8,322	−$1,407

*25 percent random sample of male faculty in survey.

SOURCE: Derived from analysis of Carnegie Commission Survey of Faculty and Student Opinion, 1969.

CHART 14 *Distribution of differences between actual salary and salary predicted from equation for the opposite sex, for male and female faculty members in selected institutions and fields, 1969*

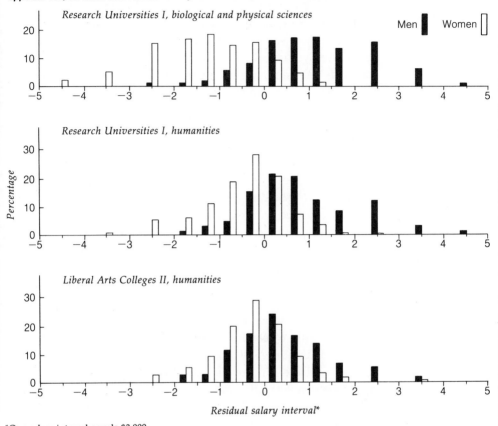

*Residual salary interval**

*One salary interval equals $3,000.

SOURCE: Adapted from Carnegie Commission Survey of Faculty and Student Opinion, 1969.

Some of Scott's most interesting results relate to men and women in selected fields in particular groups of institutions. For example, when the actual salary of each male and female faculty member was compared with the salary that would have been received on the basis of the equation for the opposite sex, it was found that the great majority of men in the biological and physical sciences in Research Universities I received salaries ranging roughly from $1,000 to $7,500 above those that would have been predicted, and small percentages received salaries $10,000 to $13,000 above these predicted amounts. Women's salaries fell below those predicted on the basis of the male equation by similar amounts (Chart 14). Each salary interval in the chart equals $3,000.

A similar pattern emerged in the humanities departments in leading research universities, but the differences were not as wide. The reasons for the more pronounced deviations in the biological and physical sciences are probably to be found in the more highly competitive job market for distinguished men in these fields. The large increase in the percentage of the gross national product expended on research and development between about 1952 and 1964 led to pronounced increases in research activity and graduate training in these fields in universities; to intensified competition among government agencies, industrial firms, and academic institutions for scientific talent; and to chronic shortages of qualified scientists. The intensified competition probably affected men more than women, partly because married women scientists were less likely to be free to move in response to a competitive job offer. In the humanities, supply and demand were in better balance, competition was less intense for talent among academic institutions, and there were practically no attractive employment opportunities outside of higher education for holders of Ph.D.'s in these fields. Even so, it is interesting to note that a few men in the humanities in leading research universities had salaries that exceeded predicted amounts by about as much as those of the most highly paid men in the biological and physical sciences. This apparently reflects the pattern at a few of these prestigious universities that make a point of paying professors in the humanities as much as those in the sciences. Where such policies did not prevail, lower relative salaries in the humanities did not usually reflect differences in salary schedules among the various fields but rather the fact that in the more competitive fields people are promoted faster and move in larger proportions to "above-scale" salaries.

An aspect of the intense competition that developed in the natural sciences, and to some extent in the social sciences, during the 1950s and 1960s was that prestigious academicians were able to negotiate large research grants from the federal government and from foundations. A university attempting to hire one of these prominent scientists would not only add to the prestige of its faculty but also to its research program, including funds for the support of graduate research assistants. Frequently a faculty member hired away from another university would bring an existing grant with him.

Results of Scott's analysis for all major groups of fields and types of institutions are included in Appendix C, Tables C-3 to C-12. The data provide evidence of a pervasive pattern of lower compensation for women that is not explained by the predictor variables. The fact that the results measure statistical tendencies must be kept in mind, of course. It is possible that a close examination of the files of these women would reveal some justification for the relatively low compensation, but the probability of so many unusual cases is very small.

IS THERE DIS-CRIMINATION? Both the Astin-Bayer and the Scott findings strongly suggest that there is discrimination against women in status and compensation in higher education. In virtually all public institutions and in many private institutions that have formal salary structures, the discrimination does not take the form of paying a woman a lower salary than a man when she is in the same step of the same rank, but it does take the form of not moving her up through the steps and ranks as quickly. Scott's analysis shows that in Research Universities I in the sciences, salaries increased with years of academic employment about twice as rapidly for men as for women. Another important factor is the retention of many women in the position of lecturer or instructor.

How does this discrimination come about? It is doubtful that it results from deliberate decisions of college and university administrators to discriminate against women, but rather from myriads of individual decisions within departments and schools that do the actual recruitment and selection of faculty members (subject to subsequent administration approval) and that initiate the recommendations for merit increases and promotions. We have earlier commented on the flexibility in the use of faculty members that departments achieve by employing women as part-time lecturers, and on the fact that some women are quite content with this type of employment, while others deeply resent it.

The charge is frequently made by academic women, with considerable justification, that the recruitment methods used by departments and schools tend to favor men. The typical procedure in prestigious departments is for the department chairman or the chairman of the department's personnel committee to visit the ten to a dozen most distinguished departments in his field in other universities and to interview advanced candidates for the Ph.D. Women charge that the candidates who are recommended for interview under these procedures tend to be the men being trained by faculty members who want to see them placed in prestigious institutions, where their performance will redound to the credit of the department in which they have been trained. Whether or not these faculty members are less interested in their women students, it is charged, they are likely to think that women will not acquire distinguished records through their future research and publication activities. Yet there are exceptions to these prevailing practices. Some faculty members and some search committees have made special efforts to recruit more broadly.

Less distinguished departments will tend to recruit among more graduate schools than leading departments do, because their chances of hiring from the most prestigious departments are less good. But, in general, academic recruitment procedures tend to be somewhat "cosy." Especially among the more prestigious departments, openings are not publicized. Interviews with prospective candidates are conducted either at the candidate's university, at the university doing the hiring (by invitation), or at professional association meetings. Even at the association meetings, however, it is frequently very difficult for jobseekers to discover which departments have openings. The United States public employment service tries to make its services available at these meetings, but the more distinguished departments are unlikely to list their openings, because they prefer to limit their interviews to candidates who have been recommended to them by the departments from which they usually hire. In fact, the representatives from leading departments who are on hand to do the interviewing conducts a steady stream of interviews, even without advertising their presence to all prospective jobseekers.

Now, not only under the impact of HEW pressure, but also as a result of the activities of the numerous committees on the status of women, the cosier methods of recruitment are breaking down. Many of the women's committees have devoted considerable energy to the development of rosters of available women. Some of these committees, and, in fact, some energetic individual women, have been systematically contacting departments to determine what openings will be available and to obtain biographical information on women who are about to receive their doctor's degrees. One of the busiest centers of activity at the 1972 annual meeting of the American Economic Association in Toronto was an office maintained by the Committee on the Status of Women in the Economics Profession. A steady stream of women who were in the job market came to fill out biographical forms, and a sizable number of potential employers came to provide information on their openings. The employers were frequently academic but were also frequently representatives of federal agencies seeking economists.

Whatever the relative influence of government pressure versus the activity of women's groups, a number of leading universities have reported stepped up hiring of women in the last few years. We shall have more to say about their policies in the next section.

Once a woman has been hired, however, the big question is whether she will have an equal opportunity to receive merit increases and promotions. Our data indicate that the situation as recently as 1969 was not at all encouraging in this respect. Some married women clearly fall behind because they take time out to have children, but this is by no means the full explanation.[7] We would suggest that departments tend to take advantage of the fact that women have less bargaining power than men, for at least three reasons:

1 First, and most important, a married woman is not usually in a position to move to another college or university at some distance unless her husband is also negotiating a move to the same area. But men tend to receive their largest salary increases when they receive attractive offers from other institutions. Either the offer is accepted, and the move is accomplished with a sizable salary increase, or a corresponding or even greater increase is negotiated at the individual's present institution. A married woman cannot convincingly negotiate on the basis of another job offer unless it is clear that her husband is also seriously considering a move to the same area. And married women are not particularly likely to receive unsolicited job offers involving a

---

[7]In fact, the latest ACE survey of teaching faculty found that in 1972–73 nearly one-fourth of all faculty had interrupted their professional careers more than one year for military or family reasons and that, moreover, a greater percentage of men than of women had done so (Bayer, 1973).

geographical move, because of the assumption that they would not be likely to accept.

It is true that these mobility constraints are changing and may change even more in the future. It is now not uncommon for academic couples to give the same, or even greater, consideration to the wife's employment status in decisions that might involve a move, and the availability of jet planes has made possible long-distance commuting that would have been unthinkable a few decades ago. There are a good many examples of both male and female faculty members who teach at some distance from home. In some cases, for example, this involves being away from home three or four days a week and returning home for long weekends.

2 As secondary earners in the family, academic women typically do not need to strive for salary increases as vigorously as men. As long as their compensation represents a comfortable contribution to the family income, they are likely in many cases to be content. Thus, in the economist's terms, secondary earners tend to have different labor supply functions from primary earners.

3 A more subtle influence is the feeling of some women that reaching a salary or career status superior to their husbands' is something to be avoided—a woman might somehow lose some of her charm and femininity in her husband's eyes if this occurred. We have earlier referred to Matina Horner's research on achievement motivation. Similar points have been made by Graham (1970), and Keniston and Keniston (1964).

To sum up, then, discrimination tends to occur at the departmental level, but college and university administrations have been guilty of indifference to the problem. Departments have not been asked whether they passed over qualified female candidates in appointments and promotions or whether their recruitment procedures included special efforts to search for qualified women. Now, under pressure from the federal government and from women's committees, institutions are developing affirmative action policies that embody intensive scrutiny of departmental procedures, but progress in developing and implementing these policies is frequently very slow.

WOMEN IN AD-MINISTRATION   If women are thinly represented on faculties, especially in traditionally male fields, they are so rarely represented in top academic administrative positions as to be practically nonexistent in the upper echelons. The Catholic women's colleges are an exception. In the latter part of 1971, virtually no four-year coeducational institution was headed by a woman. Even among the nonsectarian women's colleges there were only eight female presidents—in marked contrast with the situation in the latter part of the nineteenth century and the early years of the present century. And schools of social work, which used to have women deans quite frequently, were almost exclusively headed by men (Pifer, 1971).

Other data based on a recent survey of the representation of women among academic administrators are included in Appendix A, Table A-20. One of the factors that has contributed to a decline in the number of women holding administrative positions in coeducational institutions has been the elimination of deans of women or their subordination to deans of students.

What accounts for the fact that so few women are now serving as presidents in nonsectarian women's colleges in contrast with the situation in their earlier histories? The factors are much the same as those explaining the decline in the relative representation of women on the faculties of these institutions. Early women presidents, like M. Carey Thomas of Bryn Mawr, were unmarried. This was so much the tradition that Alice Freeman retired as president of Wellesley in 1887 when she married George Herbert Palmer of Harvard (Bernard, 1964, p. 16). In more recent years, there has been much emphasis on college or university presidency as a two-person job, with the president's wife assuming the role of first lady and chief hostess. Not many married couples—as yet, at least—would be likely to accept the recent Bennington solution of wife as president and husband as vice-president. The fact is that there have been a good many instances in which married women have declined offers of the presidency of a women's college because it would have been inconvenient for the spouses involved to give up often prestigious positions of their own to move to the neighborhood of the women's college. There have also been examples of men refusing presidencies because of the wife's employment status. The women's movement may nevertheless bring about a reversal of the downward trend in women's presidencies of women's colleges. In recent years men have replaced women as presidents at Bryn Mawr, Sarah Lawrence, and Vassar. But when Radcliffe set out to find a successor to Mary Bunting, a firm decision was made at an early stage to confine the search to women. Smith is reported to be looking for a woman to succeed its male president when he retires (Bird, 1972, p. 64).

THE PROSPECTS   As the rate of increase of enrollments in higher education declines in the 1970s, it will become increasingly difficult to correct sexual and racial imbalances on college and university faculties. Elizabeth Scott has developed projections of percentages of faculty members who will be women in future years in universities, four-year colleges, and two-year colleges, on the basis of several assumed ratios of women to men among newly hired faculty members and several projected turnover rates. The projections are presented in Appendix C, Charts C-1 to C-4 and in Table C-13. Chart C-1 shows the growth path in the percentage of faculty members of universities who will be women from 1970 to 1990 for six different initial percentages of faculty who are women, on the assumption that the proportion of new hires who are women is a constant 30 percent. This chart is particularly appropriate for assessing the situation in individual universities, because some have ratios of women to men that are considerably lower or higher than the average 15 percent for universities. Chart C-2 shows the average growth path for universities on the basis of four different assumptions about the percentage of women among new hires. Only when 100 percent of the new hires are women will the percentage of all faculty members who are women reach 50 percent in the 1980s. To reach an average percentage of 30 percent women in 1990, universities as a whole would have to maintain a constant proportion of women among new hires of 50 percent.

In practice, maintaining a hiring rate of 50 percent women is inconceivable for universities, or for any other group of institutions that normally recruits largely, or almost entirely, among holders of doctor's degrees.[8] As we have seen, women have represented only 13 to 14 percent of the recipients of doctor's degrees in the last few years. The proportion varies by field, of course, but even in such fields as English and education, women make up only 20 to 30 percent of the Ph.D. recipients (Chart 9). Only in nursing, in which the number of Ph.D.'s awarded is extremely small, and in home economics do women represent a large majority of Ph.D. recipients. In setting goals for its affirmative action program for the next five years, Columbia University mentioned pools ranging from about 2 to 5 percent women in such fields as business administration, engineering, and law to 47 percent in social work. (Women represented only 36 percent of the recipients of doctor's degrees in social work in 1970, but a good many faculty members in schools of social work, especially those who supervise field work, do not have doctor's degrees.) Intermediate between these extremes, pools of 20 percent women in the humanities, 10 percent in the social sciences, and 10 percent in the natural sciences were mentioned. In setting its actual goals, Columbia took into account not only these percentages, but also existing percentages of women among faculty members in these groups of fields (Columbia University, 1972, pp. 6–7).

The projections in Appendix C suggest that it is exceedingly important for universities and colleges to take vigorous steps to correct imbalances in the immediate future, while enrollment increases continue to stimulate modest increases in the demand for faculty members. The most rapid increases in enrollment, in fact, are occurring in two-year colleges, where sexual imbalances on faculties are least serious. As in the case of graduate students, it would have been far easier to provide increased opportunities for women on faculties a decade ago, when enrollments were rising exceedingly rapidly.

Of special interest in this connection is that, in December 1971, Stanford University announced that it was establishing a faculty Affirmative Action Fund of $75,000 of annually recurring

---

[8] A common practice in the 1950s and 1960s was to hire a young man who had completed all the requirements for the Ph.D. except for the thesis and to give him the title of "acting assistant professor" until his thesis was completed. This practice is becoming less common in the current unfavorable job market for Ph.D.'s.

"budget-base money" to "provide a special means for increasing the proportion of women and ethnic minority group members on the faculty" (Appendix D).

8. Affirmative Action

Beginning about 1968, pressure began to be applied to colleges and universities to develop affirmative action policies that would improve employment opportunities for women. Pressure had been applied relating to minority groups earlier, but the policies that had been adopted to improve employment opportunities for minority groups by no means fully met the special problems of women. For example, antinepotism rules are not especially likely to have a discriminatory impact on employment of minority men, but they do frequently bar the employment of a qualified married woman, because such women are frequently married to a person in the same field.

The initial pressure relating to sex-based discrimination often came from women's groups on campuses. The numerous committees or caucuses on the status of women in various professions were also instrumental in developing pressure. And early in 1970 the federal government moved into the situation much more actively than before, largely as a result of a complaint filed by a small, relatively unknown women's civil rights group, the Women's Equity Action League. The WEAL complaint was filed against the entire academic community, charging it with an "industrywide" pattern of sex discrimination. The charges were accompanied by about 80 pages of documentation and were later followed by more than 360 class-action complaints filed by WEAL and other women's groups against individual institutions (Sandler, 1973a, p. 8).

Before discussing the consequences of the WEAL complaint, we need to trace briefly the development of federal legislation and policy that provided a legal basis for the complaint. The first significant piece of legislation relating to sex discrimination in employment was the Equal Pay Act of 1963, although this legislation did not apply to administrative and professional employees until July 1972. Next came the prohibition of sex discrimination in employment under Title VII of the Civil Rights Act of 1964.[1] The provisions did not apply to academic employment until they were extended by the Equal Employment Opportunity Act of 1972, which included educational institutions for the first time under the 1964 Civil Rights Act ban on job discrimination because of race, color, sex, religion, or national origin. The legislation authorized the Equal Employment Opportunity Commission to take universities to court if women's complaints of sex bias in employment were considered valid after an investigation and could not be resolved by conciliation. The commission may bring charges both in individual cases and where it is alleged that a pattern of discrimination exists (Fields, 1972*a*, p. 2).

However, the WEAL action was brought under the executive order banning discrimination by employers having federal contracts. In January 1970, this order was largely unknown in the academic community, because it had been enforced only in other sectors of society. To the extent that the order was known, it was in connection with the negotiation of federal research contracts, which had to include clauses calling for nondiscriminatory policies in the employment of persons paid by the federal research funds. Sex guidelines had not been issued by the government, and Order No. 4, which included the requirements for affirmative action plans, did not apply to women, only to minorities.

Executive Order 11246, as amended by Order 11375 of October 1968, provides that all educational institutions with federal contracts of over $10,000 are prohibited from discrimination in employment on the basis of sex, as well as race, color, religion, and national origin. In addition, under Revised Order No. 4 of

[1]Caroline Bird presents a fascinating account of how Representative Howard W. Smith of Virginia, a foe of the proposed Civil Rights Act, introduced the sex amendment in an attempt to surround the debate with ridicule and laughter. If Title VII could not be beaten, perhaps it could be laughed off the floor. The idea of introducing the amendment was apparently prompted by a question directed to Smith by May Craig, a strong feminist, on "Meet the Press" several weeks earlier (Bird, with Briller, 1972, pp. 1–7).

December 1971, all institutions employing 50 or more persons and receiving $50,000 or more in federal contract or grant funds must have affirmative action plans, including numerical goals and timetables.[2] Institutions found in violation of the Order are subject to having any pending government contracts delayed and current contracts canceled; they may even be declared ineligible for future contracts. In its application to colleges and universities, the Order is enforced by the Office for Civil Rights in the Department of Health, Education and Welfare, although for other federal contractors it is enforced by the Department of Labor, so that certain types of important final decisions for colleges and universities would be made by the Secretary of Labor, on the recommendation of the Secretary of HEW.

Early attempts of the federal government to investigate the complaints brought by WEAL and other groups and to threaten withholding of funds unless certain steps were taken by the institutions were often clumsy and were rightly resented by the affected institutions. Investigators were frequently unfamiliar with the special problems of academic employment, policies followed by regional representatives varied from region to region, and some of the orders initially directed to individual institutions were crude and unworkable in an academic setting. Even some of the women who were interviewed by HEW investigators found some of the questions they were asked offensive and lacking in understanding of an academic environment.

In October 1972, the Office for Civil Rights sent to college and university presidents a detailed and explicit set of guidelines to be followed in implementing affirmative action on campuses. They apply to all educational institutions with federal contracts of over $10,000. They relate not only to women but also to members of minority groups, but we shall confine our discussion to their applicability to women. In general, the guidelines were greeted with relief in the academic community, because they showed more understanding of the special problems of academic employment than some earlier HEW actions had suggested.

Based chiefly on Executive Order 11246 (though provisions of

[2]This provision applied only to private institutions at first but was amended early in 1973 to apply, also, to public institutions.

Title VII are also pertinent), the guidelines emphasize the distinction between *nondiscrimination* and *affirmative action*. Nondiscrimination is defined as "the elimination of all existing discriminatory conditions, whether purposeful or inadvertent," on the basis of race, color, religion, national origin, or sex. Affirmative action goes beyond, ensuring "employment neutrality" in the area of deliberate and positive efforts on the part of institutions to rectify existing inequities that result from past discrimination.

To determine whether such inequities exist, and to what extent, a job analysis must be undertaken to identify "underutilization" of women, as determined by the availability of qualified women. The guidelines recognize that it is often difficult to determine figures for available academic personnel, because some faculty positions require highly specialized skills and because the recruitment pool for some institutions may be national or even international. They suggest that, in the case of senior-level positions, at least three data sources may be consulted: the National Science Foundation's National Register of Scientific and Technical Personnel,[3] the U.S. Office of Education's annual reports of earned degrees, and the National Research Council of the National Academy of Science. For junior-level positions, it is suggested that institutions consult the Office of Education's annual report of earned degrees for the past five years and data on current graduate school enrollments. In these ways, each institution can arrive at some estimate of the number of qualified women, by field, who make up the pool from which it may draw and, further, can assess the extent of their underutilization.

On the basis of this job analysis, the institution is further required to have an affirmative action plan that sets numerical goals consistent with the available pool and with projected turnover in employment and that specifies a time schedule for improving the situation. The guidelines stress that these goals are targets to be aimed at, not quotas that must be met within the specified time period.

The institution itself, not HEW, establishes the criteria for

[3]The Committee on the Status of Women in the Economics Profession has found the National Roster quite incomplete, especially because it tends to include only persons who are employed.

hiring, promotion, etc., and is required to make them "reasonably explicit" and available to applicants and employees. The individual departments or units at an institution must keep records that document reasons for employment decisions; in addition, a central institutional office must audit and monitor the departments and units, making a formal report annually to the Office for Civil Rights (OCR) on the progress of the affirmative action program. OCR is empowered to examine the relevant documents with the intention of determining whether the institution has been making "good faith" efforts to implement its program.

Other important requirements (or recommendations) covered by the guidelines are (1) that institutions take active steps to identify and recruit women by using search committees that include women, by drawing on data provided by women's groups and disciplinary and professional associations, by advertising openings through channels that will reach women, and by stating in such advertising that they are equal opportunity employers; (2) that salaries be based on qualifications and merit rather than on ascriptive qualities; (3) that antinepotism rules be abolished; (4) that policies which prohibit a department from hiring its own graduate students be reconsidered, since they have often worked to the disadvantage of women; (5) that maternity leave be granted to women and parental leave for child rearing be granted to both sexes; and (6) that sound internal grievance procedures be developed. Finally, the institution must have a written policy of nondiscrimination and must publish its affirmative action plan.

At any point during a compliance review of an individual institution, HEW can delay awarding a new contract should it find that the institution is in noncompliance and that reasonable efforts to secure compliance by conciliation and conference are not working. This delay is often for a specific number of days, within which the institution must move into compliance if it wants new contracts. The procedure for delay of a *new* contract is fairly informal, but the procedure for termination or suspension of an existing contract is much more formal, involving a hearing before the sanction is imposed (Sandler & Steinbach, 1972). In actual practice, there have been a number of decisions to delay contracts, but there has never been a termination.

SOME CASE HISTORIES In November 1970 it was reported that investigations of alleged employment discrimination against women were under way or had been completed at about 18 colleges and universities. Since then there have been many more charges and investigations. There is little need to discuss the charges in detail. Enough has been said in the preceding section to provide an indication of the status of women on college and university faculties. One point worth repeating and often made by women pressing charges is that, in general, the more prestigious the institution, the fewer women are to be found in the higher ranks of its faculty.

One of the first institutions to be extensively involved in negotiations relating to charges of sex discrimination was the University of Michigan, whose president, Robben W. Fleming, is a labor lawyer with a long record of experience in arbitration and industrial relations. Following an investigation, it was reported that a contract awarded to the institution by the Agency for International Development was being held up. Shortly thereafter HEW issued a list of nine requirements that the university would have to meet to continue its eligibility for federal contracts:

1. Achieve salary equity in every job category.

2. Compensate through payment of back wages each female employee who has lost wages due to discriminatory treatment. Payments must be retroactive to October 13, 1968 (the date of Executive Order 11246).

3. Achieve a ratio of female employment in academic positions at least equivalent to availability as determined by the number of qualified female applicants.

4. Increase ratios of female admissions to all Ph.D. graduate programs.

5. Increase the participation of women in committees involving the selection and treatment of employees.

---

[4] These included Albany State College, Georgia; Borough of Manhattan Community College; Brooklyn College; Brown University; Georgia Institute of Technology; Georgia State University; Harvard University; Loyola University, Los Angeles; New Mexico State University; St. John's University, New York; Tufts University; University of Georgia; University of Pittsburgh; University of Michigan; University of San Francisco; University of Texas Medical School in Dallas; University of Vermont; and University of Wisconsin ("HEW Probing Alleged Employment Bias," 1970).

6. Develop a written policy on nepotism which will ensure correct treatment of tandem teams.

7. Analyze the past effects of antinepotism policies and retroactively compensate (to October 13, 1968) any person who has suffered discrimination as a result.

8. Assure that female applicants for nonacademic employment receive consideration commensurate with their qualifications; also ensure that any conception of male and female job classifications is eliminated in recruitment procedures.

9. Assure that all present female employees occupying clerical and other nonacademic positions and possessing qualifications equal to, or exceeding, those of male employees occupying higher level positions be given primary consideration for promotion (Bazell, 1970).

In January 1971, it was reported that the university and HEW had reached agreement and that several contracts that had been withheld were being approved. President Fleming had protested the third requirement listed above as "unworkable because it ignores the quality of applicants and lends itself to artificially increasing the number of women who apply." According to the university, HEW had agreed that other factors in addition to the percentage of applications should be considered. On the fourth provision, it was reported that the question of the ratio of women admitted to Ph.D. programs had been submitted to then-HEW Secretary Elliot L. Richardson for a ruling. The university contended that there were no Ph.D. programs in which admissions were specifically related to employment opportunities ("U. of Michigan, HEW Agree," 1971, p. 4). We have been informed that the ruling was never issued. The legal situation relating to admission to Ph.D. programs has, of course, changed under the provisions of Educational Amendments of 1972, which ban discrimination by graduate and professional schools.

On January 4, 1971, President Fleming appointed a Commission for Women to evaluate and monitor fulfillment of the affirmative action goals. In November 1972, *Science* magazine reported that the commission was regarded by some women as too "establishment," but that it had "a secure place, an influential voice, and a no-nonsense chairwoman, lawyer Virginia Davis Nordin, who divides her time between the commission and her teaching job at the Center for Continuing Legal Education" ("Women in Michigan," 1972, p. 841). In an address to the faculty that fall, President Fleming made the following comments:

On the question of equity for women, as well as others, we have had an outside consulting agency review our professional and administrative personnel policies, and we hope by the end of the year to have made significant changes in some of our policies. We have reviewed all female salaries as compared with those of men, and a large number of adjustments have been made. We have a grievance procedure under which those who are dissatisfied may complain. We have tried to open up new classifications for women.

Our critics will say that we have done far too little, and much too late. I do not agree with that point of view, and I will gladly debate it publicly, but I certainly do not wish to silence it.

A word remains to be said about the work of our Commission for Women. Aside from a Chairwoman and a full-time secretary, most of their work is now on a voluntary basis. We do not always agree with one another's point of view, but it needs to be said for them that they have devoted untold hours and effort toward trying to better the lot of women within the University, and that their efforts have been both reasonable and constructive. When we disagree it is not, I believe, because either of us wishes to be capricious or arbitrary, but because we have genuine differences of opinion, or perhaps because we have different prejudices! (Fleming, 1972, p. 18).

We have been informed that Michigan's affirmative action plan has been revised several times, in an attempt to meet HEW objections, but that it has not yet (July 1973) received HEW approval.

Even more protracted than those of Michigan have been Columbia University's negotiations with the federal government. A series of negotiations began on January 31, 1969. Eleven months later the university submitted an affirmative action plan to the Office for Civil Rights. The plan was accepted with the condition that Columbia make a series of modifications. At that stage the concern was over employment opportunities for minority groups. It was only later, when charges were filed by a group of Columbia women, that the question of women was brought into the contention. According to J. Stanley Pottinger, then director of HEW's Office for Civil

Rights, the requested modifications were never received, and, therefore, in February 1971, his office initiated a second review of Columbia's employment practices. In November 1971, it was reported that Pottinger was asking the department's general counsel to initiate action "to terminate all existing federal contracts with Columbia University and all of its divisions and to debar the University and all of its divisions from future participation in federal contracts." The action was reported to be the first time that the OCR had initiated formal proceedings to end all federal contracts with a university, although approval of contracts with about 35 institutions had been temporarily delayed (Semas, 1971, p. 5).

In March 1972 the ban on federal contracts was lifted when Columbia submitted an interim affirmative action plan, and in September 1972 it was reported that the Office for Civil Rights was drafting a letter indicating acceptance of Columbia's "final affirmative action" plan, while "raising some areas of concern which will be negotiated out later" ("Columbia Passes U.S. Test," 1972). Excerpts from Columbia's plan, which was published in December 1972, are included in Appendix D.

However, in February 1973, it was reported that once again the federal government had held up a $1.9 million contract with Columbia, pending a meeting between the university and the OCR to determine if Columbia's affirmative action plan had been violated. A Columbia women's organization had complained to the OCR that two recent appointments had violated the plan ("Columbia Contract Withheld," 1973, p. 2).

These two case histories, as well as others, indicate that negotiations with the federal government may be very prolonged. But they also indicate, especially in the Michigan case, that federal officials were led to better understanding of the special problems of academic employment in their early negotiations with colleges and universities. The guidelines issued in the fall of 1972 reflect this improved understanding.

POLICY CONSID-ERATIONS In October 1972, at the annual meeting of the American Council on Education, which was concerned with women in higher education, President Martha E. Peterson of Barnard College charged that the hostile reaction to women's demands for equal treatment on the nation's campuses had provided a prime ex-

ample of the academic community's lack of internal leadership
She observed that the "higher education community seemed
unable to recognize and to take action in correcting injustices
until forced to do so.... The disgrace of 'affirmative action' is
that HEW had to get into it at all" (Fields, 1972b, p. 3).

We agree that it was unfortunate that most colleges and
universities did not display greater sensitivity to the charges
made by women's groups on their campuses. Federal government intervention is justified because of neglect of this significant aspect of civil rights, but it is imposing a heavy price in
terms of potential interference with the autonomy of institutions and in terms of the detailed record-keeping and reporting,
as well as the time-consuming negotiations, that are required.
However, we do believe that the guidelines issued in the fall of
1972 show a much more reasonable approach to the policies that
must be followed by institutions of higher education than had
been suggested by some earlier federal action.

In fact, there had been a good deal of confusion and misun-
derstanding about HEW's earlier policies. A rather widespread
impression in the academic community was that quotas were
being imposed. HEW officials contend, on the contrary, that
quotas were never imposed. There are indications, however,
that the distinction between goals and quotas was not really understood by some regional HEW officials.

Because this report is concerned with the special problems of
women in higher education, its recommendations relate particularly to the problem of discrimination on the basis of sex. But
many of the recommendations in this report apply equally well
to discrimination against members of minority groups, and we
support their implementation in that context as well. Minority
group women would, of course, benefit from implementation
of the recommendations.

Because the problem of discrimination in faculty appointments and promotions is the most difficult and sensitive aspect
of affirmative action policies, we shall give special consideration to these problems in the present section. Our recommendations relating to undergraduate and graduate students have
been included in earlier sections.

The Commission believes that the evidence we have presented in Section 7 relating to the representation of women on
college and university faculties, and to the lower salaries

women receive, indicates clearly that a serious problem of discrimination exists and that the problem is particularly acute in leading research universities and in the departments and schools in those universities that have traditionally had predominantly male faculties.

However, we strongly believe that colleges and universities should take the initiative, without waiting for federal pressure, to develop affirmative action policies and to see that they are carried out. Such action is long overdue in terms of fair treatment. In addition, the more progress an institution of higher education makes in achieving the goals of an affirmative action policy, the less risk there will be of federal interference and the less likely it will be to get involved in court cases.

We also believe that colleges and universities can achieve affirmative action goals without the lowering of standards that some critics of affirmative action imply will be inevitable. As we have stated elsewhere:

...a department or a college can be a better balanced and more effective institution if it draws its faculty from among members of minority groups and from among women as well as from among majority males. Such a department or college can, we believe, provide a better environment for all students while also supplying "models" for women students and members of minority groups to try to emulate—but the "models" must be worth emulating academically. Contributions to a better balanced and more effective environment for students should be considered, of course, along with the other more traditional standards of academic performance. These other standards, however, are never fully precise and are always multidimensional, and judgments are often made among people who are reasonably equal in realized and potential talent and performance rather than among a group where each person is "head-and-shoulders" above each next person with one person being clearly outstanding; there is usually a range of competent and acceptable persons for the particular job within which a choice is made.

We are not suggesting a new basic principle to be made operative in the employment of faculty members. Departments and colleges are always, and quite rightly, concerned with balance—among younger and older faculty members, as between and among fields and points of view and methodologies, as between those who have potential interests in administrative work and those who do not, as between those with special concern for student interests and those without, and in other ways. Balance, and, consequently, greater potential effectiveness for the department or college, is a standard criterion in making appointments. The standard question is not whether a candidate is the best single person regardless of field, or age, or interests. The standard question is, rather, whether a candidate is the best person for the department or college considering balance and overall effectiveness. We affirm the principle of balance, and we believe it should be extended to consideration also of race and sex where such consideration may add to the effectiveness of the department or college as a whole—where the capacity to inspire students from varied backgrounds is important, and where sensitivity to their special problems and attitudes is needed. We support academic excellence, although we define it somewhat more broadly than has been traditional. The best person should be chosen for the job, but *best* should be defined to include, along with many other characteristics, consideration for the welfare of the entire student group that will be affected.

Thus we believe that members of minority groups and women should be given special consideration in hiring when such persons have the training and the background to perform competently the teaching and research and other assignments of the university or college, and when such special consideration is essential to the creation of a more effective total academic environment. The requirements (1) that members of previously excluded groups be fully competent to perform the tasks for which they are employed and (2) that their employment adds to the effectiveness of the department or college as a whole, obviate the possibility of lowering academic standards by the employment of university and college faculty from among members of groups that were previously excluded or discriminated against (Carnegie Commission, 1973*d*, pp. 31–33).

We do not share the views of some male academic critics of affirmative action for women whose writings imply that increasing the number of women on faculties will inevitably lower quality.[5] Such views are inconsistent with the evidence on the relative ability of women holding doctor's degrees. We do believe, however, that some of this criticism has arisen because departments or schools have unwisely explained the rejection of particular white male candidates on the ground that their institution's policies force them to hire women or members of minority groups. We believe that such explanations often provide a convenient way out of informing a particular candidate that he is not the most qualified applicant for a position. They should be avoided for this reason and because they are

[5]See, for example, Van Dyne (1973, p. 4).

not consistent with the principle of balance that we have discussed above.

At the same time, we recognize the difficulties involved in developing goals and timetables that are appropriate for specific departments and schools. The sources of information mentioned in the federal guidelines are useful, but by no means all recipients of doctor's degrees in the last five years, for example, are in the job market at any given time. The concept of pools of available men and women is elusive, because it is extremely difficult to determine how many persons are actually seeking an academic position or could be moved from an existing position with proper inducements. The rosters that various groups of professional women are developing will be very useful in this connection.

Even so, it is important to recognize that pools are not legally defined as those persons who are in the job market or available at any given time, but rather, and quite properly, in terms of numbers of qualified persons regardless of availability.

Another extremely important point, which tends to be overlooked in much of the discussion of these issues, is that most women who are qualified for academic positions very much want to be considered on their merits and do not want to be given preference over a more highly qualified man.

We also believe that there is a tendency among some of the white male academic critics to exaggerate the threat to employment opportunities for white men. Granted, we are facing a situation in which the rate of increase in the number of faculty members employed is slowing down, and faculty employment may well become stationary or actually decline for a time in the 1980s. The potential job shortage for both sexes is most serious in the humanities and arts, in which women tend to be relatively well represented, but there are so few female Ph.D.'s in some of the traditionally male fields that it will be a long time before the competition of women presents any real threat. Early in 1971 it was reported that women Ph.D.'s had been hurt more than men by the deterioration in the market for Ph.D.'s ("Women Ph.D.'s Hurt More," 1971, p. 4).

Probably the most serious handicap facing married women desirous of a teaching career in higher education, especially in research-oriented universities, is that in the very age range in which men are beginning to achieve a reputation through research and publication, 25 to 35, married women are likely to be bearing and rearing their children. In some fields, in which the advancement of knowledge proceeds very rapidly, particularly the natural sciences and some of the social sciences, it may be very difficult for a woman to recover the ground lost by withdrawing from professional activity during this period. It requires an exceptional amount of self-discipline to attempt to keep up with the literature in one's field when one is primarily involved in household and child-rearing activities. However, in a follow-up study of Radcliffe Ph.D.'s, one married woman stressed the importance of doing this:

It is possible to keep up with developments in one's field even when not working, and this is important if one wants to pick up one's career when children are older (Radcliffe Committee, 1956, p. 61).

Exacerbating the difficulty for women in some fields is that the age at which creativity peaks varies considerably by field and tends to occur as early as age 28 or so in physics and mathematics. On the other hand, in some of the humanities, withdrawing from professional activity for a period may not seriously affect one's later career.

An important distinction in this context is that a woman may be equal in ability and in potential accomplishment to men who are being considered for a given appointment or promotion, without being equal in achievement. Thus, in judging a woman's research record, she should not be considered inferior if, having been held back by child rearing, her published or unpublished work is of high quality but does not measure up quantitatively to that of men with whom she is being compared. In other words, weight should be given to her research *potential* as indicated by the quality of her doctor's thesis and other available evidence. This is especially relevant to her initial appointment. At a later stage, what may be needed in connection with promotion from assistant to associate professor (the stage at which tenure is usually granted) is a somewhat longer period of time in which to build a research record for married women with children who have withdrawn from the labor force for a period or served on a part-time basis.

Related to this issue is the relative importance to be assigned to teaching and research as criteria for promotion. Especially in research-oriented universities, there has been a tendency to pay lip service to the teaching-ability criterion while in practice paying attention almost solely to the research and publication criterion, although there is variation from department to department in this respect. Even more serious has been a tendency, probably chiefly in less prestigious institutions, to place primary emphasis on quantity rather than on quality of publication. Not just in the interests of women, but in the interests of better teaching, we have elsewhere recommended and at this point emphasize again, the need to give greater relative emphasis to teaching ability as a criterion for promotion than has been typical in many highly research-oriented universities in the recent past.

In Appendix D we have included excerpts from affirmative action policy statements of selected institutions, arranged according to subject matter for ready comparison. These statements show that there is considerable variation in the extent to which individual institutions have departed from traditional policies in developing these statements. This is true with respect to the relative emphasis on and specificity of goals and timetables relating to both women and minority groups. It is also true with respect to changes in policies regarding such questions as part-time appointments and modification of antinepotism rules.

We believe that administrative and departmental policies should not bar a woman from serving on a part-time basis or from promotion to tenure even though she wishes to continue to serve part time. As her children grow older, conversion of the position to a full-time basis may be possible. Men who want to teach part time because of family circumstances should also be given the same consideration.

It is sometimes argued that two part-time faculty members are not as satisfactory as one full-time member, but this impression seems to be based on the fact that many part-time faculty members are professional men with expertise in a given specialty, and whose chief employment is in a different setting. Frequently their practice is to come onto campus only to meet a class and then to depart immediately. They are not usually available for committee service. This is often true of part-time clinical professors in medical schools, practicing lawyers givin a specialized course, and practitioners in many other profes sional fields. We believe that a woman who serves on a part time basis because of child-rearing responsibilities will be mo concerned with the welfare of the department and more readi available for committee service and other departmental respon sibilities than these busy professional men. Similar conside ations apply to men who accept part-time employment for fami ly reasons.[6]

While drawing this distinction between two different type of part-time appointments, we should add that bringing a prac ticing woman lawyer or engineer to the campus to give a spe cialized course may be a particularly promising way of increas ing the number of women on faculties and providing opportu nities for students to become familiar with able women in the fields.

It must be recognized that increasing the number of part-tim appointments does entail some added costs for institutions. Fc example, extending fringe benefits to part-time facult members, who frequently do not share in all fringe benefits a present, would entail costs, although credit for sabbaticals an contributions to pension plans would reflect the part-tim status. Some institutions have displayed care in attempting t draw distinctions between different types of part-time appoint ments.

Another set of policies in need of revision to provide mor equal opportunities for women are antinepotism rules. In som institutions, these rules apply on a campuswide basis, but i most instances they merely bar two close relatives from servin in the same department, organized research unit, or other ad ministrative unit. Because many women with doctor's degree are married to men in the same field, these policies have consti tuted one of the most significant barriers to equal opportunit for women, and their removal has sometimes been placed at th top of the list of proposals designed to improve opportunitie for women as faculty members. We believe that these rule should be relaxed, as they are now beginning to be in a numbe

[6]See the statement on "senior appointments with reduced loads" adopted k Committee W of the American Association of University Professors in Februa 1971 (Appendix D).

of institutions, but that appropriate precautions should be taken to ensure that a faculty member is not involved in a decision affecting his or her spouse and that appointments and promotions of close relatives are subject to exceedingly careful departmental and administrative scrutiny to ensure that the institution's usual standards are maintained.[7]

Careful screening of appointments of spouses will be needed beyond the departmental level. Antinepotism rules have many undesirable effects, but their removal may create situations that will have to be handled with administrative care. Perhaps the chief danger is that one member of a department will have a wife who is highly qualified and who clearly merits appointment, whereas another may have a wife with the same qualifications on paper but not in terms of actual ability. Large campuses frequently have a requirement that departmental recommendations for appointments or promotions be reviewed by an ad hoc committee, a majority of whose members are from departments other than the initiating department (usually closely related departments). We believe that such procedures are not only appropriate for all appointments, but are especially needed in connection with appointment of close relatives in the same department, because networks of friendships within departments make it especially difficult to act with complete objectivity in relation to a close relative of an individual member.

Maternity leave for a reasonable length of time is also an important concern of women's groups that are seeking to improve the status of women in academic employment. We have referred to the provision of the HEW guidelines that maternity leave be granted to women and parental leave for child rearing be granted to both sexes. The Equal Employment Opportunity Commission (EEOC) has also issued guidelines relating to rights to leave in cases of pregnancy, maternity, and childbirth.[8] We have included in Appendix D the policy statement on "leaves of absence for child-bearing, child-rearing and family emergencies" approved by Committee W of the AAUP in

---

[7]See the AAUP policy on "faculty appointment and family relationship" in Appendix D.

[8]For a convenient summary of these guidelines, see Sandler (1973*b*).

March 1973, as well as relevant excerpts from affirmative action plans of individual institutions of higher education.

Rights to maternity leave and cash benefits for specified periods of time during maternity leave have long been an accepted aspect of national sickness or temporary disability insurance schemes in most other industrial countries, although the provisions do not always apply to academic employment. Cash maternity benefits are beginning to make their way into the provisions of the six state temporary disability insurance systems[9] in the United States, but these systems do not typically cover academic employment on a compulsory basis (U.S. Social Security Administration, 1970, p. 229; and Price, 1973 pp. 20–29). Maternity leave provisions are also beginning to appear in collectively bargained health and welfare plans. However, cash maternity benefits comparable with those found in other industrial countries continue to be a rarity in the United States.

In September 1972, it was reported that the City University of New York was prepared to offer 20 days of paid leave and up to 18 months of unpaid leave for purposes of child-rearing for both men and women on its professional staff (Spiegel, 1972). We have been informed that the provisions were implemented in May 1973.

Demands for equal retirement payments present more complex problems because of the longer life expectancy of women than of men. The great majority of American institutions of higher education arrange for fixed retirement annuities through the Teachers Annuity and Insurance Association, and many have combined fixed and variable annuity plans through TIAA and the closely associated College Retirement Equities Fund (CREF). Under TIAA-CREF plans, equal pension contributions are made for men and women who earn equal salaries, and annual retirement benefits are lower for women than for men. For example, if a male and female employee reach age 65 with the same amount of accumulation, say $100,000, the man

---

[9] Puerto Rico, one of the six, is treated as a state for this purpose.

In West Germany, which has the oldest national sickness insurance scheme in the world, dating from 1883, maternity benefits have long been available, and in 1969 the provisions called for payment of 100 percent of earnings for six weeks before and eight weeks after confinement. However, coverage was limited to wage earners and to salaried employees earning less than 10,800 marks per year (U.S. Social Security Administration, 1970, pp. 80–81).

receives $10,026 a year, and the woman $9,160 a year. Over their average life expectancies, however, the man will receive a total of about $170,000, and the woman about $192,000. "Her total is the actuarial equivalent of his, even though it's larger because compound interest is at work four years longer for her" (Teachers Insurance and Annuity Association, 1972, p. 4). However, after educational institutions were brought under the jurisdiction of Title VII of the Civil Rights Act in the spring of 1972, they became subject to regulations of the Equal Employment Opportunity Commission that "it shall be an unlawful employment practice for an employer to have a pension or retirement plan . . . which differentiates in benefits on the basis of sex" (ibid., p. 1).

Unlike TIAA plans, most industry and state retirement systems contribute differential amounts for men and women who earn equal salaries, in order to provide equal benefits to men and women at the time of retirement. When the plans call for both employer and employee contributions, this difference frequently applies to both the employer and the employee amounts. One of the largest academic institutions with its own individual retirement system, not under TIAA, is the University of California. Provisions of its retirement plan formerly called for employee contributions that were somewhat larger for women than for men and that also varied directly with the age of the individual at the time of entry into the plan. Several years ago the provisions were changed to call for uniform employee contributions of 8.1 percent of covered earnings, with temporary continuation of lower contributions for members whose previous contributions had been below 8.1 percent. The regents make contributions from the university in support of regular University of California Retirement System benefits at a uniform rate of 8.36 percent of covered earnings of all members, but certain classes of academic employees receive a special regents' contribution that reduces the amount of member contributions required of them. Men and women receive retirement benefits under the same formula (University of California Retirement System, 1972). The regents' contributions are pooled, that is, not kept in separate accounts for individual members.

TIAA's position on the EEOC regulations, as stated in a special memorandum of September 1972, is that it is for EEOC and the courts to decide whether its plans are deemed an "unlawful employment practice." The memorandum contends (TIAA, 1972, p. 6) that averaging "things out for everyone at time of retirement, in effect moving some of the men's accumulations over to the women, . . . would be unfair and *cannot be done because all TIAA-CREF annuities are fully vested in the individual*" (emphasis in original). The statement concludes:

Under all TIAA-CREF retirement income options, benefits payable to a woman from a given amount of accumulation are the actuarial equivalent of benefits payable to a man of the same age. We believe this is one appropriate and equitable approach to pensions, particularly for plans that guarantee individual ownership and full funding of all retirement and survivor benefits as they are earned, and that put no economic barriers in the way of career mobility. There are other good approaches, of course, and TIAA-CREF and the colleges could provide them. It is to be hoped that the employer's present freedom of choice in meeting retirement needs will be reaffirmed at the federal level (ibid., p. 8).

Any change in TIAA plans, whether ordered by the courts or adopted voluntarily, would almost certainly have to be restricted to future contributions and thus would have relatively little effect on the retirement benefits of individuals approaching retirement age at the present time.

With respect to the problem of providing more opportunities for women in the top administration of colleges and universities, perhaps the most important point to keep in mind is that academic administrators are usually selected from among faculty members who have served ably as department chairmen or directors of research institutes, especially the former. We believe that opportunities for women to serve in such positions should be encouraged, as, in fact, they have been in some fields and some institutions.

It is sometimes implied that administrative ability is an exclusively male attribute. We do not agree. Given equal opportunity and the withering away of old prejudices, potential administrative ability is probably equally distributed among men and women. Many men, and women too, in academic life are potentially able administrators, and many are not. Among the latter are the many faculty members who are immersed in their scholarly activities and have no desire to rise in the administrative hierarchy of the institution. Then there are others who are simply not temperamentally suited to be successful administrators. On the other hand, colleges and universities probably have a reasonable share of faculty members who have the capability to become exceptionally able administrators.

An argument that is frequently advanced against selecting women for administrative positions is that men do not like to be in a position of subordination to a woman. But many women have successfully demonstrated the capacity to occupy high administrative positions with male subordinates—in government, industry, and academic life. The most conspicuous examples in academic life, of course, are the many women who have successfully served as presidents of women's colleges. There are, to be sure, women as well as men who cannot establish satisfactory relations with subordinates, in some cases because of an overly aggressive or authoritarian style of leadership. Such persons should be passed over for administrative appointments, regardless of sex. But colleges and universities should take decisive steps to open up more opportunities for women to rise to top administrative positions, not only for the sake of equitable treatment, but also because it is extremely important for students of both sexes to observe women successfully carrying out the responsibilities of top administrative positions.

In addition to opening opportunities for women to become department chairmen, colleges and universities should provide management training opportunities for both male and female academic employees for academic administrative positions and for nonacademic employees for nonacademic administrative posts. In recent years, various organizations have increasingly sponsored special summer seminars and other special programs for college and university administrators, but the individuals selected by colleges and universities for participation in such programs at the expense of the institution are usually persons who have already been appointed to administrative positions, and hence are almost invariably men. We believe that there should be greater emphasis on encouraging both men and women who might later be considered for administrative positions to participate in such special training programs.

Recommendation 17: All colleges and universities covered b
federal affirmative action requirements relating to employme
should proceed to develop adequate written statements of affi
mative action policy and should take active steps to see that th
goals of the affirmative action policy are achieved within a re
sonable period of time. To expedite achieving such goals, eve
large college or university should appoint one or more affirm
tive action officers, whose policies should be guided by an ap
propriately constituted advisory committee or council. Sma
colleges may find it preferable to assign affirmative action re
sponsibilities to an existing administrator or faculty member

Every affirmative action policy, as it concerns the employ
ment of faculty members, should include at least the followir
provisions relating to sex discrimination:

1   Departments and schools should actively recruit women ar
maintain records that indicate the steps they have taken in th
recruitment program. Efforts should be made to recruit wome
who are members of minority groups through recruitme
plans especially designed to seek them out. Serious conside
ation should be given to appointing qualified women lecture
to regular faculty positions.

2   Every department and school in an academic institution shou
establish, in consultation with the administration of the colle
or university, a goal relating to the relative representation
women on its regular faculty (assistant professor to full profe
sor). In determining these goals, every appropriate source of i
formation on the relative size of available pools of qualifi
women and men should be consulted—not just those indicat
in the federal guidelines. A reasonable timetable for achievir
the goals should be developed, but allowance should be mac
for special difficulties that may be encountered in adhering
the timetable, especially in fields in which there are current
relatively few women with doctor's degrees and in which con
petition among institutions for this limited pool of talent
likely to be intense. Special consideration should be given
women who meet the institution's standards of competence i
terms of both realized and potential ability, even though the
may have had a less substantial record of achievement in term
of research and publication than men who are being considere

for the same positions. Standards of competence vary by type of institution. In practice, however, they are often only vaguely defined. Where this is a problem, they should be made more explicit.

3 Part-time appointments should not be discouraged for men and women whose family circumstances make such appointments desirable. Institutions may find it advantageous to distinguish, as some have done, between (1) such part-time appointments and (2) appointments to the faculty of persons whose principal employment is elsewhere and who come to the campus to give one or two specialized courses. For example, fringe benefits, prorated on the basis of the proportion of a full-time appointment, are more appropriate for the first type of part-time employee.

4 Policies requiring decisions on the granting of tenure to be made with a given period of years should permit a limited extention of the time period for persons holding part-time appointments. Men and women holding part-time appointments for family reasons should be permitted to achieve tenure on a part-time basis. In such cases, tenure on a full-time basis at some future time would not be ensured, but the institution should attempt to shift the individual's status to a full-time tenured position when desired if budgetarily possible and academically appropriate.

5 Faculty members holding part-time appointments for family reasons should not be barred from service on departmental or campus committees and should, if holding an appropriate faculty rank, be eligible for membership in the academic senate.

6 There should be no antinepotism rules applying to employment within the institution or campus as a whole, or within individual units, such as departments, schools, and institutes. However, a husband or wife should not be involved in a decision relating to his or her spouse.

7 There should be equal treatment of men and women in all matters relating to salary, fringe benefits, and terms and conditions of employment.

8 Women should be entitled to maternity leave for a reasonable length of time, and affirmative action plans should include specific provisions relating to the definition of a reasonable length

of time, right to accumulated leave, and other relevant consider
ations.

Recommendation 18: The affirmative action program shoul
also provide for an effective internal grievance procedure, if th
institution does not already have one. An effective grievanc
procedure should result in minimizing litigation.

Recommendation 19: We support the objectives of federa
policies aimed at ensuring that institutions of higher educatio
having contracts with the federal government pursue effectiv
affirmative action programs, but we believe that these federa
policies should be carried out in relation to each institution wit
due regard for the sensitive characteristics of academic employ
ment, and for the difficulties that may be encountered by indi
vidual departments and schools in meeting affirmative actio
goals and timetables.

1   The power to delay or cancel contracts should not be used i
connection with complaints by individuals, which are bes
handled, as is now required, by the Equal Employment Oppor
tunity Commission under Title VII of the Civil Rights Act o
1964.[10] Institutions should be given adequate warning befor
contracts are delayed and should be entitled to a hearing, as i
now required, before any existing contract is canceled. More
over, we do not believe that any existing contracts should b
canceled unless a pattern of discrimination has persisted for
considerable period of time and the institution has failed t
take steps to correct it. The ultimate sanction of debarring an in
stitution from eligibility for future contracts should be reserve
only for the most extreme cases in which a pattern of discrimina
tion is deliberate and has persisted for a lengthy period of time
Final decisions on withholding contract funds should be mad
only by the Secretary of Labor, on the recommendation of th
Secretary of Health, Education and Welfare.

2   The lengthy delays that have sometimes characterized HEW
procedures, on the one hand, and the prolonged delays that
have been involved in the development or implementation o

---

[10] Some individual cases that were initiated with HEW are still being processed by
that department.

adequate affirmative action plans by institutions, on the other, are equally unwise and should be avoided in the future.

3 We define a pattern of discrimination as involving one or more of the following situations:

(a) Failure to develop an adequate affirmative action plan within a reasonable period of time;

(b) Lack of evidence that the institution is making an effort to achieve its affirmative action goals; or evidence of widespread faculty or administrative attitudes that are antagonistic to the achievement of the affirmative action goals;

(c) Lack of progress in achieving its affirmative action goals within a reasonable period of time.

Recommendation 20: Colleges and universities should take especially vigorous steps to overcome a pervasive problem of absence of women in top administrative positions. Women should be given opportunities by their departments to serve as department chairmen, because academic administrators are usually selected from among persons who have served ably as department chairmen. Most important is an administrative stance that is highly positive toward providing opportunities for women to rise in the administrative hierarchy. Also very important is the provision of management training opportunities for both men and women who have potential administrative ability but do not hold administrative positions.

9. Needed Campus Facilities

One of the most important recent developments in higher education has been the movement to provide increased opportunities for nontraditional study for adults. The British Open University has been a major stimulus for this movement, but steps had been taken in this country to provide for more flexible patterns of participation in higher education long before the launching of the Open University—for example, the establishment of the College of Continuing Education to administer a new bachelor of liberal studies program at the University of Oklahoma in 1960.

Women are major beneficiaries of this movement to provide more varied opportunities for adult education. We have earlier referred to the desire of many married women for continued education that became increasingly apparent in the 1960s. We believe that the recommendations that have been made in Sections 4 and 6 aimed at providing opportunities for part-time study at both the undergraduate and graduate levels are exceedingly important for married women wishing to continue their education after a period out of the labor force with young children.

The establishment of external degree programs and institutions modeled after the British Open University, such as Empire State University in New York, should not be permitted to interfere with this relaxation of rules in conventional institutions of higher education. Women who are qualified for admission to a given college or university campus on the basis of earlier high school or college records and test scores should not be barred from the opportunity to study, for example, under the distinguished faculties on major campuses. Indeed, we have referred to the recognition by some faculty members of the

unique contribution such women can make to class discussion
At the same time we strongly support the movement toward
external degree programs and other forms of nontraditiona
study and emphasize their importance in relation to the needs
of mature women. These programs will be particularly important for married women who do not live near a traditiona
campus. We would simply stress in this context, as in other
parts of this report, the need for as much freedom of choice as
possible.

A particularly interesting example of a success story in continuing education for women was reported by the *New Yorh
Times* in June 1973.

College was out of the question for Marguerite Marshall when she
graduated from high school in the nineteen-thirties. She was poor
black and orphaned and it was the Great Depression.

But recently, Mrs. Marshall, now 51 years old and the mother o
three, was graduated summa cum laude from Marymount College o
the city's East Side. Had it not been for Malcolm-King: Harlem College
Extension, from which she transferred to Marymount, Mrs. Marshal
feels she would not have resumed her long-interrupted schooling.

Malcolm-King, the only institution of higher education with degree
level work in Harlem, is little publicized and almost unnoticed by the
rest of the city. But in the five years of its existence it has offered a
growing number of adults such as Mrs. Marshall a second chance ir
life, the opportunity to pursue fully accredited college-level studies
(Maeroff, 1973).

A student may earn up to 62 course credits at Malcolm-King
and then transfer elsewhere as a junior to complete a bachelor's
degree program. However, individual success stories do not
mean that the institution does not have its problems, including
a high dropout rate. The college has also found it difficult to attract male students. Women dominate the enrollment by more
than a 3 to 1 margin.

Another significant development of the 1960s was the establishment of centers for continuing education for women on
many campuses. A U.S. Women's Bureau (1971) report lists
about 30 centers or special offices for continuing education for
women on coeducational campuses, and undoubtedly a

number of others have been started in the past two years.[1] In addition, the report listed a number of such centers on women's college campuses, as well as a large number of special women's study programs or policies designed to facilitate part-time study for mature women.

The centers for continuing education for women vary somewhat in their programs, but counseling and guidance services are central to most of them. These services are sometimes conducted in cooperation with the regular counseling service for students on the campus and sometimes are quite separate. Another feature of many of the centers is the sponsoring of a special orientation course for married women wishing to prepare for a career, but uncertain about a career choice, or simply wishing to continue their education, but uncertain about the choice of a field. This type of course is sometimes offered directly by the center and sometimes by arrangement with an extension program. Another function of many of the centers is to contact departmental or general campus offices about rules or regulations that interfere with opportunities for mature women to enroll or to take up the case of an individual woman who is encountering such obstacles. The popularity of these centers is attested by the experience of the Center for Continuing Education of Women at the University of Michigan, one of the earliest of the centers on college campuses. Established in 1964, the center had provided counseling services to about 4,000 women by early 1973. A study of a sample of these women indicated that the woman who returned to college was typically in her thirties, married, had children, and had a husband who was "well-educated and high-earning." The majority of the women received financial support for their educational expenses from their husbands, although 46 percent contributed to their own education. Most of them, moreover, had already had some college education (*University of Michigan News*, 1973). It seems likely that a university community like Ann Arbor would be especially likely to attract women whose husbands were highly educated. Scattered information on centers located in large urban areas suggests that they attract a broader group.

---

[1] We have included only centers or offices that include "for women" or "of women" in their name.

The Radcliffe Institute is somewhat distinctive from othe centers. Its program for Independent Study emphasizes gran ing support to highly talented and qualified women who wis to pursue independent study and research at critical points i their career development. The Radcliffe seminars, the continuin education arm of the Institute, has recently added to its cu ricula in the humanities and arts courses in landscape desigr

Another function that some of these centers are taking on and one that seems highly useful and appropriate in relation to the major themes of this report, is the furnishing of special kit of information to incoming freshmen women about the need to plan their educational program carefully in relation to future ca reer opportunities. Efforts are also being directed toward work ing with high schools to provide improved counseling service for female students.

It is sometimes argued that centers for continuing education at least on coeducational campuses, should not be establishe for women alone but should be open to both sexes. The com mittee that was appointed by former Chancellor Roger W Heyns to consider a proposal for establishing a center at the Uni versity of California, Berkeley, debated this question at som length and decided in favor of a center for women:

Although some of us may not have been convinced on this point whe we began our investigation, we are now unanimously persuaded tha there is a strong case for a center for women. The main reason for thi is that a center would serve as a "visible" welcome sign to women wh wish to return to higher education but who are wary of the problem and difficulties they might encounter. Here will be a place where the can count on sympathetic analysis and understanding of their prob lems. This expectation of wholehearted support will be especially sig nificant to minority group women, who in many cases may have at tended college when the doors of predominantly white institutions o higher education were not open to them and who may be fearful of the quality of their previous education (Chancellor's Advisory Committee 1972).

We believe that a campus faced with a proposal for a cente for continuing education of women should consider carefully whether a single-sex center is the preferable solution o whether it might not be more desirable to serve women in a broader center for continuing education of adults, perhaps with a special office for women. Circumstances vary, and we do not think that a single answer to this question is necessarily appropriate under all conditions.

One of the most well-known of the centers that serve women is the Claremont University Center at Claremont Colleges. It is open to both men and women, but most of those who seek its services are women.

One of the considerations in any decision about whether there should be a separate center for women is the problem of financing the center. The concept of a separate center for women tends to be an attraction to some potential private donors and a deterrent to others. But maintaining adequate financial support is a major problem for women's centers. Fees tend to be charged for enrollment in specialized orientation courses and are sometimes charged for counseling services on an ability-to-pay basis. Continuing education programs proposed by institutions of higher education may qualify for federal assistance under the Community Service and Continuing Education Programs authorized under Title I of the Higher Education Act of 1965. Between passage of the act in November 1965 and June 30, 1970, 63 programs were approved for federal funding to provide counseling, training, or academic instruction specifically for women (U.S. Women's Bureau, 1971; Appendix D). But the future of Title I funds is at present very precarious.

A primary need, in connection with the establishment of an office or center for continuing education, whether for women or for both sexes, is the appointment of an advisory committee, one of whose functions will be continuous fund-raising efforts.

One of the factors facilitating the establishment and early operations of a number of the women's centers has been the availability of enthusiastic volunteer participation, for example, by women graduate students. But the common experience of these centers is that their financing is quite precarious unless there is a regular provision in the institution's budget for the center's core staff and other essential expenses.

RECOMMENDA-
TIONS

Recommendation 21: The Commission reiterates its support of the development of external degree and other nontraditional study programs, emphasizing the need, that has not in all cases been observed, for high quality in such programs. They are especially important in relation to the special needs of mature married women for continuing education.

Recommendation 22: The existence of separate institutions for nontraditional study should not be used as an excuse for denying qualified adults of either sex the opportunity to study on traditional campuses on a full-time or part-time basis. (See Recommendations 5 and 12).

Recommendation 23: Large campuses should have an administrative officer specifically concerned with ensuring that qualified adults are given opportunities to pursue undergraduate or graduate study on a full-time or part-time basis. Whether there should be a separate center for continuing education of women should be decided in the light of the circumstances prevailing on any given campus. We believe that there is often a case for a center primarily concerned with the educational problems of mature women, but that the need for such a center may be transitional and that in the future the concept of continuing educational opportunities for mature women is likely to be so thoroughly accepted that a center especially oriented toward women's problems may no longer be desirable or necessary.

THE PROBLEM OF CHILD CARE In recent years many colleges and universities have been confronted with demands to establish child-care centers, and many have responded. Although women students and faculty members share needs for child-care services with working mothers generally, the needs of women on campuses are often for part-time care only. Students, part-time women faculty members, and other women employees who are on a part-time basis can often arrange their schedules so that they need child-care services only for a few hours a day. Frequently, also, student fathers can adjust their schedules to take responsibility for child care during certain hours. This means that the services can be provided at considerably less cost than full-time child-care services.

Programs that provide child-care services are not new to American college campuses. For several decades, many academic departments have operated laboratory schools or nursery schools that enroll children under six. The primary purpose of these programs, however, has not been to free student or faculty parents from child care but to give students enrolled in certain psychology, education, or home economics courses practical training in child-care and child-development problems. On research-oriented campuses, the centers have frequently been designed primarily to facilitate research on problems of child development.

Child-care centers are of more recent origin; they tend to emphasize services to student-parents and are less likely to be under the control of a particular academic department or of the institution itself. According to a 1971 survey of 310 four-year colleges and universities (Greenblatt & Eberhard, 1973), about one-fourth of these institutions offered at least one preschool program, and many offered two or more. Larger institutions were more likely to have such programs than smaller ones, as would be expected. About one-fourth were day-care programs, 32 percent were nursery schools, 18 percent were laboratory schools, and the rest were either some combination of these types or of an indeterminate type. The great majority of the programs charged fees, sometimes on a sliding scale according to income.

In contrast with the nursery and laboratory schools, which had been started at the initiative of faculty members, slightly more than one-half of the child-care programs had been initiated by student-parents. Moreover, student-parents managed close to one-half of the day-care centers, had hiring authority in 30 percent, and were included as staff members at 30 percent. The great majority of the child-care centers were located in facilities owned by the institution, although they were somewhat more likely to be located off-campus than were the nursery or laboratory schools.

Child-care centers were much less likely to receive their major financial support from the college or university than were nursery or laboratory schools. Only one in four of the child-care centers received its major support from the institution. In the other three-fourths of these centers, the sources of financial support were as follows:

Sources of financial support for campus child-care centers not supported primarily b the institution, 1971

Fees	51.0%
Public funds	21.6
Federal	13.7
State	3.9
Local	3.9
Student government	13.7
Private gifts developed through fund-raising efforts	9.8
Foundations and churches	3.9

Although federal funds provided, on the average, a relatively small proportion of the funds received by these centers, thei relative importance as a source of support was larger in some situations than in others. When it was announced that the fed- eral government was about to enforce much more restrictive regulations in allocating funds for child-care centers early in 1973, it was widely reported in the press that this would force the closing down of a number of existing centers, including some on college and university campuses. Because the campus centers tended to have some private sources of support, they would have been especially affected by a proposed provision cutting off federal funds from any center that was partially sup- ported from private sources. The proposed regulations were later modified, but, among other things, the family income eli- gibility conditions for federal support under new regulations announced on May 1, 1973, were highly restrictive.

Nationally, the issue of federal support for child-care services is a matter of controversy and has tended to be closely tied to the issue of welfare reform. As a commission concerned with higher education, we are not in a position to make specific rec- ommendations about child-care policies, except as they relate specifically to the problems of colleges and universities.

We believe that colleges and universities should seek to meet the needs of their students and employees for satisfactory child- care arrangements. On large campuses, it may be appropriate to attempt to provide child-care arrangements on or near the campus, whereas on small campuses, cooperation with community groups to ensure adequate child-care services elsewhere in the community may be more suitable.

Child-care centers of the conventional type may not necessarily be the most satisfactory. Especially because many members of campus communities need child-care services during only part of the day, other arrangements should be considered. Many college-educated mothers have long been active, for example, in sponsoring and participating in cooperative nursery schools. These schools are often sponsored by groups of parents, and each mother, or sometimes a father, is expected to spend one session a week at the school assisting the director in supervising the children. The schools are typically open only in the morning, or sometimes have morning sessions for the younger children and afternoon sessions for four-year-olds, who no longer need an afternoon nap. Mothers frequently feel that shy children are likely to adjust better to the strange nursery school environment if the mother is intimately involved, and they also recognize that they come to understand their own child's problems better if they are seen in the perspective of the behavior of other children in the same age group. Most of these schools have a professionally trained director, and sometimes, trained assistant directors, but mothers, and sometimes fathers, find it a very satisfying activity, not only to participate in the school but also to serve for a time as an officer or board member.

Where there are careful licensing provisions,[2] care for a small group of children by a woman in her own home may be a more satisfactory and a more economical arrangement than a large day-care center, especially for very young children who find it difficult to adjust to large groups.

We believe that colleges and universities should be responsive and cooperative in relation to requests or demands for child-care services and that they have a responsibility to ensure that child-care arrangements associated with the campus are of high quality. However, as we have recommended in an earlier

---

[2] For a discussion of licensing provisions in California, and for a most enlightening discussion of existing child-care services and child-care needs, see Pacific Training and Technical Assistance Corporation (1970).

report,[3] we believe colleges and universities should avoid direct sponsorship of services that are peripheral to their central functions. In developing child-care services, cooperation with other community agencies to see that such services are provided under broader community auspices would generally be preferable. If a need is felt for child-care services on or near the campus, especially in the case of large campuses, we believe it would ordinarily be preferable to see that these services are under the control of a separate board of trustees, formed for the purpose, rather than under direct control of the institution.

In any case, the most appropriate initial step when requests for child-care services are presented by campus groups is to appoint a committee to make a careful study of various alternative ways of providing such services. Such committees should include interested parents and faculty members with special expertise on child-development problems, drawn from such departments as education, home economics, and psychology.

Student government organizations, private gifts, and foundations and churches have provided some of the funds for child-care arrangements on or near campuses. We do not believe that direct financing by the institution should be provided. On the other hand, there is no reason why individuals associated with the campus should not be actively involved in fund-raising efforts.

Recommendation 24: Colleges and universities should be responsive to campus groups seeking to develop child-care services. An essential step is to appoint a carefully selected committee to study various possible types of child-care services, including those already available in the community, and to recommend a plan for making such services available to students and employees of the institution. The committee should include faculty members drawn from appropriate departments, parents, and persons knowledgeable about community resources.

We believe that in most situations, especially for smaller campuses, it will be preferable for the academic institution to cooperate with other community groups in ensuring the availability of adequate child-care services in the community. If campus fa-

---

[3] Carnegie Commission (1973d, Section 11).

cilities are desired on or near large campuses, we believe, consistent with our general view that an academic institution should not assume functions that are not central to its main purposes, that it will usually be preferable to seek an arrangement under which the child-care services will be provided under the auspices of a separate board of directors and not as a direct function of the academic institution. The board of directors would be expected to ensure adequate financing and adequate standards for the child-care services.

We believe that student-parents should be expected to pay for child-care services on the basis of sliding scale fees according to their incomes and that parents who are employees of the institution would normally be expected to pay for the full cost of services. Subsidies to meet the needs of low-income student-parents should be sought from extramural public and private sources and should not normally be sought from the academic institution's regular budget.

10. Concluding Remarks

Throughout this report, we have referred in a variety of contexts to the need for broader options and greater freedom of choice for women to make maximum use of their abilities. We do not see a future in which every woman will aspire to become a research scientist, a physician, or an engineer. In fact, we think this is not at all likely. But we do believe strongly that the various barriers that have existed in the paths of women, who might have such aspirations and who have the ability to realize them, should be removed.

These barriers begin in the early acculturation of female children. We have recommended various specific measures, such as improved high school counseling, to provide a more encouraging environment in relation to the career aspirations of women. But we see the most important need as a change in attitude all the way along the line—on the part of parents, schoolteachers, school counselors, college admissions officers and other administrators, faculty members, and college counseling staffs. These changes will come slowly, and federal pressure for affirmative action and pressure from campus and professional women's groups are needed in the interim. But we hope that these types of pressures are a transitional need, and that, as attitudes change, aspirations of women toward participation in higher education on a basis of equal opportunity with men will come to be taken for granted.

Attitudes of people toward sex roles are changing rapidly, especially among the college-educated, but no one can envisage exactly how sex roles and family structure will evolve in the future. There might even be a swing of the pendulum away from the liberalized attitudes displayed by many people today, as there was a backward swing of the pendulum following the granting of women's suffrage. We hope and expect, instead, a steady trend toward full equality of opportunity for women in academic life.

Appendix A: Statistical Tables

TABLE A-1 *Percentages of women in the labor force by educational attainment and marital status, selected age groups, 1970*

Age and educational attainment	Total	Married, husband present		Other marital status	
		With own children under 6	Without own children under 6	With own children under 6	Without own children under 6
Age 25–29 years					
TOTAL	45.7	28.3	63.1	55.5	77.5
8 years of school	35.2	24.9	44.9	36.0	53.9
High school, 4 years	44.3	27.9	63.0	64.6	82.5
College, 1–2 years	47.9	27.5	68.5	71.0	85.2
College, 4 years	59.1	30.5	80.7	71.0	91.5
College, 5 years	70.6	39.6	81.9	80.8	87.1
College, 6 years or more	75.7	42.9	85.8	84.4	92.8
Age 30–34 years					
TOTAL	44.6	27.5	52.4	51.3	73.5
8 years of school	38.7	25.0	44.8	36.8	57.0
High school, 4 years	44.7	26.7	53.2	60.0	80.1
College, 1–2 years	43.2	24.7	50.2	66.0	81.3
College, 4 years	47.1	28.5	64.2	73.8	88.4
College, 5 years	63.4	37.9	78.1	80.3	91.7
College, 6 years or more	70.9	45.4	81.7	83.9	93.6
Age 35–44 years					
TOTAL	50.6	28.0	51.6	51.2	72.4
8 years of school	45.0	26.1	46.1	40.1	60.4
High school, 4 years	51.7	26.7	53.1	60.0	79.4
College, 1–2 years	50.5	27.0	49.5	63.4	81.8
College, 4 years	52.5	29.2	53.8	69.2	85.0
College, 5 years	69.0	38.8	70.6	79.7	91.1
College, 6 years or more	78.1	47.6	77.1	89.1	94.7

SOURCE: U.S. Bureau of the Census (1973*b*, pp. 126–127).

TABLE A-2 *Percentages of nonwhite women in the labor force by educational attainment and marital status, selected age groups, 1970*

Age and educational attainment	Total	Married, husband present		Other marital status	
		With own children under 6	Without own children under 6	With own children under 6	Without own children under 6
Age 25–29 years					
TOTAL	58.9	51.8	66.7	49.3	69.8
8 years of school	43.4	36.8	54.8	34.2	52.7
High school, 4 years	63.5	54.2	69.8	59.5	77.2
College, 1–2 years	72.9	62.1	73.7	78.4	83.1
College, 4 years	83.1	73.7	87.6	82.4	90.1
College, 5 years	83.6	77.1	89.1	87.9	84.7
College, 6 years or more	87.3	75.4	92.3	78.8	95.1
Age 30–34 years					
TOTAL	59.5	49.8	65.8	47.8	68.2
8 years of school	47.2	39.1	49.7	39.1	56.2
High school, 4 years	64.5	50.8	69.3	59.7	77.7
College, 1–2 years	71.0	57.8	74.5	69.3	82.4
College, 4 years	83.7	78.4	86.2	91.1	88.5
College, 5 years	86.2	73.9	95.3	88.1	90.2
College, 6 years or more	84.8	76.0	89.4	77.4	88.6
Age 35–44 years					
TOTAL	61.1	47.6	77.1	48.8	67.2
8 years of school	52.9	38.6	53.6	40.8	60.9
High school, 4 years	67.0	51.0	66.9	60.6	76.4
College, 1–2 years	74.5	56.2	74.4	67.3	84.5
College, 4 years	85.4	78.9	86.0	92.1	88.2
College, 5 years	88.8	82.7	89.8	88.4	91.1
College, 6 years or more	91.6	81.5	93.3	96.0	93.9

SOURCE: U.S. Bureau of the Census (1973*b*, pp. 130–131).

Occupational group	Number of women (in thousands)		
	1950	1960	1970
TOTAL*	16,481.9	22,303.7	30,601.0
Professional and technical workers	1,896.9	2,723.9	4,397.6
Accountants	57.0	81.9	187.0
Architects	.9	.8	2.0
Engineers	6.7	7.2	20.3
Farm and home management advisers	5.0	6.4	6.5
Lawyers and judges	7.0	7.5	13.4
Librarians	50.7	64.6	101.5
Life and physical scientists	12.6	15.2	29.2
Personnel and labor relations workers	15.0	34.2	91.7
Pharmacists	7.4	7.2	13.3
Physicians, medical and osteopathic	12.3	16.2	26.1
Dietitians	21.7	24.8	37.8
Registered nurses	399.2	613.7	819.3
Therapists	†	16.4	48.5
Health technicians	46.3	88.0	184.1
Clergymen	7.3	4.7	6.3
Other religious workers	28.7	38.6	20.1
Social scientists	11.3	15.1	32.0
Social workers	54.0	59.4	138.9
Recreation workers	7.7	14.9	22.5
Teachers, elementary	†	851.2	1,199.4
Teachers, secondary	†	280.5	498.7
Teachers, college and university	27.8	46.5	140.4
Engineering and science technicians	†	43.5	68.7
Draftsmen	7.2	12.3	23.6
Radio operators	1.7	3.1	7.6
Authors	5.8	7.3	7.7
Dancers	†	3.9	5.7
Designers	10.7	13.4	27.2
Editors and reporters	29.4	39.0	61.5
Musicians and composers	†	29.8	33.5

Women as a percentage of all persons in occupation		
1950	*1960*	*1970*
28.1	32.8	38.0
39.0	38.4	39.9
14.9	16.5	26.2
3.8	2.1	3.6
1.3	.8	1.6
46.1	47.2	49.7
4.1	3.5	4.9
88.8	85.4	82.0
11.0	9.2	13.7
28.3	33.1	30.9
8.7	7.5	12.0
6.7	6.9	9.3
96.5	92.7	92.0
97.6	97.5	97.3
†	63.4	63.5
57.4	68.2	69.7
4.4	2.3	2.9
69.9	63.3	55.7
32.9	25.4	23.2
69.3	62.8	62.8
45.4	51.2	42.0
†	85.8	83.7
†	49.3	49.3
22.4	23.9	28.6
†	11.1	12.9
6.0	5.6	8.0
10.2	16.7	25.9
36.5	25.5	29.1
†	86.0	81.3
26.7	19.3	24.2
32.1	36.6	40.6
†	38.6	34.8

TABLE A-3
(continued)

Occupational group	Number of women (in thousands)		
	1950	1960	1970
Photographers	8.6	6.5	9.5
Other professional, technical, and kindred workers	†	270.1	513.9
Managers and administrators, except farm	680.8	844.5	1,034.3
Managers and administrators, salaried ‡	329.7	482.6	844.1
Managers and administrators, self-employed ‡	347.1	297.4	211.3
Sales workers	1,374.7	1,736.0	2,096.7
Clerical and kindred workers	4,343.4	6,407.0	9,910.0
Craftsmen	247.3	295.3	524.1
Operatives	3,190.8	3,521.2	4,222.6
Laborers, except farm	134.1	193.1	294.6
Farm workers	602.2	394.8	222.3
Service workers	3,564.1	4,890.3	5,751.9
Occupation not reported	447.6	1,297.7	2,147.1

* Detail may not add to totals because of rounding.
† Data are not available because of changes in classification.
‡ Not elsewhere classified.
SOURCE: Adapted from table in *Economic Report of the President* (1973, pp. 155–159).

Women as a percentage of all persons in occupation		
1950	*1960*	*1970*
16.2	12.2	14.2
†	33.9	32.9
13.7	14.8	16.6
13.8	13.9	16.1
15.6	17.2	18.7
34.2	36.2	38.6
61.9	67.9	73.6
3.1	3.1	5.0
27.4	28.7	31.5
3.6	5.1	8.4
8.8	9.6	9.5
58.1	61.9	60.0
35.2	37.6	41.5

TABLE A-4 Probable career choices of college freshmen, by sex (weighted national norms), 1966 to 1972

Career choice	1966	1967	1968	1969	1970	1971	1972
Men							
TOTAL*	100.3%	100.1%	100.1%	99.8%	100.1%	100.0%	100.0%
Businessman	18.6	17.5	17.5	16.9	17.4	16.1	15.4
Lawyer	6.7	5.8	5.5	5.6	6.2	6.8	7.1
Engineer	16.3	15.0	14.6	14.5	13.3	9.7	9.6
College teacher	2.1	1.4	1.3	1.3	1.2	0.8	0.7
Teacher, elementary and secondary	11.3	11.2	12.7	10.9	9.6	7.5	5.7
Physician or dentist	7.4	6.4	5.6	4.9	5.9	6.4	7.9
Other health professions	3.2	2.7	2.9	2.8	3.0	4.1	4.8
Research scientist	4.9	3.9	3.8	3.3	3.5	3.3	3.1
Farmer or forester	3.2	3.3	2.9	3.0	3.1	4.8	4.8
Clergyman	1.2	1.9	1.1	1.4	1.3	1.0	1.0
Artist (including performer)	4.6	4.1	4.2	4.3	5.1	4.9	5.2
Other choice	15.8	16.7	16.7	19.3	19.0	21.7	21.3
Undecided	5.0	10.2	11.3	11.6	11.5	12.9	13.4

Career choice	1966	1967	1968	1969	1970	1971	1972
Women							
TOTAL*	99.8%	99.8%	99.9%	100.1%	100.2%	100.0%	99.9%
Businesswoman	3.3	3.3	3.3	3.6	4.2	4.4	4.8
Lawyer	0.7	0.6	0.6	0.8	1.0	1.4	2.0
Engineer	0.2	0.2	0.2	0.3	0.4	0.2	0.3
College teacher	1.5	0.9	0.9	0.8	0.9	0.6	0.6
Teacher, elementary and secondary	34.1	36.4	37.5	36.5	31.0	24.8	19.5
Physician or dentist	1.7	1.5	1.3	1.3	1.5	2.0	2.8
Nurse	5.3	5.4	6.1	6.0	8.7	8.6	9.8
Other health professions	6.6	6.3	5.7	6.0	6.4	8.8	10.4
Research scientist	1.9	1.6	1.7	1.4	1.6	1.5	1.5
Farmer or forester	0.2	0.1	0.1	0.2	0.4	0.7	0.7
Clergywoman	0.8	0.3	0.2	0.3	0.2	0.2	0.2
Artist (including performer)	8.9	8.1	7.8	7.6	7.6	7.2	8.0
Other choice	31.0	25.2	23.7	24.3	24.5	26.1	24.9
Undecided	3.6	9.9	10.8	11.0	11.8	13.5	14.4

* Totals may differ from 100.0 because of rounding.
SOURCE: American Council on Education (annual).

TABLE A-5 *Women as a percentage of persons employed in selected occupations, selected countries, specified years*

Occupation	Australia (1966)	Denmark (1965)	Finland (1960)	France (1965)	Germany (FR) (1965)
Engineers	0.6*				
Lawyers	4.6	7.0–8.0†	7.0–8.0†		5.5
Life scientists	8.4				
Physical scientists	8.9				
Physicians and dentists	9.7				
Physicians		16.4	23.4	12.8	20.0
Dentists		25.0	76.9		13.0
University faculty members			17.7	20.6	2 3
Full professors					0.6
Salaried managerial workers	12.4				

* Architects, engineers, and surveyors.
† Range for several countries, not precise figures.
‡ Data exclude two–year colleges.

SOURCES: Australia (1968, p. 1158); Epstein (1971*b*, p. 12); Fogarty, Rapoport, and Rapoport (1971, p. 543); Galenson (1973, pp. 24–27); New Zealand (1972, p. 855); and U.S. Bureau of the Census (1972*c*, Tables 1 and 8).

Great Britain (1966)	New Zealand (1966)	Norway (1960)	Poland (1964)	Sweden (1965)	United States (1970)	USSR (1963)
1.0	0.3*		11.0		1.6	28.0
5.0	1.3			7.0–8.0†	4.9	36.0
}7.0	11.1				}13.7	}38.0
	5.2					
	6.6					
18.0		10.3	44.0	17.4	9.3	75.0
10.6		20.1	80.0	23.6	3.4	83.0
10.8		1.7		10.0	19.0‡	
2.0					8.6	
15.0	12.2				16.4	

	Men	Women	Total
TABLE A-6 *Type of institution and source*			
Source of financing			
undergraduate *Total, all institutions*			
years: the 1971			
survey responses Support from your parents	60.6	74.5	66.6
of 1967 college			
freshmen Support from your spouse	7.6	10.8	9.0
(weighted			
percentages) Federal scholarship, fellowship, or grant	10.6	9.3	10.1
State scholarship, fellowship, or grant	13.8	17.7	15.5
Other scholarship, fellowship, or grant	15.6	17.3	16.3
Federal loan	18.7	19.3	19.0
Other loan	12.9	13.3	13.0
College work-study program	11.3	14.2	12.5
Research assistantship	0.6	0.3	0.5
Teaching assistantship	0.9	0.7	0.8
Employment	61.4	49.3	56.1
Other sources (savings, etc.)	35.4	30.1	33.1
Two-year colleges			
Support from your parents	46.4	59.3	51.6
Support from your spouse	8.5	11.5	9.8
Federal scholarship, fellowship, or grant	7.5	6.0	6.9
State scholarship, fellowship, or grant	10.3	12.2	11.0
Other scholarship, fellowship, or grant	9.5	13.0	10.9
Federal loan	15.7	13.5	14.8
Other loan	12.3	12.1	12.2
College work-study program	7.5	11.3	9.0
Research assistantship	0.1	0.1	0.1
Teaching assistantship	0.8	0.5	0.7
Employment	61.7	47.0	56.0
Other sources (savings, etc.)	35.4	30.7	33.6

Type of institution and source	Men	Women	Total
Four-year colleges			
Support from your parents	65.7	78.6	71.9
Support from your spouse	6.1	10.0	7.9
Federal scholarship, fellowship, or grant	12.1	11.2	11.7
State scholarship, fellowship, or grant	19.1	24.2	21.5
Other scholarship, fellowship, or grant	18.3	19.0	18.7
Federal loan	20.8	22.2	21.5
Other loan	15.9	16.4	16.2
College work-study program	15.2	17.1	16.1
Research assistantship	0.6	0.3	0.4
Teaching assistantship	1.0	0.9	0.9
Employment	58.7	48.8	54.0
Other sources (savings, etc.)	33.8	29.3	31.6
Universities			
Support from your parents	69.5	82.5	74.8
Support from your spouse	8.5	11.4	9.7
Federal scholarship, fellowship or grant	12.1	9.5	11.0
State scholarship, fellowship or grant	10.8	12.3	11.4
Other scholarship, fellowship or grant	18.8	18.7	18.8
Federal loan	19.4	20.3	19.8
Other loan	9.7	9.1	9.4
College work-study program	10.5	12.2	11.2
Research assistantship	1.1	0.6	0.9
Teaching assistantship	1.0	0.4	0.8
Employment	64.3	52.3	59.4
Other sources (savings, etc.)	37.3	30.8	34.7

SOURCE: Bayer, Royer, and Webb (1973, p. 21).

TABLE A-7 *Highest degree* *now held: the* *1971 survey* *responses of 1967* *college freshmen* *(weighted* *percentages)*	*Type of institution in which originally* *enrolled and highest degree now held*	*Men*	*Women*	*Total*

Type of institution in which originally enrolled and highest degree now held	Men	Women	Total
Total, all institutions			
None	40.8	32.8	37.3
Associate (or equivalent) (A.A., A.S., etc.)	16.9	14.7	15.9
Other	0.9	1.9	1.4
Bachelor's degree (A.B., B.A., B.S., etc.)	41.2	50.6	45.4
Two-year colleges			
None	39.7	35.7	38.1
Associate (or equivalent) (A.A., A.S., etc.)	41.7	40.8	41.3
Other	1.7	2.8	2.1
Bachelor's degree (A.B., B.A., B.S., etc.)	16.8	20.7	18.3
Four-year colleges			
None	39.2	29.3	34.3
Associate (or equivalent) (A.A., A.S., etc.)	5.4	5.0	5.2
Other	0.7	1.5	1.1
Bachelor's degree (A.B., B.A., B.S., etc.)	54.5	64.1	59.2
Universities			
None	44.1	35.7	40.6
Associate (or equivalent) (A.A., A.S., etc.)	4.7	5.5	5.0
Other	0.5	1.8	1.0
Bachelor's degree (A.B., B.A., B.S., etc.)	50.6	56.8	53.2

SOURCE: Bayer, Royer, and Webb (1973, p. 24).

Type of institution and activities expected	Men	Women	Total
Total, all institutions			
Attending college, full time (undergraduate)	27.5	15.5	22.3
Attending college, part time (undergraduate)	7.0	5.8	6.5
Attending graduate school	12.9	9.8	11.6
Having a temporary college interruption (illness, etc.)	2.3	2.0	2.2
Attending night school, adult education	3.0	4.0	3.5
Attending a school other than a college or university	2.0	1.9	2.0
Working part time	15.4	12.6	14.2
Working full time	35.5	49.4	41.5
In military service, active duty	12.9	0.4	7.5
Being a housewife	0.1	23.9	10.4
Being unemployed, looking for a job	5.7	9.1	7.2
Being unemployed, not looking for a job	2.5	4.5	3.4
Two-year colleges			
Attending college, full time (undergraduate)	28.0	16.3	23.5
Attending college, part time (undergraduate)	10.7	8.7	10.0
Attending graduate school	3.7	3.3	3.5
Having a temporary college interruption (illness, etc.)	2.6	3.1	2.8
Attending night school, adult education	5.0	5.5	5.2
Attending a school other than a college or university	2.3	1.5	1.9
Working part time	14.7	11.2	13.3
Working full time	39.0	47.1	42.2
In military service, active duty	14.2	0.5	8.8
Being a housewife	0.3	27.7	11.0
Being unemployed, looking for a job	5.3	6.0	5.6
Being unemployed, not looking for a job	1.9	5.0	3.1

TABLE A-8
Activities expected during latter part of year (September–December): the 1971 survey responses of 1967 college freshmen (weighted percentages)

TABLE A-8
(continued)

Type of institution and activities expected	Men	Women	Total
Four-year colleges			
Attending college, full time (undergraduate)	25.4	13.9	19.8
Attending college, part time (undergraduate)	5.7	4.4	5.1
Attending graduate school	16.5	12.5	14.6
Having a temporary college interruption (illness, etc.)	2.1	1.7	1.9
Attending night school, adult education	2.5	3.6	3.0
Attending a school other than a college or university	1.9	2.1	2.0
Working part time	14.0	12.8	13.4
Working full time	36.6	51.1	43.6
In military service, active duty	12.4	0.4	6.7
Being a housewife	0.1	21.6	10.4
Being unemployed, looking for a job	5.9	11.2	8.4
Being unemployed, not looking for a job	2.2	3.9	3.0
Universities			
Attending college, full time (undergraduate)	29.7	17.4	24.7
Attending college, part time (undergraduate)	4.7	5.0	4.8
Attending graduate school	18.2	11.8	15.6
Having a temporary college interruption (illness, etc.)	2.3	1.5	2.0
Attending night school, adult education	1.7	3.3	2.3
Attending a school other than a college or university	1.8	1.9	1.8
Working part time	17.9	13.9	16.3
Working full time	30.4	49.0	38.0
In military service, active duty	12.2	0.5	7.4
Being a housewife	0.1	24.0	9.8
Being unemployed, looking for a job	6.0	8.8	7.1
Being unemployed, not looking for a job	3.4	5.2	4.1

SOURCE: Bayer, Royer, and Webb (1973, p. 21).

TABLE A-9
Percentages
dicating events
experienced
since entering
ollege: the 1971
rvey responses
of 1967 college
freshmen
(weighted
percentages)

Type of institution and event	Men	Women	Total
Total, all institutions			
Got married	26.8	36.2	30.9
Changed major field	44.4	37.1	41.3
Changed career choice	43.7	38.2.	41.3
Failed one or more courses	43.2	24.5	35.2
Graduated with honors	9.5	14.0	11.4
Was elected to a student office	13.4	16.6	14.8
Joined a social fraternity, sorority, or club	33.0	33.5	33.2
Authored or co-authored a published article	6.8	5.1	6.1
Was elected to an academic honor society	10.5	15.0	12.4
Participated in student protests or demonstrations	24.5	21.4	23.2
Dropped out of college temporarily (exclude transferring)	29.5	24.4	27.3
Dropped out of college permanently	6.6	10.7	8.4
Transferred to another college before graduating	26.3	25.0	25.7
Two-year colleges			
Got married	30.2	39.8	34.0
Changed major field	40.4	27.7	35.4
Changed career choice	40.2	33.6	37.6
Failed one or more courses	39.9	21.0	32.5
Graduated with honors	5.7	9.9	7.3
Was elected to a student office	8.7	12.3	10.1
Joined a social fraternity, sorority, or club	21.2	25.5	22.9
Authored or co-authored a published article	4.5	3.4	4.1
Was elected to an academic honor society	5.5	9.2	7.0
Participated in student protests or demonstrations	14.3	9.1	12.2
Dropped out of college temporarily (exclude transferring)	40.5	29.9	36.4
Dropped out of college permanently	10.9	15.8	12.8
Transferred to another college before graduating	40.0	34.4	37.8

TABLE A-9
(continued)

Type of institution and event	Men	Women	To■
Four-year colleges			
Got married	25.2	33.4	29■
Changed major field	44.5	38.3	41
Changed career choice	44.6	37.9	41
Failed one or more courses	44.9	24.7	35■
Graduated with honors	10.6	14.5	12■
Was elected to a student office	17.7	20.3	19
Joined a social fraternity, sorority, or club	39.3	37.3	38
Authored or co-authored a published article	8.7	6.2	7
Was elected to an academic honor society	11.6	16.1	13
Participated in student protests or demonstrations	28.6	27.0	27
Dropped out of college temporarily (exclude transferring)	23.8	20.3	22
Dropped out of college permanently	4.5	9.0	6
Transferred to another college before graduating	21.3	22.5	21.
Universities			
Got married	25.0	37.6	30
Changed major field	48.7	44.3	46
Changed career choice	46.3	43.2	45.
Failed one or more courses	44.7	27.8	37.
Graduated with honors	12.2	17.2	14.
Was elected to a student office	12.9	14.6	13.
Joined a social fraternity, sorority, or club	37.7	35.0	36
Authored or co-authored a published article	6.8	5.1	6.
Was elected to an academic honor society	14.4	18.8	16.
Participated in student protests or demonstrations	30.1	24.5	27.
Dropped out of college temporarily (exclude transferring)	25.0	25.7	26.
Dropped out of college permanently	4.5	8.6	6.
Transferred to another college before graduating	18.0	19.6	18.

SOURCE: Bayer, Royer, and Webb (1973, p. 21).

TABLE A-10 *Reasons for leaving college of matriculation, reported in 1965 by students who had entered college four years earlier*

Reasons	Men		Women	
	Major reason	*Minor reason**	*Major reason*	*Minor reason**
Reasons related to career plans or interests and goals	<u>48.5</u>	<u>37.8</u>	<u>43.1</u>	<u>29.8</u>
Changed career plans	22.1	15.4	20.7	13.6
Wanted time to reconsider interests and goals	26.4	22.4	22.4	16.2
Academic and related reasons	<u>53.5</u>	<u>59.4</u>	<u>34.1</u>	<u>44.8</u>
Dissatisfied with college environment	26.7	22.3	22.3	19.7
Academic record unsatisfactory	15.5	20.8	5.8	11.1
Tired of being a student	11.3	16.3	6.0	14.0
Financial reasons	<u>26.4</u>	<u>18.7</u>	<u>19.2</u>	<u>15.2</u>
Scholarship terminated	2.8	3.1	1.4	2.5
Could not afford cost	23.6	15.6	17.8	12.7
Personal reasons	<u>8.9</u>	<u>3.7</u>	<u>37.2</u>	<u>9.6</u>
Marriage	7.8	3.1	29.0	6.1
Pregnancy	1.1	0.6	8.2	1.4
Draft	<u>1.4</u>	<u>0.9</u>	<u>0.0</u>	<u>0.1</u>

*A third alternative, "unrelated to my decision," is not shown.

SOURCE: Astin and Panos (1969, p. 31). Subgroups of reasons were developed by the Carnegie Commission staff.

TABLE A-11 Degrees awarded to men, by level and field, 1948 and 1970

Field	Bachelor's and first-professional		Master's		Doctor's		Total	
	1948	1970	1948	1970	1948	1970	1948	197
Total number (in thousands)	176.0	486.9	28.9	126.1	3.7	25.9	208.6	639
Total percent	100.0	100.0	100.0	100.0	100.0	100.0	100.0	100
Mathematical sciences	1.5	3.5	1.9	3.2	3.2	4.4	1.6	3
Mathematics	n.a.	3.4	n.a.	2.9	n.a.	3.8	n.a.	3
Statistics	n.a.	0.1	n.a.	0.3	n.a.	0.6	n.a.	0
Computer sciences		0.3		1.1		0.4		0
Physical sciences	5.0	3.8	7.7	4.0	21.0	15.7	5.6	4
Chemistry	3.0	2.0	4.0	1.3	14.6	7.7	3.3	2
Earth sciences	n.a.	0.1	n.a.	0.3	n.a.	1.5	n.a.	0
Physics	1.1	1.0	2.3	1.6	5.2	5.4	1.4	1
Other physical sciences	0.9	0.7	1.4	0.8	2.1	1.1	0.9	0
Life sciences	8.4	7.8	7.4	4.5	14.5	14.0	8.4	7
Biological sciences	4.6	5.6	3.5	3.1	9.4	10.9	4.6	5
Agriculture	3.3	1.8	3.2	1.1	4.8	2.7	3.3	1
Forestry	0.5	0.4	0.7	0.3	0.3	0.4	0.5	0
Engineering	17.6	9.1	14.5	12.2	7.0	14.1	16.9	9
Health professions	6.4	3.8	2.6	1.8	2.5	1.2	5.8	3
Dentistry	0.9	0.8	0.3				0.8	0
Medicine	3.6	1.6	0.8		0.3		3.1	1
Other health professions	1.9	1.4	1.5	1.8	2.2	1.2	1.9	1
Social sciences	10.2	18.7	11.0	11.8	11.1	14.8	10.3	17.
Anthropology	*	0.3	0.1	0.3	0.4	0.6	0.1	0.
Economics (including agricultural economics)	4.4	3.4	2.8	1.7	2.9	3.6	4.0	3.
Political science	2.1	4.3	2.3	1.3	2.4	1.8	2.2	3.
Psychology	1.6	3.9	2.3	2.0	3.3	5.0	1.7	3.
Sociology	1.0	2.6	1.0	0.9	1.5	1.7	1.0	2.
Other social sciences	1.1	4.2	2.5	5.6	0.6	2.1	1.3	4.

	Bachelor's and first-professional		Master's		Doctor's		Total	
Field	1948	1970	1948	1970	1948	1970	1948	1970
Arts and humanities	9.2	15.0	13.5	10.6	12.2	12.4	9.9	14.0
English	2.5	3.8	3.6	2.6	3.4	3.2	2.7	3.6
Fine and applied arts	2.0	3.2	4.0	3.3	1.9	2.3	2.3	3.2
Foreign languages	0.7	1.2	1.5	1.5	2.0	2.2	0.8	1.3
History	3.2	5.8	3.7	2.7	3.7	3.5	3.3	5.0
Philosophy	0.8	1.0	0.7	0.5	1.2	1.2	0.8	0.9
Professional fields (other than health and education)	28.8	27.9	13.0	21.4	12.8	4.4	26.4	25.7
Architecture	0.5	0.8	0.5	0.5	0.1	*	0.5	0.7
Business and commerce	18.2	19.8	6.7	16.3	1.0	2.3	16.3	18.4
Journalism	1.2	0.7	0.7	0.5		0.1	1.1	0.6
Law	6.0	3.1†	1.3	0.7	6.5	0.1†	5.4	2.5
Religion and theology	1.7	1.9	2.8	1.8	5.0	1.5	1.9	1.9
Other professions	1.2	1.6	1.0	1.6	0.2	0.4	1.2	1.6
Education	6.6	8.5	25.5	28.3	11.7	18.1	9.3	12.8
Broad and general curricular and miscellaneous	6.3	1.6	2.9	1.1	3.1	0.5	5.8	1.5

*Less than 0.05 percent.

†Data for 1948 and 1970 are not comparable, because a J.D. was classified as a doctor's degree in 1948 and as a first-professional degree in 1970.

SOURCES: U.S. Office of Education (annual).

TABLE A-12 *Degrees awarded to women, by level and field, 1948 and 1970*

Field	Bachelor's and first-professional 1948	1970	Master's 1948	1970	Doctor's 1948	1970	Total 1948	1970
Total number (in thousands)	96.2	246.4	13.5	83.2	0.5	4.0	110.2	433.6
Total percent	100.0	100.0	100.0	100.0	100.0	100.0	100.0	100.0
Mathematical sciences	1.7	3.0	1.1	2.0	2.0	2.4	1.6	2.8
Mathematics	n.a.	3.0	n.a.	1.9	n.a.	1.9	n.a.	2.8
Statistics	n.a.	*	n.a.	0.1	n.a.	0.5	n.a.	*
Computer sciences		0.1		0.2		0.1		0.1
Physical sciences	2.5	0.9	2.1	1.0	8.2	5.9	2.5	0.9
Chemistry	2.1	0.6	1.6	0.5	6.0	4.2	2.1	0.6
Earth sciences		0.1		0.2		0.4		0.1
Physics	0.2	0.1	0.3	0.2	1.2	0.9	0.2	0.1
Other physical sciences	0.2	0.1	0.2	0.1	1.0	0.4	0.2	0.1
Life sciences	4.9	3.2	3.2	2.4	16.0	12.5	4.7	3.1
Biological sciences	4.7	3.1	3.1	2.3	15.4	11.8	4.5	3.0
Agriculture	0.2	0.1	0.1	0.1	0.6	0.7	0.2	0.1
Forestry	*	*	0.0	*	0.0		*	*
Engineering	0.2	0.1	0.1	0.2	0.0	0.6	0.2	0.1
Health professions	5.2	5.2	2.8	2.9	4.6	1.5	4.9	4.7
Dentistry	0.1	*	0.0	0.0	0.0	0.0	*	*
Medicine	0.8	0.2	0.2	0.0	0.8	0.0	0.7	0.2
Nursing	3.4	3.2	1.5	1.8	0.0	0.3	3.2	2.9
Other health professions	0.9	1.8	1.1	1.1	3.8	1.2	1.0	1.6
Social sciences	13.3	16.9	16.5	10.1	13.6	18.4	13.7	15.6
Anthropology	0.1	0.6	0.1	0.4	0.4	1.5	0.1	0.6
Economics (including agricultural economics)	1.4	0.6	0.9	0.3	2.0	1.3	1.3	0.5
Political science	1.2	1.5	1.0	0.5	1.8	1.4	1.2	1.3
Psychology	3.7	4.3	3.9	1.9	6.4	9.4	3.8	3.9
Sociology	4.7	5.2	1.1	0.8	2.4	2.6	4.2	4.4
Other social sciences	2.2	4.7	9.5	6.2	0.6	2.2	3.1	4.9

ield	Bachelor's and first-professional		Master's		Doctor's		Total	
	1948	1970	1948	1970	1948	1970	1948	1970
Arts and humanities	24.0	26.1	20.8	16.7	27.1	24.8	23.6	24.3
English	8.6	11.0	7.3	6.2	10.3	9.3	8.4	10.0
Fine and applied arts	8.2	5.9	6.7	4.4	4.2	3.6	8.0	5.6
Foreign languages	3.2	4.6	3.0	3.9	6.0	7.4	3.2	4.5
History	3.7	4.3	3.6	2.0	5.4	3.4	3.7	3.9
Philosophy	0.3	0.3	0.2	0.2	1.2	1.1	0.3	0.3
Professional fields (other than health and education)	18.1	7.5	10.5	10.5	6.0	3.2	17.2	8.1
Business and commerce	6.4	2.8	2.6	0.9	0.6	0.3	5.9	2.4
Journalism	1.4	0.7	0.4	0.4	0.0		1.3	0.6
Home economics	7.5	2.8	4.0	1.5	2.4	2.0	7.0	2.7
Law	0.4	0.3†	0.2	0.1	1.6	0.1†	0.4	0.2
Library science	1.2	0.3	0.7	6.5	0.2	0.4	1.2	1.5
Religion and theology	1.0	0.5	2.5	0.9	1.2	0.3	1.2	0.6
Other professions	0.2	0.1	0.1	0.2	0.0	0.1	0.2	0.1
Education	24.3	35.9	40.7	53.0	17.5	30.1	26.2	39.2
Broad and general curricula and miscellaneous	5.8	1.1	2.2	1.0	5.0	0.5	5.4	1.1

ess than 0.05 percent.

)ata for 1948 and 1970 are not comparable, because a J.D. was classified as a doctor's degree in 1948 and as a first-professional degree in 1970.

sources: U.S. Office of Education (annual).

TABLE A-13 Percentage of Woodrow Wilson fellows beginning graduate study from 1958 to 1963 who had dropped out by 1966, by sex and fields of study

Field	Men	Women	Total
TOTAL	44%	64%	49%
Humanities	52	66	58
Social sciences	46	64	51
Natural sciences	26	54	30

SOURCE: Sells (1973).

TABLE A-14 Percentage of Woodrow Wilson fellows beginning graduate study from 1958 to 1963 who had dropped out by 1966, by sex, field, and whether or not second year financial support was received

Field	No support		Some support	
	Men	Women	Men	Women
Humanities	57%	72%	43%	43%
Social sciences	51	69	38	52
Natural sciences	33	66	16	26

SOURCE: Sells (1973).

TABLE A-15 Percentage of Woodrow Wilson fellows beginning graduate study from 1958 to 1963 who had dropped out by 1966, by sex, field, and parenthood

Field	No children		Any children	
	Men	Women	Men	Women
Humanities	52%	64%	54%	77%
Social sciences	46	63	49	74
Natural sciences	26	49	27	80

SOURCE: Sells (1973).

TABLE A-16 *Percentage of Woodrow Wilson fellows beginning graduate study from 1958 to 1963 who had dropped out by 1966, by sex, field, and graduate rating*

Field	Excellent		Very good		Average to dreadful	
	Men	Women	Men	Women	Men	Women
TOTAL	32%	58%	44%	67%	61%	80%
Humanities	42	63	54	65	67	85
Social sciences	39	54	47	75	61	77
Natural sciences	12	50	23	50	51	67

SOURCE: Sells (1973).

TABLE A-17 *Median salaries of faculty members, by sex, and percentage of faculty members who were women, by type, control, and size of institution, 1971-1972*

Type, control, and size of institution	Median salary			*Percentage of faculty who were women*
	Men	*Women*	*Difference*	
All four-year institutions	$13,359	$11,026	$2,333	19.0
Public universities				
Enroll 10,000 or more	14,342	11,519	2,823	15.6
Enroll 5,000–9,999	13,112	11,140	1,972	19.7
Enroll less than 5,000	12,887	10,960	1,927	23.5
Nonpublic universities				
Enroll 5,000 or more	14,944	11,367	3,577	13.6
Enroll less than 5,000	13,127	10,787	2,340	15.6
Public colleges	12,648	11,421	1,227	22.5
Nonpublic colleges				
Enroll 1,000 or more	11,841	10,283	1,558	21.6
Enroll 500–999	10,773	9,580	1,193	29.1
Enroll less than 500	10,388	8,925	1,463	29.6
Two-year institutions				
Public two-year institutions	12,337	11,118	1,219	31.2
Enroll 2,000 or more	13,668	12,397	1,271	31.3
Enroll 1,000–1,999	10,966	10,047	919	31.5
Enroll fewer than 1,000	10,450	9,452	998	30.4
Private two-year institutions	n.a.	n.a.		41.1

SOURCE: National Education Association (1972, pp. 11 and 62).

TABLE A-18   *Religion of faculty members in public and private universities and colleges, by type of institution and sex, 1969*

Type of institution and sex	Total Number (000)*	Total Percent	Protestant	Catholic	Jewish	Other	None
Public							
Total men	210.1	100.0	53.6	11.2	4.6	6.8	23.8
Total women	48.3	100.0	60.3	12.9	4.5	5.8	16.5
Research universities I and II							
Men	79.3	100.0	51.3	8.8	5.7	6.8	27.4
Women	11.7	100.0	59.0	11.6	3.1	5.7	20.6
Doctoral-granting universities I and II							
Men	24.9	100.0	52.9	9.6	4.1	7.9	25.6
Women	3.8	100.0	60.7	11.1	2.8	6.5	19.0
Comprehensive universities and colleges							
Men	62.5	100.0	55.0	11.8	4.5	6.6	22.1
Women	20.2	100.0	60.9	10.1	7.1	6.1	15.8
Liberal arts colleges							
Men	1.4	100.0	65.4	16.6	4.6	1.6	11.7
Women	0.4	100.0	76.1	7.2	7.2	9.4	0.0
Two-year colleges							
Men	39.4	100.0	56.7	15.1	2.5	6.6	19.1
Women	12.2	100.0	60.3	19.5	1.6	5.3	13.3

Type of institution and sex	Total Number (000)*	Percent	Protes-tant	Catholic	Jewish	Other	None
Private							
Total men	126.8	100.0	43.6	17.9	9.7	6.1	22.6
Total women	36.1	100.0	43.1	33.6	5.4	4.6	13.4
Research universities I and II							
Men	47.3	100.0	32.9	10.7	17.3	6.0	33.2
Women	6.0	100.0	37.4	16.6	13.2	5.3	27.5
Doctoral-granting universities I and II							
Men	17.7	100.0	44.0	16.1	12.1	6.3	21.4
Women	4.3	100.0	46.4	23.6	7.6	5.9	16.4
Comprehensive universities and colleges							
Men	12.5	100.0	33.3	41.6	6.4	5.3	13.3
Women	3.3	100.0	32.9	48.7	5.2	3.2	10.0
Liberal arts colleges							
Men	42.0	100.0	57.3	19.2	2.2	5.2	16.0
Women	18.2	100.0	44.0	38.5	2.8	3.7	11.0
Two-year colleges							
Men	5.6	100.0	51.9	18.5	3.3	16.8	9.5
Women	3.7	100.0	58.4	24.9	4.1	8.0	4.6

*Total includes respondents from other types of institutions not reported separately here.

SOURCE: Carnegie Commission Survey of Faculty and Student Opinion, 1969. The question relates to present religious preference, not to religion in which raised.

TABLE A-19 *Racial characteristics of faculty members in public and private universities and colleges, by type of institution and sex, 1969*

Type of institution and sex	Total Number (000)*	Percent	White	Black	Other
Public					
Total men	217.6	100.0	95.7	2.6	1.7
Total women	49.9	100.0	91.7	6.3	2.0
Research universities I and II					
Men	81.9	100.0	97.3	0.4	2.3
Women	12.1	100.0	97.0	1.3	1.7
Doctoral-granting universities I and II					
Men	25.9	100.0	97.6	0.3	2.1
Women	3.9	100.0	98.0	0.7	1.4
Comprehensive universities and colleges					
Men	64.9	100.0	91.5	6.9	1.5
Women	21.0	100.0	85.3	12.8	1.9
Liberal arts colleges					
Men	1.5	100.0	76.7	22.8	0.5
Women	0.4	100.0	63.8	28.9	7.2
Two-year colleges					
Men	40.9	100.0	98.7	0.7	0.6
Women	12.5	100.0	96.0	1.5	2.5

'ype of institution and sex	*Total* Number (000)*	Percent	White	Black	Other
'rivate					
Total men	130.9	100.0	95.4	2.6	1.9
Total women	37.1	100.0	93.4	5.7	0.9
Research universities I and II					
Men	48.9	100.0	96.8	0.5	2.7
Women	6.1	100.0	96.7	1.4	1.8
Doctoral-granting universities I and II					
Men	17.8	100.0	92.7	5.1	2.2
Women	4.4	100.0	90.3	8.8	0.9
Comprehensive universities and colleges					
Men	12.9	100.0	98.1	0.4	1.5
Women	3.3	100.0	99.0	0.5	0.5
Liberal arts colleges					
Men	43.3	100.0	93.7	5.0	1.4
Women	18.7	100.0	90.4	8.6	1.0
Two-year colleges					
Men	5.6	100.0	98.7	1.3	0.0
Women	3.7	100.0	100.0	0.0	0.0

*Total includes respondents from other types of institutions not reported separately here.
SOURCE: Carnegie Commission Survey of Faculty and Student Opinion, 1969.

TABLE A-20 *Women as a percentage of academic administrators in four-year colleges and universities, 1969–70*

Administrative officers	Total (454 institutions)	Public colleges	Private colleges	Over 1,000 students	Under 10,000 students	Women's colleges
Presidents	11	3	8	0	13	47
Vice-presidents	4	0	4	0	8	17
Directors of development	4	1	3	0	3	6
Business managers	9	1	9	2	4	32
College physicians	8	9	7	10	5	13
Financial aid directors	23	9	23	12	32	67
Placement directors	28	14	30	10	33	73
Counseling directors	19	9	20	5	32	67
Deans of students	23	9	18	5	26	81
Head librarians	35	22	37	8	62	61
Academic deans	18	8	14	17	15	62
Associate or assistant academic deans	17	11	16	12	20	44
Counselors	25	19	22	16	26	51

SOURCE: Oltman (1970, p. 16).

Appendix B: Retention Rates

The annual retention rate—a measure of the proportion of students who return to college the following year—has tended to be somewhat lower for women than for men (Chart B-1).[1] Although the male rate has clearly been affected to a greater extent at certain times by such developments as the return of veterans from the Korean conflict and changes in the impact of the draft, fluctuations in the rates for men and women have been somewhat similar.

Despite their lower annual retention rates, women have tended to have slightly higher graduation rates in recent years (measuring the graduation rate as the ratio of bachelor's degree recipients to first-time degree-credit enrollment four years earlier).[2] Other evidence pointing to a similar conclusion is the fact that the proportion of bachelor's degrees awarded to women in 1970 (43 percent of the total) slightly exceeded their proportion of total undergraduate degree-credit students in the preceding four years (40 to 42 percent).

[1]The annual retention rate $= [U(t) - F(t)]/[U(t - 1) - B(t)]$, where $U(t)$ denotes undergraduate degree-credit and first-professional enrollment in year t, $F(t)$ is the corresponding first-time enrollment, and $B(t)$ is the number of bachelor's and first-professional degrees awarded during the academic year ending in year t.

[2]Because many high school graduates do not enter college immediately after graduating from high school. Haggstrom's measure of first-time enrollment (developed from various sources of existing information) is a weighted average—$.6F(t - 4) + .3 F(t - 5) + .1 F (t - 6)$.

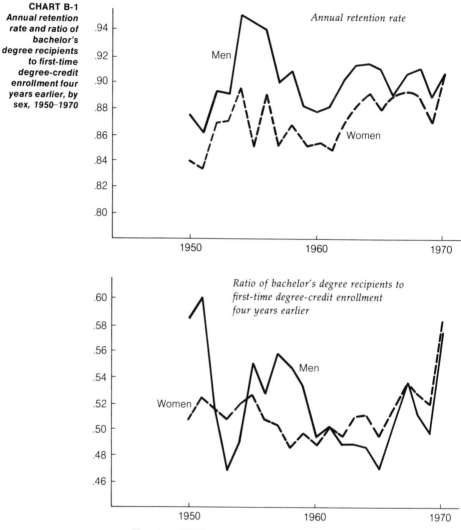

CHART B-1
Annual retention rate and ratio of bachelor's degree recipients to first-time degree-credit enrollment four years earlier, by sex, 1950–1970

Annual retention rate

Men

Women

Ratio of bachelor's degree recipients to first-time degree-credit enrollment four years earlier

Women

Men

SOURCE: Haggstrom (1971*b*).

Appendix C: Statistical Analyses Based on Carnegie Commission Survey of Faculty and Student Opinion, 1969

TABLE C-1   *Classification of fields used in tables based on Carnegie Commission Survey of Faculty and Student Opinion, 1969*

Engineering	Business	Law, medicine, etc.
Biological sciences	Accounting	New professions
Biochemistry and biophysics	Business administration	Health technology
Botany	Secretarial	Nursing
Zoology	Other business fields	Pharmacy
Other biological sciences	Education	Therapy
Physical sciences	Fine arts	Architecture and environmental design
Chemistry	Art and art history	Journalism
Computer science	Music	Social work, welfare, criminology
Geology, astronomy	Speech and drama	
Mathematics	Humanities	Agriculture
Statistics	English literature	Ethnic studies
Physics	Modern languages	Electronic technology, communications
Other physical sciences	Other languages and classics	
Social sciences		Forestry
Anthropology	Philosophy	Home economics
Economics	Theology	Industrial arts
Geography	History	Library science
Political science	Other humanities	
Psychology		
Sociology		
Other social sciences		

TABLE C-2   Women as a percentage of persons at successive levels of higher education, by field and type of institution, 1969

Field and type of institution	Under-graduate	Graduate student	Lecturer	Instruc-tor	Assistant Professor	Associate Professor	Professor
Research Universities I							
Engineering	1	1	1	1	0	1	0
Physical sciences	21	11	9	9	4	3	1
Biological sciences	22	22	25*	40	12	9	2
Social sciences	35	27	26	22	9	7	3
Business	16	3	2	5*	3	2	0
Education	65	47	18	40	19	19	15
Fine arts	66	42	31	32	20	13	6
Humanities	46	44	40	33	14	9	3
Medicine, law, etc.	20	8	10*	17	9	5	2
New professions	61	40	24	50	31	21	12
Other Universities							
Engineering	2	1	0*	0	1	0	0
Physical sciences	23	11	23	22	4	3	1
Biological sciences	27	15	39*	29	12	9	4
Social sciences	30	27	27	18	10	7	5
Business	14	3	3*	20	6	4	2
Education	86	46	41*	43	26	22	17
Fine arts	59	62	23*	34	17	13	8
Humanities	46	40	39	42	17	10	4
Medicine, law, etc.	20	7	0	13	6	5	3
New professions	60	36	24	60	37	26	15
Comprehensive Universities and Colleges							
Engineering	3	1*	0*	20*	3	1	0
Physical sciences	35	9*	21*	18	9	9	4
Biological sciences	33	11	45*	20*	18	7	14
Social sciences	49	42	21*	22	18	18	13
Business	26	0	14*	27	23	14	10
Education	87	44	37*	47	32	21	13
Fine arts	63	68*	59*	33	25	22	11
Humanities	67	47	55*	47	29	24	12
Medicine, law, etc.	27	7*	0*	†	12*	0*	6*
New professions	57	59	36*	71	44	35	21

TABLE C-2 (continued)

Field and type of institution	Under-graduate	Graduate student	Lecturer	Instruc-tor	Assistant Professor	Associate Professor	Professor
Liberal Arts Colleges I							
Engineering	7	†	†	0*	74*	0*	0*
Physical sciences	42	100*	31*	27	9	7	7
Biological sciences	47	100*	93*	66*	22	18*	23
Social sciences	54	77*	20*	27	12	9*	8*
Business	21	†	†	5*	18*	0*	0*
Education	84	56*	53*	58	46*	35	14
Fine arts	79	89*	42*	47	28	9	22
Humanities	64	0*	60*	36	26	18	18
Liberal Arts Colleges II and Two-Year Colleges							
Engineering	1			0	0*	0*	0*
Physical sciences	25			22	16	14	9
Biological sciences	37			35	25	27*	20
Social sciences	45			24	24	32	14
Business	37			30	23	48*	22*
Education	75			29	54	38	29
Fine arts	58			32	31	31	13
Humanities	53			4 2	33	31	23

* Based on fewer than 50 respondents.
† No respondents.

MULTILINEAR REGRESSION ANALYSIS OF FACULTY SALARY
DIFFERENCES

Table 8 and Chart 14 in Section 7 showed selected results of the
multilinear analysis of salary differences between male and
female faculty members. Additional findings are included in
this appendix.

Coefficients for each of the variables entering into the regression equations in the biological and physical sciences in
Research Universities I are included in Table C-3. The third and
fourth columns give the coefficients for men and women
separately. Some of the coefficients are very similar, while
others are quite different. In the first place, the constant term,
the intercept, is lower for women than for men by 2.27 salary in-
tervals, that is, by almost $7,000. Salary increases tend to occur
with increasing number of years in academic employment
about 1.7 times as rapidly for men as for women. The number of
articles published is slightly more important as an influence on
salary for women than for men, but the number of books
published has nearly twice the positive effect on compensation
for women as for men. (The fact that the number of articles is
relatively more important as an influence on salary than the
number of books probably reflects the fact that articles are an
especially frequent form of publication in the sciences.)

Somewhat surprisingly, some of the relationships shown in
Table C-3 are not what would be expected. The most striking
example is that receiving one's graduate degree from a prestigious institution had a negative effect on salaries of women of
about $1,000. However, this unexpected relationship did not
show up in any of the other fields or types of institutions studied. In a search for possible explanations, we found that about
one-half of the 59 women in the high salary brackets did not
have doctorates from prestigious American universities; in
even higher brackets, the ratio was more than half. Six of the
fifty-nine had foreign doctorates; four of these were among the
higher paid women in the group.

In Table C-4 we have included the codes that were used in
classifying the variables in the predictor equations as a guide
to the reader in interpreting the analysis.

The weighted average coefficients in the predictor equations
for each sex for all respondents in all types of institutions are

TABLE C-3
Coefficients of
the multilinear re-
gression equa-
tion for predicting
faculty salaries,
biological and
physical scien-
ces, Research
Universities I

Variable	Men and women	Men	Women
Constant	2.62	2.21	−.06
1. Sex	−.60‡		
2. Date of birth	.11*	.12	.15*
3. Married versus single	.23	.13	−.24
4. Number of children	.40‡	.21†	.46*
5. Highest degree	.73‡	.80‡	.73‡
6. Year of highest degree	−.15‡	−.16‡	−.10*
7. B.A. from prestigious school	.12	.11	.07
8. Graduate degree from prestigious school	−.12	−.08	−.32†
9. Support toward highest degree	.07	.08	.00
10. Rank (variable omitted)			
11. Years employed in higher education	.23‡	.26‡	.15*
12. Years employed in present institution	−.13‡	−.15‡	−.09
13. Quality of present institution	−.07	−.09*	.04
14. Number of articles	.40‡	.37‡	.44‡
15. Number of books	.13†	.10*	.19
16. Association with a research institute	.06	.08	−.00
17. Number of sources of research support	.03	.01	.20*
18. Number of sources of paid consulting	.25‡	.23‡	.36*
19. Research versus teaching inclination	−.08*	−.12*	.02
20. Administrative activity	.19‡	.20‡	.12*
21. Consulting	.01	.02	−.03
22. Outside professional practice	−.10*	−.10*	−.16
23. Hours taught per week	−.13‡	−.15‡	−.01
24. Salary base (whether 9-month or 11-month)	.78‡	.78‡	.84‡
27. Interaction variable: date of birth and number of articles	−.04‡	−.03†	−.06‡
28. Interaction variable: sex and number of children	−.11		
29. Interaction variable: date of birth and number of children	−.03†	−.03	−.08*
30. Interaction variable: sex, marital status, and age	.03	.17*	.10
31. Part-time by rule 5	−.69‡	−.69‡	−.42†

* Individual coefficient differs from zero at 0.05 significance level (two sided);

† Differs from zero at 0.01 significance level;

‡ Differs from zero at 0.001 significance level.

NOTE: Sample includes 1,183 men and 312 women; one salary interval is $3,000. For codes used for each variable, see Table C-4.

SOURCE: Adapted from Carnegie Commission Survey of Faculty and Student Opinion, 1969.

TABLE C-4 *Codes used in classifying variables in multilinear regression equations*

1. Sex, 1 = male, 2 = female

2. Date of birth, 1 = 1908 or before to 9 = 1944 or later

3. Married versus single, 1 = never married, 2 = married or formerly married

4. Number of children, 1 = none to 4 = 3 or more

5. Highest degree, 0 = Bachelor's or less, 1 = Master's, 2 = doctorate or other advanced degree

6. Year of highest degree, 11 = 1928 or before to 21 = 1967 or later

7. B.A. from prestigious school, 0 = no, 1 = yes

8. Graduate degree, if any, from prestigious school, 0 = no, 1 = yes

9. Support toward highest degree, 0 = none to 2 = teaching assistantship/research assistantship plus fellowship

10. Rank (variable omitted in all equations)*

11. Years employed in higher education, 1 = one year or less to 8 = 30 years or more

12. Years employed in present institution, 1 = one year or less to 8 = 30 years or more

13. Quality of present institution, 1 = high to 7 = low

14. Number or articles, 1 = none to 6 = more than 20

15. Number of books, 1 = none to 4 = five or more

16. Association with a research institute, 1 = yes, 2 = no

17. Number of sources of research support, 0 to 6

18. Number of sources of paid consulting, 0 to 6

19. Research/teaching inclination, 1 = heavily research to 4 = heavily teaching

20. Administrative activity, 1 = none to 7 = 81 to 100 percent time

21. Consulting, 1 = none to 7 = 81 to 100 percent time

22. Outside professional practice, 1 = none to 7 = 81 to 100 percent time

23. Hours taught per week, 1 = none to 9 = 21 or more

24. Salary base, 1 = 9 to 10 months, 2 = 11 to 12 months

25. Institution type (variable omitted in all equations)

26. Field (variable omitted in all equations)

27. Interaction: date of birth and number of articles

28. Interaction: sex and number of children

29. Interaction: date of birth and number of children

30. Interaction: sex, married versus single, and age, 1 = male, never married, under 30 to 8 = female, married or formerly married, 30 or older

31. Part-time, 1 = full-time, 2 = part-time

TABLE C-4 (*continued*)

Salary codes: for question, "What is your basic institutional salary, before tax and deductions, for the current academic year?"

1. Below $7,000
2. $7,000–$9,999
3. $10,000–$11,999
4. $12,000–$13,999
5. $14,000–$16,999
6. $17,000–$19,999
7. $20,000–$24,999
8. $25,000–$29,999
9. $30,000 and over

* Rank was not used as a predictor variable because it is highly correlated with salary and also with such variables as number of years in academic employment. In addition, the use of rank as a control variable obscures the influence of relatively slow promotion of women or of lengthy service as a lecturer without promotional opportunities.

included in Table C-5. Some of the relationships are of considerable interest. For example, having been married had a negative effect on women's salaries but a positive effect on men's. Similarly, there is a positive relationship between male salaries and number of children (up to three children), whereas women's salaries are not significantly affected by number of children.

Advanced degrees are important for both men and women, but much more so for men. Having held an advanced degree for many years had a positive effect on male salaries but no significant effect on female salaries. Similarly, having received a graduate degree from a prestigious institution had a positive effect on male salaries, but no significant effect on women's compensation.

Both men and women can expect salary increases with increasing numbers of years of academic employment, but the effect is relatively more important for men by about 50 percent. Male salaries varied directly with the quality of the institution in which they were employed, within any given type of institution, but women's salaries were relatively little affected by quality of institution.

The effect of number of publications was about the same for both sexes, while association with a research institute had a positive effect on men's salaries, but no significant effect on women's. This probably reflected the fact that male scientists, with their relatively high salaries, were especially likely to be associated with a research institute. On the other hand, women appeared to benefit relatively more from having more than one source of research support and from having several sources of paid consulting. Not unexpectedly, male salaries were inversely related to the number of hours taught per week, as were women's, but the influence on female salaries was somewhat less important. Relatively distinguished faculty members are more likely to have released time for research and also are more likely to serve on time-consuming departmental or campus committees with compensating time off from teaching. Formal hours of teaching also tend to be somewhat misleading in the case of senior faculty members in universities, who frequently serve on many Ph.D. thesis committees and spend many hours outside the classroom in consultation with doctoral candidates on whose committees they serve.

	Variable	Men	Women
	Constant		
1.	*Sex*		
2.	*Date of birth*	−0.08	−0.02
3.	*Married versus single*	0.28	−0.26
4.	*Number of children*	0.33	−0.03
5.	*Highest degree*	0.62	0.41
6.	*Year of highest degree*	−0.13	0.02
7.	*B.A. from prestigious school*	0.24	0.29
8.	*Graduate degree from prestigious school*	0.12	−0.02
9.	*Support toward highest degree*	0.13	0.08
10.	*Rank (variable omitted)*		
11.	*Years employed in higher education*	0.23	0.15
12.	*Years employed in present institution*	−0.08	0.01
13.	*Quality of present institution*	−0.13	−0.04
14.	*Number of articles*	0.32	0.37
15.	*Number of books*	0.25	0.25
16.	*Association with a research institute*	−0.13	0.01
17.	*Number of sources of research support*	0.08	0.22
18.	*Number of sources of paid consulting*	0.16	0.25
19.	*Research versus teaching inclination*	−0.04	0.01
20.	*Administrative activity*	0.18	0.18
21.	*Consulting*	−0.07	−0.07
22.	*Outside professional practice*	−0.15	−0.14
23.	*Hours taught per week*	−0.14	−0.09
24.	*Salary base (whether 9-month or 11-month)*	0.71	0.42
27.	*Interaction variable: date of birth and number of articles*	−0.03	−0.05
28.	*Interaction variable: sex and number of children*		
29.	*Interaction variable: date of birth and number of children*	−0.04	0.03
30.	*Interaction variable: sex, marital status, and age*	0.06	0.06
31.	*Part-time by rule 5*	−0.53	−0.57

TABLE C-5
Grand weighted average coefficients of the multilinear regression equations for predicting faculty salaries*

*One salary interval is $3,000 (or $2,000 or $5,000).

NOTE: For codes used for each variable, see Table C-4.

SOURCE: Adapted from Carnegie Commission Survey of Faculty and Student Opinion, 1969.

In Tables C-6 to C-10, we have included the coefficients in selected fields in five types of institutions. These tables also include data providing information on the reliability of the results. The number of observations used, the corresponding number of degrees of freedom, and the multiple R-squared—usually about 0.7—are shown. The last two lines of the tables give the mean residual for each category, that is, the average difference between the actual salary of an individual and that predicted by the multilinear regression equation for the opposite sex. The standard deviation of the residuals is also shown.

We note that the mean residual for men is almost always positive. In Research Universities I, it tends to amount to about $3,000 in a number of fields. Conversely, the mean residuals for women are almost always negative. On the average, after controlling for the predictor variables, actual salaries of women tend to fall below those predicted on the basis of the male equation by amounts that are somewhat similar to the positive mean residual differences for men.

As we have observed in Section 7, patterns of sexual differences in salaries vary by type of institution. They also clearly vary by field. The effect of sex is considerably less important in both the humanities and sciences in Comprehensive Universities and Colleges than in other types of institutions. It is also relatively unimportant in humanities in Liberal Arts Colleges I, but relatively important in the natural sciences in these colleges. The number of years in academic employment has a relatively less important influence in Comprehensive Universities and Colleges than in universities, but the number of years in one's present institution has a positive influence as against a negative influence in universities. In other words, it appears to be advantageous to move around in universities but to "stay put" in Comprehensive Universities and Colleges. It seems likely that seniority exerts relatively more influence, as compared with other factors, in the latter group of institutions.

It is important to recognize that our study of salary differences between men and women is *retrospective*, utilizing salaries and prediction equations of faculty members actually employed in 1969. Discrimination that takes the form of failing to employ women is not reflected in the data. Furthermore, for those who are employed, we utilize the observed predictor variables. If there is discrimination against women in connection with admission to graduate school or in obtaining the Ph.D., it is not revealed in our data. To the extent that there is such discrimination, as suggested in the discussion in Section 6, our mean salary residuals associated with sex are underestimated.

It is of interest to compare differences in faculty salaries associated with race as well as with sex. However, the numbers of nonwhite faculty members in specific fields and types of institutions are too small to permit the same type of analysis as was undertaken for sex differences. Even so, we can observe the residuals in salaries for each race separately. Do black men tend to have negative mean residuals when their salaries are estimated from the equation for all men (and thus essentially for all white men, who are overwhelmingly predominant), for each field and type of institution? Do black women tend to have negative residuals when their salaries are estimated from the equation for all women? The same questions can be asked for Asian-Americans and for other races (chiefly Native Americans and those of Spanish origin). Furthermore, by examining the distribution of residual salaries of black men when their salaries are estimated from the equation for all women in the same field and type of institution—and similarly for other combinations of race and sex—we can determine whether race or sex is the more important in reducing salary.

The results were clear and consistent, even though there were the irregularities to be expected from very small samples. There was a slight tendency for black men to have negative mean residuals when their salaries were predicted on the basis of the equation for all men, while there was a slight tendency for black women to have positive mean residuals when their salaries were predicted on the basis of the equation for all women. Somewhat similar relationships prevailed for Asian-Americans, but more irregularly. However, these differences were not statistically significant. On the other hand, the difference associated with sex persisted and was strong. Not only were the mean residuals for white men substantial and positive, but this was also true for black men, Asian-American men, and men of "other" races, and the mean residuals tended to be similar in amount to those for all men. Conversely, the residuals for women, regardless of race, tended to be negative in every field and type of institution.

TABLE C-6
Coefficients of the multilinear regression equations for predicting faculty salaries in Research Universities I, by sex and field

Variable	Biological and physical sciences		Education	
	Men	Women	Men	Women
Constant	2.21	−.06	2.34	5.19
2. Date of birth	.12	.15*	−.02	−.05
3. Married versus single	.13	−.24	.08	−.14
4. Number of children	.21†	.46*	.18	.11
5. Highest degree	.80‡	.73	.86	.76
6. Year of highest degree	−.16‡	−.10*	−.11*	−.14‡
7. B.A. from prestigious school	.11	.07	−.04	−.09
8. Graduate degree from prestigious school	−.08	−.32†	−.15	.12
9. Support toward highest degree	.08	.00	−.01	−.04
11. Years employed in higher education	.26‡	.15*	.12	.11*
12. Years employed in present institution	−.15‡	−.09	−.06	−.07
13. Quality of present institution	−.09*	.04	.05	.08
14. Number of articles	.37‡	.44‡	.19	.14*
15. Number of books	.10*	.19	.10	−.02
16. Association with a research institute	.08	−.00	−.18	−.04
17. Number of sources of research support	.01	.20*	.17*	.13
18. Number of sources of paid consulting	.23‡	.36*	.25‡	.19‡
19. Research versus teaching inclination	−.12*	.02	−.01	−.08
20. Administrative activity	.20‡	.12*	.09*	.13*
21. Consulting	.02	−.03	−.08	−.12*
22. Outside professional practice	−.10*	−.16	.09	−.03
23. Hours taught per week	−.15‡	−.01	−.15‡	−.14‡
24. Salary base (whether 9-month or 11-month)	.78‡	.84‡	1.02‡	.52‡
27. Interaction: date of birth and number of articles	−.03†	−.06‡	−.02	−.01
29. Interaction: date of birth and number of children	−.03	−.08*	−.03	−.02
30. Interaction: sex, marital status, and age	.17*	.10	.10	−.03
31. Part-time by rule 5	−.69‡	−.42†	−.34*	−.65‡

	Fine arts		Humanities		Social sciences		New professions	
	Men	Women	Men	Women	Men	Women	Men	Women
	8.01	3.27	3.27	3.92	5.18	2.54	5.48	2.56
	−.02	−.05	.04	−.08*	−.01	−.07	−.04	−.04
	.23	.10	.02	−.08	.05	−.21	.16	−.16
	.27	−.20	.22†	−.29*	.33†	−.21	.16	−.12
	.51‡	.68‡	.45‡	.33‡	.52‡	.49†	.48‡	.68‡
	−.25‡	−.09*	−.15‡	−.01	−.18‡	−.07	−.18‡	−.07‡
	−.08	.05	.01	−.01	−.01	.02	.05	.17*
	.14	−.20	.23†	.08	−.11	.06	−.04	.00
	−.02	−.04	.10	.07	.02	−.04	.11	.03
	.09	.15	.29‡	.13‡	.24‡	.27†	.01	.13‡
	−.01	−.05	−.12‡	−.03	−.13‡	−.13	−.08	−.06*
	−.19	−.34†	.10	−.12*	.16*	.01	−.22*	−.08
	.03	.17	.27‡	.18†	.31‡	.10	.16*	.23‡
	.08	.07	.34‡	.26‡	.04	.11	.21‡	.05
	−.21	.10	−.07	−.17	−.09	−.08	−.14	−.03
	.05	.09	.02	.13	.00	.02	.03	.18‡
	.27†	.08	.09	.18†	.15‡	.07	.21‡	.19‡
	−.14	−.00	−.09	−.06	−.16†	.08	−.09	.03
	.16†	.13	.16‡	.16‡	.14‡	.19†	.22‡	.18‡
	−.08	−.01	−.14†	−.02	.06	.07	−.13†	.01
	−.14†	−.01	−.13*	−.19‡	−.21‡	.01	−.31‡	−.09*
	−.06	.02	−.12‡	−.17‡	−.18‡	−.09	−.03	−.05‡
	.34*	.26	.28‡	−.01	.63‡	.56‡	.96‡	.52‡
	.01	−.03	−.02*	−.01	−.02	−02	−.00	−.02
	−.06*	.03	−.03	.04	−.04*	.03	−.02	.01
	.02	−.06	.06	−.01	−.00	.03	.08	.02
	−.89‡	−.29	−.38‡	−.72‡	−.54‡	−.23	−.60‡	−.31‡

TABLE C-6
(continued)

Variable	Biological and physical sciences		Education	
	Men	Women	Men	Women
Number of observations	1,183	312	320	381
Number of variables	26	26	26	26
Residual degrees of freedom	1,156	285	293	354
Multiple R-squared	.71	.69	.69	.70
Residual mean square	1.16	.92	1.00	.63
Mean opposite sex residual	1.17	−1.04	.58	−.48
Standard deviation: opposite sex residual	1.19	1.12	1.06	.94

* Individual coefficient differs from zero at 0.05 significance level (two sided).
† Individual coefficient differs from zero at 0.01 significance level.
‡ Individual coefficient differs from zero at 0.001 significance level.

TABLE C-7
Coefficients of the multilinear regression equation for predicting faculty salaries in Research Universities II and Doctoral-Granting Universities I and II, by sex and field

Variable	Biological and physical sciences		Education	
	Men	Women	Men	Women
Constant	3.47	−.35	3.00	2.98
2. Date of birth	.02	.09	−.12	−.13†
3. Married versus single	−.23	−.19	−.02	−.03
4. Number of children	.28‡	−.57†	.16	−.35
5. Highest degree	.77‡	.63‡	.54‡	.49‡
6. Year of highest degree	−.15‡	−.05	−.11*	.03
7. B.A. from prestigious school	.12	.05	.19	.07
8. Graduate degree from prestigious school	.12	.08	.09	.05
9. Support toward highest degree	.02	−.04	−.00	.10
11. Years employed in higher education	.23‡	.17†	−.01	.08
12. Years employed in present institution	−.16‡	−.09	−.04	−.03
13. Quality of present institution	.03	.03	.07	−.05
14. Number of articles	.27‡	.41‡	.32‡	.21†
15. Number of books	.15†	.31*	.25‡	.04
16. Association with a research institute	.03	.03	.04	−.20
17. Number of sources of research support	.01	.04	−.03	.13
18. Number of sources of paid consulting	.17‡	.11	.14†	.07
19. Research versus teaching inclination	−.08	−.06	−.13	−.02
20. Administrative activity	.21‡	.21‡	.12‡	.06*

Fine arts		Humanities		Social sciences		New professions	
Men	Women	Men	Women	Men	Women	Men	Women
264	192	712	520	581	215	700	1,029
26	26	26	26	26	26	26	26
237	165	685	493	554	188	673	1,002
.69	.60	.78	.70	.73	.56	.60	.63
.99	.71	.84	.50	.94	1.11	1.39	.83
.84	−.77	.72	−.58	.97	−.50	.79	−.69
1.17	.99	1.11	.87	1.11	1.10	1.28	1.06

Fine arts		Humanities		Social sciences		New professions	
Men	Women	Men	Women	Men	Women	Men	Women
1.28	2.84	2.07	1.31	5.17	.80	2.48	1.21
−.09	−.17†	−.05	.00	−.03	.05	−.08	−.04
−.12	.08	.41†	−.22*	−.13	−.58	.80†	−.31*
.27	−.15	.18*	−.11	.17	−.47*	.18	−.08
−.01	.57‡	.34‡	.34‡	.79‡	.46†	.77‡	.78‡
.06	−.02	−.03	.00	−.19‡	.07	−.13‡	−.02
.16	.36	.07	.09	−.23*	.09	−.18	.08
.18	−.21	.24†	.10	.11	.14	.28*	−.03
−.01	.09	−.00	.03	.15	−.13	.03	.01
.24‡	.12	.36‡	.10†	.18‡	.33‡	.06	.12‡
−.03	−.03	−.11‡	.05	−.20‡	−.29‡	−.03	−.01
−.01	−.24	−.01	.02	.01	−.07	−.16	.02
.06	.10	.15†	.56‡	.18*	.34*	.15*	.07
.15	−.05	.24‡	.03	.07	.06	.03	.16†
−.29	−.23	.09	.27	−.09	−.08	−.04	.10
.13	.39*	.02	.02	.07	.07	−.05	.16†
.18*	.17	.12	.16†	.05	.13	.28‡	.24‡
.04	.08	−.08	−.09	.04	−.09	−.04	−.00
.19‡	.14*	.11‡	.15‡	.14‡	.19†	.24‡	.16‡

		Biological and physical sciences		Education	
TABLE C-7 **(continued)**					
Variable		Men	Women	Men	Women
21.	Consulting	.09	.05	−.07	−.05
22.	Outside professional practice	−.21‡	−.08	−.19†	−.13†
23.	Hours taught per week	−.12‡	−.05	−.05	−.09‡
24.	Salary base (whether 9-month or 11-month)	.69‡	.72‡	1.10‡	.43‡
27.	Interaction: date of birth and number of articles	−.02*	−.03	−.03	−.01
29.	Interaction: date of birth and number of children	−.03*	−.10†	−.01	.04
30.	Interaction: sex, marital status, and age	−.03	.04	.05	.01
31.	Part-time by rule 5	−.46‡	−.37	−.09	−.48†
Number of observations		941	254	368	468
Number of variables		26	26	26	26
Residual degrees of freedom		914	227	341	441
Multiple R-squared		.69	.64	.67	.55
Residual mean square		.87	.84	.83	.79
Mean opposite sex residual		.60	−.34	.84	−.50
Standard deviation: opposite sex residual		.98	.93	1.07	1.04

*Individual coefficient differs from zero at 0.05 significance level (two sided).

†Individual coefficient differs from zero at 0.01 significance level.

‡Individual coefficient differs from zero at 0.001 significance level.

	Fine arts		Humanities		Social sciences		New professions	
	Men	Women	Men	Women	Men	Women	Men	Women
	−.12	−.02	−.07	−.08†	−.03	.10	.05	−.01
	−.08	.00	.04	−.04	−.04	−.13	−.14†	−.15‡
	−.04	.01	−.20‡	−.08†	−.22‡	−.05	.03	−.04†
	.56†	.31	.27†	.05	1.11‡	.18	.59‡	.51‡
	.01	−.01	−.00	−.08‡	−.02	−.03	−.00	.01
	−.04	.03	−.02	.01	−.01	.08*	−.04	−.00
	.08	−.11	−.09	.02	−.00	.17*	−.06	.06
	−.61*	.24	−.61‡	−.58‡	−.60‡	−.43	−.08	−.25†
	241	204	602	553	499	189	500	883
	26	26	26	26	26	26	26	26
	214	177	575	526	472	162	473	856
	.59	.49	.76	.61	.69	.56	.60	.63
	.89	.80	.71	.42	.88	.98	1.06	.68
	.12	−.59	.76	−.09	1.14	−.71	.98	−.27
	1.05	1.03	1.05	.80	1.22	1.23	1.12	.97

		Biological and physical sciences		Education	
	Variable	Men	Women	Men	Women
	Constant	3.06	0.60	5.27	1.16
2.	Date of birth	−.06	−.01	−.10	.05
3.	Married versus single	.06	.23	.25	−.08
4.	Number of children	.09	−.44	−.05	.26
5.	Highest degree	.77‡	.59†	.71‡	.88‡
6.	Year of highest degree	−.08	−.04	−.14†	−.02
7.	B.A. from prestigious school	−.08	.06	.41	.30
8.	Graduate degree from prestigious school	.24	−.24	−.18	.11
9.	Support toward highest degree	.14	−.08	.08	.02
11.	Years employed in higher education	.04	−.10	.13	.14†
12.	Years employed in present institution	−.04	.26*	−.08	.03
13.	Quality of present institution	−.26‡	−.06	−.16†	−.16‡
14.	Number of articles	.52‡	.53†	.15	.40†
15.	Number of books	.23*	.12	.18	.31†
16.	Association with a research institute	.43*	.72	−.33	−.07
17.	Number of sources of research support	−.20*	.18	.06	−.18
18.	Number of sources of paid consulting	.19	−.16	.14	.09
19.	Research versus teaching inclination	−.10	−.11	.05	−.07
20.	Administrative activity	.19‡	41‡	.11*	.07*
21.	Consulting	−.03	−.14	−.03	−.01
22.	Outside professional practice	−.04	−.03	−.15	−.10
23.	Hours taught per week	−.08*	−.10	−.08	−.04
24.	Salary base (whether 9-month or 11-month)	.92‡	.82†	.58‡	.59‡
27.	Interaction: date of birth and number of articles	−.07‡	−.05	−.01	−.06*
29.	Interaction: date of birth and number of children	.00	.08	.02	−.07
30.	Interaction: sex, marital status, and age	−.09	−.02	−.01	.03
31.	Part-time by rule 5	−.63†	−.65	−.21	−.40*

TABLE C-8 Coefficients of the multilinear regression equation for predicting faculty salaries in Comprehensive Universities and Colleges I and II, by sex and field

Fine arts		Humanities		Social sciences	
Men	Women	Men	Women	Men	Women
4.37	2.07	5.78	2.31	5.62	1.34
−.11	.11	−.02	.01	−.08	.04
.16	−.52	.11	.10	.31	−.13
−.11	−.23	.57‡	−.22	.44	−.24
.79†	.28	.44‡	.63‡	.64†	.54†
−.06	−.04	−.14†	−.02	−.14	−.02
.39	.31	.07	.29*	.01	−.02
.22	−.11	.01	−.03	.47*	.23
−.06	.07	.24†	.02	−.03	.01
.20	.23†	.04	.10	−.03	.14
−.04	.01	.12*	.14†	−.03	.10
−.23†	−.07	−.11*	−.09*	−.25‡	−.16†
.03	.19	.05	.33‡	−.08	.77‡
.25	.68‡	.37‡	.14	.43†	.12
−.33	−.17	−.09	−.24	−.16	.06
.16	.68‡	−.16	−.07	.07	.16
.03	.21	.13	−.01	.14	−.01
−.01	.10	−.04	−.03	−.03	−.03
.27‡	−.08	.00	.13†	.17*	.26‡
−.07	−.12	−.18*	.03	.06	−.07
−.02	−.09	−.04	−.10	−.12	−.08
.06	−.07	−.26‡	−.12*	− 19*	−.04
−.20	.57†	.14	.43‡	.37	.23
.01	−.03	−.00	−.06†	.02	−.11‡
.04	.02	−.08	.04	−.07	.05
−.16	.16*	−.01	.00	.06	.01
−.43	−.94‡	−.65†	−.59†	−.31	−.38

	Biological and physical sciences		Education	
Variable	Men	Women	Men	Women
Number of observations	253	124	194	303
Number of variables	26	26	26	26
Residual degrees of freedom	226	97	167	276
Multiple R-squared	.75	.73	.67	.66
Residual mean square	.70	.97	.90	.73
Mean opposite sex residual	−.01	.05	.55	−.15
Standard deviation: opposite sex residual	1.06	1.07	.99	.96

TABLE C-8 (continued)

* Individual coefficient differs from zero at 0.05 significance level (two-sided).
† Individual coefficient differs from zero at 0.01 significance level.
‡ Individual coefficient differs from zero at 0.001 significance level.

TABLE C-9 Coefficients of the multilinear regression equation for predicting faculty salaries in Liberal Arts Colleges I, by sex and field

	Biological and physical sciences		Education	
Variable	Men	Women	Men	Women
Constant	−1.30	0.95	2.74	1.00
2. Date of birth	−.14	.00	−.48	−.02
3. Married versus single	.21	−.08	1.49	−.03
4. Number of children	−.08	.01	.11	−.19
5. Highest degree	.26	.70†	−.18	.35*
6. Year of highest degree	.21‡	.04	.17	−.02
7. B.A. from prestigious school	−.00	−.30	1.35*	.65†
8. Graduate degree from prestigious school	−.04	−.06	.24	.13
9. Support toward highest degree	.16	.12	.28	.22*
11. Years employed in higher education	.34‡	.10	.14	.17*
12. Years employed in present institution	.01	.21*	−.02	−.12
13. Quality of present institution	−.31†	−.19	−.27	−.01
14. Number of articles	.54‡	.06	−.37	.26
15. Number of books	.04	.60†	−.28	−.13
16. Association with a research institute	−.43	−.48	−.98	.56
17. Number of sources of research support	−.01	−.10	1.04	−.23
18. Number of sources of paid consulting	.27*	.74‡	−.46	.16
19. Research versus teaching inclination	−.07	.13	−.01	.21
20. Administrative activity	.08	.26†	−.09	.24‡

Fine arts		Humanities		Social sciences	
Men	Women	Men	Women	Men	Women
123	153	238	347	177	139
26	26	26	26	26	26
96	126	211	320	150	112
.64	.68	.70	.68	.67	.78
1.01	.60	.77	.62	1.07	.68
.90	.17	.27	−.18	.40	−.37
1.22	1.00	1.03	.97	1.25	1.08

Fine arts		Humanities		Social sciences	
Men	Women	Men	Women	Men	Women
3.10	3.09	5.99	4.71	2.23	4.00
−.09	−.08	.02	−.06	.04	−.10
−.37	−.20	.52	−.01	.51	−.62
.21	−.28	.51‡	.20	.03	−.63
.12	.05	.36†	.36‡	.13	.12
−.00	.05	−.22‡	−.05	−.10	.08
.70	.34	.07	−.06	−.07	.12
.37	.16	.22	−.09	.09	.13
.12	.01	−.04	.12	.01	.21
.07	.09	.10	.22‡	.31*	.04
.21	.04	.09	−.00	−.20	−.01
.11	−.19	−.33‡	−.31‡	−.26	−.26
.45	.19	.08	.26†	.34	.36
.46*	.07	.27†	.04	.35*	.38
−.91	.54	−.38	−.36	.11	−.18
.45*	−.06	−.02	.05	.20	−.00
−.10	.18	.12	.36	−.01	.18
.15	−.06	−.10	.07	.28	.04
−.10	.23*	.20‡	.21‡	.29†	.18

TABLE C-9
(continued)

Variable	Biological and physical sciences		Education	
	Men	Women	Men	Women
21. Consulting	.08	−.07	.31	−.04
22. Outside professional practice	.19	−.36*	−.34	.00
23. Hours taught per week	−.12†	.02	−.15	−.10*
24. Salary base (whether 9-month or 11-month)	.48*	−.43*	1.17*	−.15
27. Interaction: date of birth and number of articles	−.06†	−.01	.13	−.01
29. Interaction: date of birth and number of children	.01	−.03	−.04	.02
30. Interaction: sex, marital status, and age	.11	.05	.03	.04
31. Part-time by rule 5	−.22	−.41	−.15	−.76†
Number of observations	156	140	47	108
Number of variables	26	26	26	26
Residual degrees of freedom	129	113	20	81
Multiple R-squared	.78	.76	.83	.76
Residual mean square	.52	.73	.80	.38
Mean opposite sex residual	.59	−.61	.75	−.36
Standard deviation: opposite sex residual	1.04	1.16	1.21	1.56

* Individual coefficient differs from zero at 0.05 significance level (two sided).

† Individual coefficient differs from zero at 0.01 significance level.

‡ Individual coefficient differs from zero at 0.001 significance level.

	Fine arts		Humanities		Social sciences	
Men	Women	Men	Women	Men	Women
09	−.10	−.06	−.12*	.01	−.08
28	−.01	−.09	−.01	−.17	.11
24†	−.12	−.05	−.06	−.09	−.07
59	−.22	.21	.19*	.12	−.53*
08	.01	−.00	−.03*	−.03	−.05
06	.01	−.07†	−.03	.03	.09
26	.05	−.07	−.11*	−.04	.09
02	−.86*	−.11	−.64‡	−.45	−.72†
54	93	221	292	127	81
26	26	26	26	26	26
27	66	194	265	100	54
35	.70	.79	.72	.60	.78
57	.64	.62	.56	1.09	.36
70	−1.38	.09	.06	1.14	−.11
13	1.30	.89	.95	1.25	.85

TABLE C-10
Coefficients of the multilinear regression equation for predicting faculty salaries in Liberal Arts Colleges II and Two-Year Colleges, by sex and field

Variable	Biological and physical sciences		Education	
	Men	Women	Men	Wom
Constant	−2.17	.94	2.18	−.1
2. Date of birth	−.04	.00	.13	.0
3. Married versus single	.04	.08	.52	.0
4. Number of children	.24	.99‡	.27	.0
5. Highest degree	.35*	.30	.50	.0
6. Year of highest degree	.07	−.00	−.08	−.0
7. B.A. from prestigious school	.22	.59	.09	.5
8. Graduate degree from prestigious school	.19	−.14	−.17	−.0
9. Support toward highest degree	.04	−.17	−.08	.2
11. Years employed in higher education	.26‡	.14	.29*	.1
12. Years employed in present institution	−.02	−.07	−.22	−.0
13. Quality of present institution	.20*	.07	.17	.4
14. Number of articles	−.09	.36	−.10	.1
15. Number of books	.09	−.36	.43*	−.1
16. Association with a research institute	.05	−.18	−.23	−.4
17. Number of sources of research support	−.06	−.07	−.61	−.2
18. Number of sources of paid consulting	.09	.75†	.20	.1
19. Research versus teaching inclination	.15	−.07	−.15	.1
20. Administrative activity	.19‡	.12	−.08	.0
21. Consulting	−.15	−.09	−.12	−.0
22. Outside professional practice	−.21†	−.31*	−.02	−.1
23. Hours taught per week	−.03	.06	−.03	−.0
24. Salary base (whether 9-month or 11-month)	.18	.04	.44	.0
27. Interaction: date of birth and number of articles	.04	−.01	.01	.0
29. Interaction: date of birth and number of children	−.02	−.16†	−.05	−.0
30. Interaction: sex, marital status, and age	.10	−.07	−.04	.0
31. Part-time by rule 5	−.11	−.06	−.69	−.1

Fine arts		Humanities		Social sciences		New professions	
Men	Women	Men	Women	Men	Women	Men	Women
2.31	.13	−3.03	−.93	2.36	−2.90	5.75	−1.85
−.01	.15†	.13	.05	−.00	−.05	.12	−.04
−.42	−.40	−.06	−.12	−.02	.13	−1.28	−.01
.51	−.22	.50†	.13	−.12	.01	.48	−.16
.78*	.54†	.37†	.39‡	.59*	.11	1.08†	.31*
.07	−.04	−.01	−.01	−.15	.17*	−.11	.02
−.49	.08	.17	.39†	−.19	−.15	−.29	.44*
.07	−.22	.31	.20*	−.29	.13	−1.00	.01
−.02	−.12	.01	.14*	.39*	.09	−.29	.13
.06	.11	.18*	.14†	.24	.19	.14	−.01
.12	.13	.08	.05	−.05	.07	−.08	.11
.50*	.01	.25*	.20‡	.39†	.26	−.45	.54‡
−.28	.31	.03	.10	.45	.05	1.67	−.02
.00	.09	.29*	.09	−.07	−.02	−.47	.09
−.42	−.18	.51	.21	−.62	.46	1.10	−.20
.62	.08	.20	−.00	−.08	.75†	.13	.58*
−.17	−.07	.15	.17	.12	.17	.16	−.19
.14	.18	.11	.09	.06	.03	−.12	−.13
.17	.12	.13*	.08*	.23*	.07	.06	.14†
−.13	−.08	.05	−.05	−.21	.03	−.61	−.05
−.10	−.02	−.12	−.06	.00	−.24*	−.26	−.07
−.11	−.04	−.03	−.02	−.06	−.20*	.03	.00
.43	.04	−.05	−.03	.46	.06	.67	.22
.10	−.08	.00	−.01	−.08	.02	−.20	.02
−.05	.03	−.08*	−.03	.02	−.05	−.04	−.01
.09	.16*	.11	.04	.04	.11	.12	.12
−.23	−.19	−.51*	−.51†	−.37	−.58	−.71	−.14

	Biological and physical sciences		Education	
Variable	Men	Women	Men	Wome
Number of observations	250	180	88	207
Number of variables	26	26	26	26
Residual degrees of freedom	223	153	61	180
Multiple R-squared	.48	.35	.51	.32
Residual mean square	.79	1.04	.95	.96
Mean opposite sex residual	.10	−.53	.96	−.23
Standard deviation: opposite sex residual	1.14	1.17	1.11	1.21

TABLE C-10 (continued)

* Individual coefficient differs from zero at 0.05 significance level (two sided).

† Individual coefficient differs from zero at 0.01 significance level.

‡ Individual coefficient differs from zero at 0.001 significance level.

To sum up, the apparent discrimination in faculty salaries a sociated with sex was strong and prevailed for every rac Perhaps surprisingly, the apparent discrimination associate with race was small and not statistically significant.

Our analysis of salary differences was complicated by the fa that the questionnaire addressed to faculty members did not d rectly ask for information about part-time or full-time status. was therefore necessary to attempt to identify part-time facul members from other information provided in the response This was an important part of the study, because the possibili that women were more likely to be employed on a part-tin basis could not be excluded as a perhaps significant explanatic of their lower compensation. Once having identified the par time faculty members, they could either be eliminated from tl analysis or a variable could be introduced as a predictor of the lower salaries. The latter procedure provided more significa results.

Our method was to investigate the effect of using each of s rules for identifying part-time faculty members (Table C-1

Fine arts		Humanities		Social Sciences		New professions	
Men	Women	Men	Women	Men	Women	Men	Women
93	139	241	469	112	124	47	223
26	26	26	26	26	26	26	26
66	112	214	442	85	97	20	196
.43	.48	.46	.38	.63	.48	.75	.41
.19	.59	.95	.73	1.16	1.13	1.22	.75
.26	−.81	.57	−.61	.97	−.73	1.06	−1.18
.15	.95	.98	.91	1.29	1.32	1.55	1.61

ABLE C-11 *Rules used to determine part-time status*

Not teaching this year, or

Never worked full time, or

Rank below Assistant Professor and teaching less than nine hours per week

Not teaching this year, or

Never worked full time, or

Teaching less than nine hours per week and earning less than $7,000

Not teaching this year, or

Never worked full time, or

Salary less than $7,000 and

Teaching less than eleven hours per week in a two-year college or in the fields of education or fine arts, or

Teaching less than five hours per week in the fields of medicine and law or new and semiprofessions, or

Teaching less than nine hours per week in any other field

Not teaching this year, or

Never worked full time, or

Salary less than $7,000

Not tenured and

Teaching less than seven hours per week in a research university or doctoral–granting university, or

Teaching less than nine hours per week in a comprehensive college or university or liberal arts college, or

Teaching less than eleven hours per week in a two-year college

Visiting or acting appointment, or

Teaching less than nine hours per week

NOTE: Rule 5 was devised by Allan Cartter and John Ferguson; rule 6 was used by H. S. Astin and A. E. Bayer. Whenever a case was determined to be a part-time employee, either predictor variable number 31 was assigned the value 2 or the case was omitted from a study of full-time employees only.

The coefficients for biological and physical sciences in Research Universities II are shown in Table C-12. It was thought that this group of institutions might have a relatively large proportion of part-time faculty members. The results indicate that the influence of sex on salaries was not reduced either by eliminating the part-time employees or by introducing a part-time variable. Moreover, controlling for the possible influence of part-time employment had no appreciable effect on the distribution of salary residuals. Charts derived from the investigation of the effect of controlling for part-time employment closely resemble Chart 14 in Section 7.

There appear to be two components underlying the differences between male and female salaries: (1) a general shift (to the right, as in Chart 14, Section 7) of the entire distribution of male salary residuals, amounting to about $2,000 (so that a man of specified qualifications tends to earn about $2,000 more than a woman of the same qualifications); and (2) an excess of men with exceptionally high salary deviations. Both the shift and the skewness tend to be relatively large in Research Universities I. The components are noticeable in Chart 14. Each distribution is approximately normal, but the men's curve is shifted to the right in relation to the women's curve, and there is an excess of men who are "special" in the sense that they earn much more than their qualifications predict. A more careful study of the percentiles in the salary residual distributions confirms these impressions.

Fulton (1973) has used different methods for analyzing the same data with very similar results. By cross-classifying the data, he shows that the differing proportions of doctorates among men and women cannot explain the differences in salaries, nor can the age distribution or the differing marital status distribution.

Elizabeth Scott has developed projections of percentages of faculty members who will be women in future years in universities, four-year colleges, and two-year colleges on the basis of several assumed ratios of women to men among newly hired faculty members and several projected turnover rates. The analysis drew on Cartter's (1971) projections of student enrollment and on Balderston and Radner's (1971, pp. 1–66) data on student-faculty ratios and the future behavior of enrollment in

BLE C-12 *Comparison of coefficients of the multilinear regression equations for predicting faculty aries for men and women in biological and physical sciences, Research Universities II (434 men, 104 men), using various part-time rules.*

rt-time rule	None	1	3	4	5	6	5	6
mple	All	All	All	All	All	All	All	All
ll-time only?	No	No	No	No	No	No	Yes	Yes
nstant	.44	.83	.82	.85	1.90	−.10	1.43	.32
. Sex	−.47	−.46	−.46	−.46	−.49	−.48	−.48	−.45
. Date of birth	−.04	−.04	−.04	−.03	−.05	−.04	−.02	−.04
. Number of children	.37	.38	.39	.39	.22	.36	.26	.72
. Highest degree	.49	.44	.46	.44	.55	.49	.52	.82
. B.A. from prestigious school	−.02	−.02	−.02	−.02	.00	−.01	−.00	.17
. Graduate degree from prestigious school	.14	.11	.11	.10	.12	.13	.07	−.26
. Years employed in higher education	.25	.24	.24	.24	.22	.25	.26	.06
. Years employed in present institution	−.11	−.10	−.10	−.10	−.12	−.11	−.13	−.04
. Quality of present institution	−.05	−.05	−.04	−.04	−.04	−.05	−.08	−.32
. Number of articles	.35	.36	.36	.37	.32	.35	.28	.38
. Number of books	.23	.22	.22	.22	.24	.22	.22	.18
. Number of sources of paid consulting	.12	.12	.12	.12	.11	.12	.13	−.12
. Administrative activity	.22	.22	.22	.22	.20	.22	.20	.14
. Consulting	.06	.06	.06	.06	.08	.06	.18	.08
. Outside professional practice	−.22	−.21	−.21	−.20	−.24	−.22	−.30	−.12
. Hours taught per week	−.05	−.07	−.07	−.07	−.12	−.01	−.14	−.00
. Salary base	.61	.64	.64	.64	.61	.63	.51	1.10
. Interaction: date of birth and number of articles	−.02	−.02	−.02	−.02	−.01	−.02	−.01	−.05
. Interaction: sex and number of children	−.10	−.10	−.10	−.10	−.01	−.10	−.07	−.20
. Interaction: date of birth and number of children	−.03	−.04	−.04	−.04	−.03	−.03	−.03	−.08
. Interaction : sex, marital status, and age	−.01	−.01	−.01	−.01	−.01	−.01	−.02	−.01
. Part-time		−.24	−.28	−.30	−.60	.22		
umber of observations	538	538	538	538	538	538	365	116
umber of variables	21	22	22	22	22	22	21	21
esidual degrees of freedom	516	515	515	515	515	515	343	94
ultiple R-squared	.67	.67	.67	.67	.68	.67	.68	.73
esidual mean square	1.01	1.00	1.00	1.00	.96	1.01	1.05	.83

TABLE C-12 *(continued)*

Part-time rule	5	5	6	6	5	5	6	
Sample	Men	Women	Men	Women	Men	Women	Men	Wo
Full-time only?	No	No	No	No	Yes	Yes	Yes	Y
Constant	2.16	−.44	.16	−2.80	1.52	−.56	.58	−3.7
1. Sex								
2. Date of birth	−.12	−.02	−.11	−.01	−.07	−.05	−.08	.3(
4. Number of children	.14	.28	.19	.23	.14	.14	.62	−.4
5. Highest degree	.70	.55	.63	.58	.64	.54	.84	.4
7. B.A. from prestigious school	−.02	.05	−.01	−.02	−.00	−.36	.15	.6(
8. Graduate degree from prestigious school	.17	−.09	.18	−.12	.13	−.34	−.14	.2
11. Years employed in higher education	.23	.20	.28	.18	.27	.25	.01	.2(
12. Years employed in present institution	−.14	−.13	−.13	−.08	−.14	−.15	−.10	.1
13. Quality of present institution	−.07	.11	−.08	.11	−.08	.02	−.38	−.0
14. Number of articles	.25	.46	.28	.51	.21	.54	.40	.6
15. Number of books	.22	.36	.21	.35	.23	.25	.20	−.4
18. Number of sources of paid consulting	.16	−.45	.17	−.38	.18	−.40	−.04	−.3
20. Administrative activity	.20	.14	.22	.16	.19	.22	.13	.2
21. Consulting	.06	.13	.04	.10	.15	.20	.04	.0
22. Outside professional practice	−.23	−.19	−.21	−.14	−.30	−.01	−.10	−.1
23. Hours taught per week	−.14	−.07	−.03	.10	−.17	−.03	−.08	.1
24. Salary base	.61	.67	.64	.67	.51	.62	1.28	.5
27. Interaction: date of birth and number of articles	−.01	−.03	−.01	−.04	−.00	−.03	−.06	−.1(
28. Interaction: sex and number of children								
29. Interaction: date of birth and number of children	−.01	−.06	−.02	−.06	−.02	−.03	−.11	.0
30. Interaction: sex, marital status, and age	−.10	.04	−.09	.04	−.06	−.06	.10	.1
31. Part-time	−.63	−.53	.25	.46				
Number of observations	434	104	434	104	302	63	80	3
Number of variables	20	20	20	20	19	19	19	19
Residual degrees of freedom	413	83	413	83	282	43	60	1
Multiple R-squared	.63	.68	.61	.67	.58	.73	.68	.8
Residual mean square	1.03	.68	1.08	.70	1.13	.69	1.05	.2

Part-time rule	5	5	6	6	5	5	6	6
Sample	Men	Women	Men	Women	Men	Women	Men	Women
Full-time only?	No	No	No	No	Yes	Yes	Yes	Yes
Mean opposite sex residual	.88	−.21	.99	−.25	.56	−.34	1.41	−.82
Standard deviation: opposite sex residual	1.14	.88	1.18	.90	1.24	.84	1.42	.83

the three types of institutions. Rates of retirement, death, and withdrawal were assumed to be the same for men and women. Data on these rates are not very reliable and do not take account of possible future pressures for earlier retirement. The analysis also drew on projections of turnover rates and of the age distribution of faculty members developed by Cartter, and another set of projections developed by Maslach on the basis of faculty data for the College of Engineering, University of California, Berkeley (see Charts C-1 to C-4 and Table C-13).

Chart C-1   *Women as a percentage of faculty members, projected 1970–1990 in universities; constant hiring 30 percent women. Comparison of different initial percentages in 1969.*

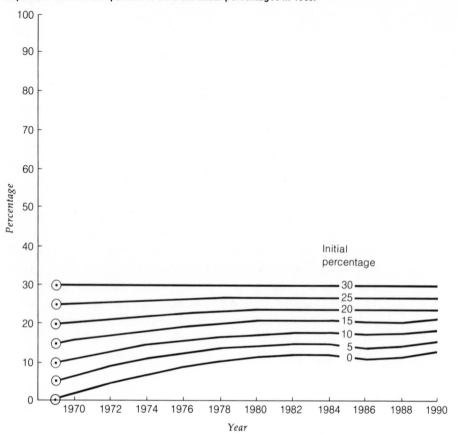

CHART C-2 *Women as a percentage of faculty members, projected, 1970 to 1990, in universities; initial percentage in 1969 equal to 14.67. Comparison of different rates of hiring women.*

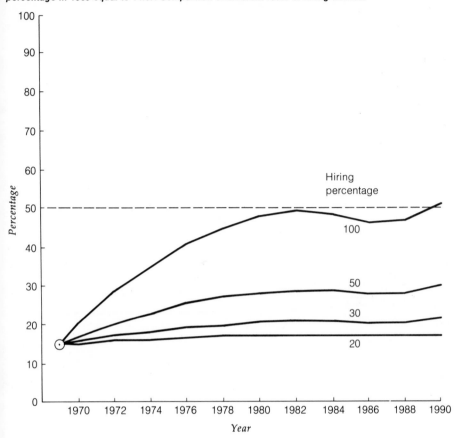

CHART C-3 *Women as a percentage of faculty members, projected, 1970 to 1990, in four-year colleges; initial percentage in 1969 equal to 24.41. Comparison of different rates of hiring women.*

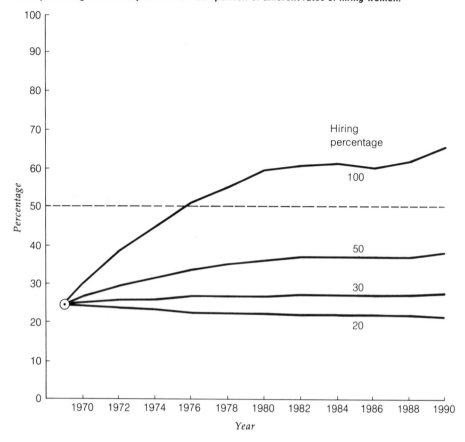

CHART C-4 *Women as a percentage of faculty members, projected, 1970 to 1990, in two-year colleges; initial percentage in 1969 equal to 26.19. Comparison of different rates of hiring women.*

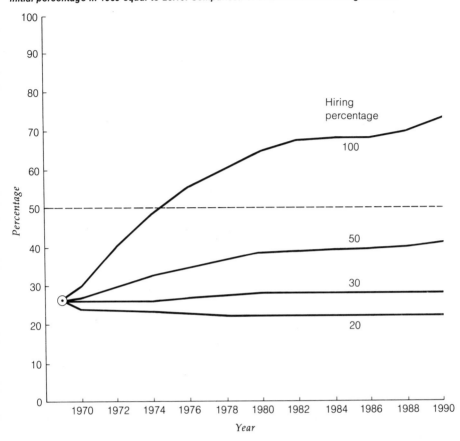

TABLE C-13 *Women as a percentage of faculty members in universities in selected future years, on the basis of varying assumptions about the percentage of women among "new hires" and among faculty members in 1969*

Data used in projection and year	Women are 20 percent of new hires						Women are 30 percent of new hires					
Women as a percentage of faculty members in 1969	5	10	15	20	25	30	5	10	15	20	25	30
Cartter												
1975	9.4	12.9	16.5	20.0	23.5	27.1	12.3	15.8	19.4	22.9	26.5	30.0
1980	11.0	14.0	17.0	20.0	23.0	26.0	14.9	18.0	21.0	24.0	27.0	30.0
1985	10.5	13.6	16.8	20.0	23.2	26.4	14.1	17.3	20.5	23.6	26.8	30.0
1990	10.6	13.7	16.9	20.0	23.1	26.3	14.4	17.5	20.6	23.7	26.9	30.0
Carnegie												
1975	9.1	12.8	16.4	20.0	23.6	27.2	11.9	15.5	19.1	22.8	26.4	30.0
1980	10.8	13.9	16.9	20.0	23.1	26.1	14.7	17.8	20.8	23.9	26.9	30.0
1985	10.7	13.8	16.9	20.0	23.1	26.2	14.6	17.7	20.7	23.8	26.9	30.0
1990	11.4	14.3	17.1	20.0	22.9	25.7	15.7	18.5	21.4	24.3	27.1	30.0
Constant two percent												
1975	9.7	13.1	16.6	20.0	23.4	26.9	12.9	16.3	19.7	23.1	26.6	30.0
1980	11.5	14.4	17.2	20.0	22.8	25.6	15.9	18.7	21.5	24.4	27.2	30.0
1985	11.4	14.3	17.1	20.0	22.9	25.7	15.6	18.5	21.4	24.3	27.1	30.0
1990	11.6	14.4	17.2	20.0	22.8	25.6	16.1	18.9	21.6	24.4	27.2	30.0
Maslach												
1975	9.1	12.7	16.4	20.0	23.6	27.3	11.8	15.4	19.1	22.7	26.4	30.0
1980	11.1	14.1	17.0	20.0	23.0	25.9	15.2	18.2	21.1	24.1	27.0	30.0
1985	12.2	14.8	17.4	20.0	22.6	25.2	17.1	19.7	22.2	24.8	27.4	30.0
1990	13.6	15.7	17.9	20.0	22.1	24.3	19.3	21.4	23.6	25.7	27.9	30.0

Rates of Retirement and Death

Cartter (1972)		*Carnegie (1969)*		*Maslach*	
1970	1.61%	–1973	1.0%	1970–1978	1%
1975	1.36	1974–1978	1.3	1979–1980	3
1980	1.28	1979–1983	1.8	1981–1990	5
1985	1.37	1984–1988	2.7		
1990	1.87	1989–1990	3.1		

Women are 50 percent of new hires						Women are 100 percent of new hires					
5	10	15	20	25	30	5	10	15	20	25	30
18.2	21.7	25.2	28.8	32.3	35.8	32.8	36.3	39.9	43.4	46.9	50.5
22.9	25.9	28.9	31.9	34.9	38.0	42.8	45.8	48.8	51.8	54.8	57.9
21.4	24.6	27.8	30.9	34.1	37.3	39.7	42.8	46.0	49.2	52.4	55.5
21.8	25.0	28.1	31.2	34.4	37.5	40.5	43.7	46.8	49.9	53.1	56.2
17.4	21.0	24.6	28.3	31.9	35.5	31.2	34.8	38.4	42.1	45.7	49.3
22.5	25.6	28.6	31.7	34.7	37.8	42.0	45.1	48.1	51.2	54.2	57.3
22.2	25.3	28.4	31.5	34.6	37.7	41.4	44.4	47.5	50.6	53.7	56.8
24.2	27.1	30.0	32.8	35.7	38.5	45.6	48.5	51.3	54.2	57.1	59.9
19.1	22.6	26.0	29.4	32.9	36.3	34.9	38.3	41.7	45.1	48.6	52.0
24.6	27.5	30.3	33.1	35.9	38.7	46.5	49.3	52.1	54.9	57.7	60.6
24.2	27.0	29.9	32.8	35.6	38.5	45.4	48.3	51.2	54.0	56.9	59.8
24.9	27.7	30.5	33.3	36.1	38.9	47.1	49.9	52.7	55.5	58.2	61.0
17.2	20.8	24.5	28.1	31.8	35.4	30.8	34.4	38.1	41.7	45.3	49.0
23.3	26.3	29.3	32.2	35.2	38.2	43.7	46.7	49.7	52.6	55.6	58.5
26.7	29.3	31.9	34.5	37.1	39.7	50.9	53.5	56.1	58.6	61.2	63.8
30.7	32.8	35.0	37.1	39.3	41.4	59.3	61.4	63.5	65.7	67.8	70.0

Appendix D: Selected Documents

RESOLUTION OF THE AMERICAN PERSONNEL GUIDANCE ASSOCIATION, ADOPTED MARCH 1972

Whereas, the Strong Vocational Interest Blanks (SVIB) provide different occupational scores for men and women, that is, women cannot be scored on occupations like certified public accountant, purchasing agent, public administrator, and men cannot be scored on occupations such as medical technologists, recreation leader, physical education teacher; and whereas, when the same person takes both forms of the SVIB, the profiles turn out differently: for example, one woman scored high as a dental assistant, physical therapist, occupational therapist on the woman's profile, and physician, psychiatrist and psychologist on the man's form; and whereas, the SVIB manual states: "Many young women do not appear to have strong occupational interests, and they may score high only in certain 'premarital' occupations: elementary school teacher, office workers, stenographer-secretary. Such a finding is disappointing to many college women, since they are likely to consider themselves career-oriented. In such cases, the selection of an area of training or an occupation should probably be based upon practical considerations, fields providing backgrounds that might be helpful to a wife and mother, occupations that can be pursued part time, are easily resumed after periods of nonemployment and are readily available in different locales" (Campbell, rev. 1966, 13); therefore, be it resolved, that APGA commission duly authorize members to petition and negotiate with the SVIB publishers to revise their instruments, manuals and norm groups so as to eliminate discrimination; and be it further resolved, that this duly authorized commission develop with the test publishers an explanatory paper to circulate among all purchasers of SVIB materials including answer sheets a statement which outlines the possible limitations inherent in the current SVIB with suggestions for ways to minimize the harm; and be it further resolved, that the commission in cooperation with the test publisher set a deadline for the new forms to be published and distributed.

EXCERPTS FROM STANFORD UNIVERSITY, COMMITTEE ON THE EDUCA
TION AND EMPLOYMENT OF WOMEN: *The Stanford Woman in 197*
November 1972, pp. 6–7.

Experience with discrimination

When asked, "Do you feel you have been discouraged from any
academic or occupational goals by a member of the Stanford
community because of your sex?" 29 of the 128 women who re
sponded said yes. This generalizes to 23 percent of all Stanford
women. Another 5 percent of the women experienced discrimi
nation but were not discouraged by it. Most of these women
were discouraged by contacts with faculty members.

In all, almost one-quarter of Stanford women are discouraged
by discrimination. The forms which this discrimination takes
range from explicit discouragement from a professor to more
subtle environmental cues. The observations of some of the
women respondents illustrate this quite clearly. The following
quotations drawn from survey responses illustrate overt dis
couragement of women by their advisers:

Dr. X, a pre-med adviser, had a dim view of the possibility of women
actually making it through all the work necessary to be a doctor, and
later of her juggling work, children, etc. . . . There were 2 other girls i
our advisee group. He said he didn't expect to see us the next year...

Not only my major adviser, but several of my professors in my depart
ment failed to offer any encouragement or assistance and in some case
actively discouraged me from further study in mathematics—both
when I sought advice and approval for advanced study and when
sought assistance and consultation in courses I was taking. A largely
negative reaction (at best, I was ignored) from male peers in math and
science classes was also quite evident.

My history adviser specifically discouraged me from going on to grad
school. He kept suggesting high school teaching as "more flexible for a
woman." And he did this even after I took several courses from him in
which I did very well. He even urged me to take on the honors thesis
program.

Other women described comments made by professors during
lectures as a source of discouragement:

I took a class [in chemistry] from Dr. X—a required course for many med schools. He began his first lecture by saying there were 2 things he couldn't stand—premeds and women who thought they could be scientists. His actions were consistent with his prejudices.

One art teacher, XX, believes that women make better art teachers than artists—his suggestions to this effect have been to classes as a whole, not to me individually, but I think that his underlying sexism affects his relationship with me although he shows a respect for my work.

Some women found assessments of the employment situation for women in some fields more discouraging than helpful:

I have been told of personal experience of the bias against women in university level teaching. I would not seek employment as a member of an academic community [university].

. . . advisers have given me "realistic" appraisals which were very discouraging.

Finally, some women did not describe a direct communication at all, but a sense they had from what was around them:

It's difficult to be specific—one carries with him the prejudices; I wish now I had gone premed; I would like to be a doctor but women weren't doctors; and women didn't go on to be English professors—I didn't look much beyond teaching—and no one suggested anything else.

Though discouragement has not been overt (except in a couple of cases where people couldn't understand why I couldn't be happy teaching in high school) there is a lot of subtle discouragement: (1) The lack of female professors which really presents a problem in terms of role identity, (2) the number of professors that give only a negative account of their role (I don't understand why they're still in it), (3) a disbelief from both professors and students that I can combine being a woman with being a professor, (4) the way I see female professors now being treated (i.e. difficulty in obtaining tenure, refusal to see their courses as anything but "fun" (both professors and students), insinuations about their teaching ability and/or intelligence related to sex, etc.).

CAMPUSES OFFERING WOMEN'S STUDY PROGRAMS DECEMBER 1972

Alverno College (Wisconsin)

Barnard College (New York)

Berkeley (University of California)

Buffalo (State University of New York)

Cambridge—Goddard Graduate School for Social Change (Massachusetts)

Cornell University (New York)

Douglass College of Rutgers University (New Jersey)

Five-College Women's Studies Committee (Amherst, Hampshire, Mount Holyoke, Smith, and the University of Massachusetts)

Fresno (California State University)

George Washington University (District of Columbia)

Goddard College (Vermont)

Governors State University (Illinois)

Laney Community College (California)

Long Beach (California State University)

Mundelein Collge (Illinois)

Northeastern Illinois University

Old Westbury (State University of Ne York)

University of Pennsylvania

University of Pittsburgh

Portland State University

Richmond College (City University of New York)

Rockland Center of the Roger William College "University Without Walls" (New York)

Sacramento (California State University)

San Diego (California State University

San Francisco (California State University)

San Jose (California State University)

Sarah Lawrence College (New York)

Sonoma State College (California)

University of South Carolina

University of South Florida

Towson State College (Maryland)

University of Washington

SOURCE: Robinson (1973, pp. 13–14).

GUIDELINES FOR "AFFIRMATIVE ACTION PLANS" TO END
DISCRIMINATION AGAINST WOMEN, AMERICAN ASSOCIATION OF
UNIVERSITY WOMEN, SEPTEMBER 1971 (as summarized in the *Chronicle
of Higher Education*, September 27, 1971, p. 6)

For students, the Association recommended:

- That admission standards and procedures be the same for men and women and that no quotas—"written or practiced"—be used.
- That "requirements and procedures for residency, full-time employment, credit transfers, and full-time or part-time enrollment" be flexible enough to allow students to combine education with family responsibilities.
- That colleges offer a "women's studies program, departmental or interdepartmental, with specific programs to develop leadership potential and opportunities for women."
- That "special counseling [be] available to meet the needs of the diverse woman student population" in educational and career planning.
- That "health counseling [be] available to all students regarding birth control, pregnancy, and knowledge of community resources."
- That women students have self-government, including control over their own social regulations and activities.
- That financial aid programs not discriminate against women or part-time students.
- That "placement policies make available the same recruiting opportunities to both men and women students, reject all recruiting literature and firms which discriminate against women or which advertise positions with specifications of sex of applicants."
- That married and graduate student housing be available equally to men and women.

For faculty and administrators, the Association recommended

- That colleges provide "equality....in salary, contract status, and fringe benefits for men and women in the same job categorie
- That policies on hiring, promotion, and tenure be the same for men and women and that colleges make special efforts toward "correcting the imbalance of men and women" on their staff.
- That antinepotism policies be abolished.
- That colleges offer maternity leave for women employees.
- That women be appointed to all committees and other campus decision-making bodies in proportion to the percentage of women students enrolled by the institution.
- That "regularly employed part-time employees receive professional benefits and [be] employed at ranks and salaries commensurate with full-time personnel."
- That women be given "equal consideration in making assignments to teaching at all levels, research and administrative projects, and writing of publications."
- That "the number of women trustees [be] in proportion to the percentage of women in the student body."

The Association also recommended that colleges include data on sex in statistics they collect on students and staff, provide child-care facilities, and not discriminate against women in hiring nonacademic employees.

Colleges should have a commission on women, the Association said, to oversee programs for women, handle complaints of discrimination, and see that the other recommended policies are implemented.

AMERICAN ASSOCIATION OF UNIVERSITY PROFESSORS, *Senior Appointments with Reduced Loads:* **Statement of Committee W on the Status of Women in the Profession, approved February 1971**

American colleges and universities would benefit from policies and practices that open senior academic appointments and tenure to persons other than those giving full-time service. Both men and women should be eligible for such appointments. These policies would provide flexibility by permitting a limited number of persons to assume senior faculty positions with reduced loads and salaries but with full perquisites, by meeting special needs of individuals, especially those with child-rearing and other personal responsibilities, and by increasing the options available both to individuals and to institutions. These appointments would not normally be encouraged if the individual is seeking reduction of the academic commitment in order to accept another position. Promotion criteria from one rank to another should be the same for all appointees, including those with reduced loads. Maximum opportunities should be available for men and women to shift from full load to reduced and back again, depending on personal and institutional needs.

FACULTY APPOINTMENT AND FAMILY RELATIONSHIP

The following statement prepared initially by the Association's Committee W on the Status of Women in the Academic Profession, was approved by that Committee and by Committee A on Academic Freedom and Tenure. The statement was adopted by the Council of the American Association of University Professors in April 1971, and endorsed by the Fifty-seventh Annual Meeting as Association policy. It was endorsed by the Board of Directors of the Association of American Colleges at its June 1971, meeting.

In recent years, and particularly in relation to efforts to define and safeguard the rights of women in academic life, members of the profession have evidenced increasing concern over policies and practices which prohibit in blanket fashion the appointment, retention, or the holding of tenure of more than one member of the same family on the faculty of an institution of higher education or of a school or department within an institution (so-called "antinepotism regulations"). Such policies and practices subject faculty members to an automatic decision on a basis wholly unrelated to academic qualifications and limit them unfairly in their opportunity to practice their profession. In addition, they are contrary to the best interests of the institution which is deprived of qualified faculty members on the basis of an inappropriate criterion, and of the community which is denied a sufficient utilization of its resources.

The Association recognizes the propriety of institutional regulations which would set reasonable restrictions on an individual's capacity to function as judge or advocate in specific situations involving members of his or her immediate family. Faculty members should neither initiate nor participate in institutional decisions involving a direct benefit (initial appointment, retention, promotion, salary, leave of absence, etc.) to members of their immediate families.

The Association does not believe, however, that the proscription of the opportunity of members of an immediate family to serve as colleagues is a sound method of avoiding the occasional abuses resulting from nepotism. Inasmuch as they constitute a continuing abuse to a significant number of individual members of the profession and to the profession as a body, the Association urges the discontinuance of these policies and practices, and the rescinding of laws and institutional regulations which perpetuate them.

SOURCE: Reprinted from Summer 1971 AAUP *Bulletin*.

AMERICAN ASSOCIATION OF UNIVERSITY PROFESSORS, *Leaves of Absence for Child-Bearing, Child-Rearing and Family Emergencies* **(Approved by Committee W, March 1973)**

INTRODUCTION The joint *Statement of Principles on Leaves of Absence,* adopted in 1972 by the American Association of University Professors and the Association of American Colleges, recommends that leaves of absence be granted for professional growth and intellectual achievement, for public or private service outside the institution, and for "illness, recovery of health, and maternity." The following statement on Leaves of Absence for Child-Bearing, Child-Rearing and Family Emergencies, prepared by Committee W on the Status of Women in the Academic Profession, supplements and amplifies this latter provision of the *Statement of Principles on Leaves of Absence.*

PURPOSE OF Committee W recommends that colleges and universities
THE LEAVES provide leaves of absence to faculty members for child-bearing, child-rearing and family emergencies. Such leaves are to assist faculty members with parental responsibilities in meeting their obligations both to their professional careers and to their families, and to prevent the loss to the institution and to the academic community of substantial professional skills.

Career patterns of academic men and women vary. Academic women differ in their desire to continue or to interrupt their professional careers during the child-bearing and child-rearing years. Couples differ in the extent to which they wish to share family responsibilities. Some faculty members may wish to take a leave of absence from their professional positions to care for their children, others wish to combine parental and professional responsibilities, while still others prefer to retain their professional affiliation on a full-time basis throughout their child-bearing and child-rearing years.

An institution's policies on faculty appointments should be sufficiently flexible to permit faculty members to combine family and career responsibilities in the manner best suited to them as professionals and parents. This flexibility requires the availability of such alternatives as longer-term leaves of absence, temporary reductions in workload with no loss of professional status, and retention of full-time affiliation throughout the child-bearing and child-rearing years.

Institutional policies which require the termination of the appointment of a woman faculty member because she becomes pregnant penalize the individual unfairly. Moreover, policies which mandate the timing and duration of a leave of absence for pregnancy and childbirth do not take cognizance of particular medical needs or individual circumstances. Institutions which customarily or by policy allow paid absences for illness or temporary disability, but which deny equivalent absences for disabilities resulting from pregnancy or childbirth, discriminate against women.[1] Allowing leaves of absence for illness or temporary disability only in cases where faculty members are themselves ill or temporarily disabled disregards the need to provide short-term care for family members in serious emergencies. In addition, it may prevent fathers from assuming responsibilities in connection with the birth of children.

SHORT-TERM LEAVES OF ABSENCE FOR CHILD-BEARING AND FAMILY EMERGENCIES

Most colleges and universities provide for paid short-term leaves of absence, through formal or informal arrangements, for faculty members who are ill or temporarily disabled. The conditions and duration of compensation for short-term leaves for pregnancy, childbirth, or family emergencies involving spouse, parents or children, should be analogous to those for leave granted for temporary disability or personal emergencies. The timing and duration of absence in such cases should be determined by mutual agreement between the faculty member and the institution, and should be based on medical need, the requirements of the educational program, and individual circumstances. Compensation during short-term leaves of absence for child-bearing or the serious illness of a family member should be consistent with customary institutional practices in cases of illness or temporary disability.

LONGER-TERM LEAVES OF ABSENCE FOR CHILD-REARING

The rearing of children should be considered appropriate grounds for a leave of absence of a semester or more, and such leaves should be available to both men and women faculty members. The timing and duration of such leaves should be determined by mutual agreement between the faculty member and the institution. Faculty members on child-rearing leaves

---

[1]See the 1972 Sex Discrimination Guidelines of the Equal Employment Opportunity Commission.

should receive the same considerations with respect to salary increments, insurance coverage, retirement annuities, and the like, as are received by faculty members on leave for public or private service outside the institution.

The alternative of a temporarily reduced workload should be available to faculty members with child-rearing responsibilities (see Committee W's Statement on *Senior Appointments with Reduced Loads*).

Individual and institutional obligations in connection with such leaves, including the timing of a tenure decision, should be those set forth in the applicable provisions of the *Statement of Principles on Leaves of Absence*.

SELECTED PROVISIONS OF AFFIRMATIVE ACTION PLANS OR COMMIT TEE RECOMMENDATIONS ON AFFIRMATIVE ACTION, SELECTED COL LEGES AND UNIVERSITIES

Sources:

1. *Columbia University Affirmative Action Program (Condense Version)*, December 1972.

2. Harvard University, University News Office, *Release*, Ma 4, 1973.

3. "The Status of Women at Oberlin," (excerpts and sum maries from the *Report and Recommendations from the Ad Ho Committee on the Status of Women at Oberlin, Oberlin Alum Magazine*, pp. 6–13, March–April 1973 (most of the recommen dations have been adopted).

4. *Affirmative Action Plan of Stanford University*, November 1. 1972.

5. New York State Education Department: *Equal Opportunit for Women: A Statement of Policy and Proposed Action by th Regents of the University of the State of New York*, Albany, N.Y. April 1972.

6. "University of California Affirmative Action Personnel Pro gram: Policy and Guidelines," *University Bulletin*, vol. 21, pp 88–94, January 22, 1973.

GOALS AND TIMETABLES

Columbia:

In the following pages, goals for faculty recruitment are stated as targets for good faith efforts over a period of five years, because Columbia operates on a basis of five-year projections, annually updated under the master-planning requirements of New York State as well as under our own planning and budgetary policies. Annual changes in the composition of faculties and professional research staff will be identified, goals will be revised accordingly, and where there is opportunity to do so, attempts will be made to accelerate progress.

Goals are expressed in terms of new appointments only, not in terms of the composition of any faculty or school. For each of the schools or faculties, the number of new appointments has been estimated from projected terminations due to retirements, resignations, and expiration of terms of appointment, as adjusted for planned changes in faculty size. The University's goals are directly tied to the number of recruiting opportunities which result from the normal processes of faculty growth and attrition and which are possible to achieve through non-discriminatory, nonpreferential hiring practices.... University policy proscribes recruitment efforts limited to any sex or ethnic group as well as faculty employment decisions based upon the treatment of sexual or ethnic identification alone as a qualification. . . .

Possible deficiencies are identified by comparing the percentage of women . . . in the nation's potential professoriate, by specialty, with the percentage on the various schools and faculties at Columbia utilizing that specialty. Where statistical discrepancies appear, the problem arises as to whether or not they are deficiencies indicative of discrimination requiring corrective action. Two possibilities exist: that the discrepancy arises primarily from a practice within the University or that it results from a cause external to the University, such as, perhaps, an occupational mobility pattern in which women leave good positions to accommodate changes in the job location of husbands or a traditional family pattern which has impeded professional advancement. The University's goals are therefore expressed not in terms of single or fixed numbers but as a range of possible actions on new appointments resulting from recruitment policies which include active search for talent among women and minorities. One point on this range is the number of new appointments that would result if the current profile of a given school or faculty were to continue unchanged; the other point on this range is the number of new appointments that would result if appointment at the rate of availability in the national pool were accomplished.

In schools or faculties whose profiles indicate that Columbia's recruitment meets or exceeds the national pool availability rate, the University's goals range from a "low option"—appointment of women and minorities at less than Columbia's profile but still at the national pool average—to a "high option"—such appointments at Columbia's traditionally high rate of utilization of women and minorities.

In schools or faculties whose profiles suggest underutilization of women or minorities, the range of possible personnel actions similarly reflects a "low option"—appointments which maintain the current rate of utilization—and a "high option"—new appointments at the national pool rate. In these cases, where women or minorities have been attracted to Columbia at a rate less than their availability in the national pool, Columbia's stated goal is to move toward parity of utilization by employing the "high option".

Columbia undertakes these "high option" goals with the specific understanding that goals are targets for good faith effort and are not inflexible quotas....

The numerical goals required by Executive Order 11246 which result from the application of these principles have been calculated by school or faculty....

For the faculty of Philosophy . . . 28 tenured and 79 nontenured full-time faculty openings are projected to occur from 1972 to 1977. With a national pool of approximately 20 percent women and a 1971–72 full-time faculty composition of 24 percent women, the goal for this faculty ranges from 19 to 25 appointments of women over the next five-year period, of which three to six would be in the tenure ranks.

For the faculty of Political Science...it is estimated that approximately 28 tenured and 41 nontenured full-time positions will be filled in the next 5 years.... With a national pool of approximately 10 percent women, a goal of seven new appointments of faculty women is indicated, three to tenure rank.

For the faculty of Pure Science...approximately 30 tenured and 42 nontenured full-time faculty openings are projected to occur. On the basis of a national pool of 10 percent women scientists, this faculty has a goal of seven appointments of women to full-time positions, of which as many as three may be to tenure rank.

The School of Social Work is projected to have four tenured and 32 nontenured full-time faculty openings through 1977. With a current composition of 55.4 percent women as against a national pool of 47.1 percent women, the School's goals range from 17 to 20 appointments of women in tenured and non-tenured ranks of the faculty over the five-year period.

Three other large professional schools—Business, Engineering, and Law—have far smaller national pools of women, varying from 1.9 percent to 5.5 percent, on which to draw for faculty recruitment. With an aggregate of 23 tenured and 48 non-tenured full-time positions opening up in the next five years, a goal of six tenured or nontenured appointments of women to these faculties is projected.

The Health Sciences Divisions have faculty profiles which equal or exceed pool percentages for women and minorities.... The goal...for these divisions is to make 18 to 32 appointments of women to the full-time faculty, within a total of 111 new appointments estimated to be made over the next five years. (Tenure and nontenure distinctions do not carry the same meaning in the Health Sciences as elsewhere in the University....)

The remaining schools—Architecture, Arts, Journalism, and Library Service—are small in size, having a combined full-time faculty of 53. While Journalism and the Arts recruit from pools which are difficult to specify, it is projected that seven appointments of women will be made out of 35 faculty openings expected to occur through 1977.

Columbia's profile for part-time faculty and for full-time officers of research equals or exceeds the pool percentages for women.... Our goal here is to continue present practices of appointing women...at a rate which equals or exceeds pool percentages.

Harvard:

Harvard University has completed a comprehensive affirmative action program report establishing University wide goals for hiring women and minority-group members during the next two academic years, and promising updated goals every two years....

Outlined for the first time in this report are the "utilization analyses"—procedures now used by the University's academic and administrative departments to determine the size of the labor pools in their areas and the percentage of women and minorities in these pools....

The detailed charts of hiring goals through June 30, 1975 include annual projections of how many women and members of minority groups will hold jobs in a specific category, how many such jobs there will be and how many of this total will become available over the two-year period, through turnover and expansion.

For instance, 14 women and 32 members of minority groups now hold full professorships, out of a total of 743 professorships in all faculties. By June of 1974, the number of professorships is projected to rise to 757, including one more woman professor and two more from minority groups. By June of 1975, projections show 18 women and 36 minority group professors out of a total of 761.

The number of women in the rank of Associate Professor—now 14 of 280—is projected to increase by half, to 21 (of 294) by 1974 and to 24 (of 302) by 1975....

Of the 109 Assistant Professorships expected to become available by 1974–75, 17 are expected to go to women and members of minority groups, bringing the 1975 projected totals at this rank to 57 women and 35 minority group members out of 566 posts....

"While there has been an increase over the past three years in the number of minority and women professors at Harvard, the numbers still remain small," the report states. "Indeed, some of the faculties do not have any women or minority professors."

Oberlin:

Recommendation 4: The faculty must commit itself to the goal of increasing the rate of hiring women for regular positions on the faculty such that, within a three-year period, the percentage of women on the faculty will reflect *as a minimum* the percentage of women in the candidate pool. Further, as positions become available, *each department* will make strong efforts to hire one or more women.

Stanford:

An analysis has been made of the representation of women, Blacks, Chicanos, and Orientals on the professorial faculty. . . . The results are summarized here.

There will be eighteen Blacks, nine Chicanos, and nineteen Orientals on the professorial faculty in the 1972–73 academic year, as counted in July. . . . While these numbers are small in comparison to the total faculty of approximately one thousand, they are not disproportionate with the number of available Ph.D.'s. The figure of eighteen Blacks is consistent with estimates that fewer than two percent of the Ph.D. degrees awarded in the decade beginning in 1960 were received by Blacks. Similarly, the figure of nine Chicanos is appreciable considering that there are fewer than two hundred Chicano Ph.D. degree holders in the United States. The figure of nineteen Orientals cannot currently be analyzed, since there are no appropriate statistics.

There will be sixty-four women on the professorial faculty in 1972–73. Analysis suggests that some departments may have fewer women than might be expected based on a statistical analysis of female Ph.D. holders in the field.

The faculty affirmative action officer met with individual deans and department chairmen in spring 1972 to discuss problem areas and goals. Six departments were identified as problem areas, so far as numbers of women were concerned, and specific five-year hiring goals were established.

Stanford has a substantial number of women employed in nonprofessorial academic positions, such as lecturer or instructor. An analysis of the number of women and ethnic minorities in these positions is a high priority item for 1972–73. The question is being considered in three different ways. A faculty committee on the professoriate is currently reviewing the entire faculty structure. The faculty affirmative action officer has been assigned responsibility to review procedures for making certain that appointments and salary scales of given individuals are appropriate for them. And the faculty affirmative action officer, and other members of the provost's staff, are examining the ongoing appointment procedures with particular concern for new nonprofessorial appointments.

University of California:

Underutilization may exist when the number of minorities or women employed is significantly fewer than would reasonably be expected based on the availability of qualified persons for employment. When underutilization is identified for appropriate organization units and occupational categories, goals and timetables are established by each Chancellor and Laboratory Director and for the Office of the President as a means of increasing the employment of minorities and women at the earliest possible time.

Goals are targets for increasing the employment of minorities and women in appropriate organization units and occupational categories of the University workforce. Goals are not rigid targets nor are they quotas.

Specific goals are reasonable estimates of what is attainable and are established separately for minorities and women. If a substantial disparity is found in the employment of a particular minority group, or in the number of either men or of women of a particular minority group, separate goals may be established for that group and sex.

Timetables are estimates of the time required to meet specific goals. In formulating timetables, account shall be taken of anticipated appointments each year for each occupational category.

Goals and timetables are reviewed at least annually and are adjusted as the availability of minorities and women and as their employment in the University workforce change.

SEARCH PROCEDURES

Columbia:

The availability of documentation to establish that non-discriminatory procedures have been followed, and positive steps have been taken to include qualified women and minority groups in academic recruitment efforts, is necessary for approval of the proposed offers of appointments. The required documentation consists of the following: (1) Statement of standard search and evaluation procedures. A general statement describing the standard procedures followed by the school or department in identifying and evaluating candidates for appointment should be filed.... This general statement should indicate school or department practice concerning the use and selection of search committees, how the school or department makes position openings known, whether seminar or class appearances and student reports are used to evaluate candidates, and the manner in which the department or school decides upon particular candidates.... (2) Search report. A brief report of the specific search for the candidate for whom clearance is requested should accompany each clearance request. This report...should identify the institutions and professional groups canvassed, the relevant professional files or registries utilized and the names and institutional affiliations of the individuals consulted, including women and minority professionals in the discipline. The report should also identify the media communication utilized in making the position opening known.

Harvard:

"In order to increase the representation of minority persons and women in the professorial ranks, the various faculties have been expanding their candidate searches and have instituted measures to ensure that all sources of potential minority and women professors are sought out. . . ."

These measures include checking such information sources as learned and professional societies and examining information issued by the President's Office on women and minorities with the appropriate qualifying degrees. The report also suggests consultation with "female and minority scholars," and the inclusion of "women and minority-group members in the department" on the committees screening candidates for tenured appointments.

Oberlin:

Recommendation 3: Departments must be required to include qualified women among the candidates interviewed for faculty positions or to show convincing evidence that it was not possible for them to do so.

Stanford:

The faculty search is central to faculty affirmative action. Search committees at Stanford are encouraged to consult with their University resources—women and minority group members on campus—for advice on candidates who might otherwise be missed.

Search committees are expected to inform all universities with significant activity in the field for which a vacancy exists of a faculty position for which they seek candidates. In addition, search committees are expected to inform committees for minorities and women within appropriate professional societies of the opening. Finally, search committees have been and will be encouraged to advertise the opening for which they seek candidates in appropriate professional journals.

University of California:

Current methods of recruitment and search for candidates for appointment shall be reviewed, and new or modified methods shall be introduced in order to broaden the scope of the search. Priority shall be given to the effective recruitment of minority and women applicants for those occupational categories and employing units where underutilization has been determined to exist.

SPECIAL AFFIRMATIVE ACTION FUNDING

Stanford:

Because the Stanford University faculty is not expected to grow appreciably during the next decade, it is particularly important to provide a special means for increasing the proportion of women and ethnic minority group members on the faculty. The Faculty Affirmative Action Fund serves that purpose exclusively. It is especially useful for the general purpose of hiring individuals who are outstanding scholars and teachers who may be expected to contribute significantly to the University's educational needs, but who do not fit exactly the specifications for an existing faculty opening. The Fund may be used:

(a) to supplement existing departmental or school budgets so that a highly desirable individual can be hired, when appropriate, at a higher rank than was anticipated when the position was defined.

(b) to allow departments and schools to anticipate retirements in taking advantage of available talent. The Fund can finance the appointment of outstanding individuals whom departments and schools want to add to their faculties but for whom no budgeted position will exist until a faculty member retires—perhaps three or four years.

(c) to allow departments and schools to create new positions when special opportunities arise.

...The Fund was announced in December 1971 with a budget of $75,000 of annually recurring ... "budget-base money." Once the funds are allotted to support an appointment they continue within the budget of a given department for the duration of the individual's appointment. The Fund was used to support partially or completely the appointment of sixteen faculty members [in 1971–72] and involved considerably more than the designated $75,000 because of special opportunities.

SALARY EQUITY

Columbia:

Average salaries of officers of instruction and officers of research as of 1971 were analyzed to identify salary differences between men and women and between minority groups and others. Among full-time officers of instruction, 57 cases were found out of a possible 111 in which there were salary differences larger than 5% among members of the identified groups holding the same rank. . . . Twenty-two of these cases were discrepancies in favor of women or minority groups. Of the remaining 35, in which the difference was in favor of men or majority group members, the large majority were accounted for by differences in length of time in rank or by merit considerations. The small remaining number of differences has been corrected or will be corrected by salary adjustments in the next fiscal year (1972–73).

Columbia's nondiscriminatory salary policies are strongly evident also in part-time faculty salaries. Here, the mean salaries of men and women and minority group members approach absolute equality, with all discrepancies favoring women and minorities. . . .

Oberlin:

Recommendation 1: That the appropriate bodies of the College undertake immediately to determine what members of the Faculty have suffered salary and rank inequities, to take positive steps to eliminate those inequities within a two-year period, and to consider ways of compensating for past inequities.

Stanford:

During the 1971–72 academic year, the salary of every female faculty and teaching staff member was reviewed to assure that it was equal to that of males with equal duties and accomplishments. Where discrepancies were found, salaries were increased accordingly.

PART-TIME EMPLOYMENT

Oberlin:

Recommendation 6: It is recommended that there be created a category of part-time full status faculty described as follows: to have responsibility for at least one credit-bearing course approved by the department or by EPPC, to be hired through the regular hiring process, to have no employment elsewhere; to hold a regular academic rank appropriate to training and experience; to receive a salary proportionate to the fraction of responsibility at the rank held and to be eligible for full or prorated support for research and other professional activities; to assume all normal faculty non-teaching responsibilities, including participation in departmental and faculty meetings with the right to vote, prorated advising, service on committees, and other administrative duties; to be eligible for multiple year contracts, and for tenure; to be considered as eligible candidates for full-time positions as they become available.

Recommendation 7: Departments, deans, and councils are strongly urged to be open to the possibilities of creating part-time full status faculty who may wish part-time full status employment for reasons such as health, family, research, or the desire for partial retirement.

Stanford:

In September 1971, the provost reaffirmed existing University policy: "There is no University wide policy which prohibits the appointment of regular faculty members—tenured or non-tenured—at any rank on a part-time basis.". . . This clarification of existing policy was important to affirmative action for women . . . . the memorandum specifically notes". . . regular part-time appointments offer the possibility of appointing noted scholars who are not available full time, faculty members who wish to assume an active role in child rearing. . . ."

University of the State of New York:

Colleges and universities should encourage adequate career opportunities for women faculty members and administrators by such arrangements as. . . permitting faculty members to continue their full faculty status with appropriate adjustments in salary during periods when family commitments temporarily limit their ability to teach a full schedule. . . .

LECTURERS

Oberlin:

Recommendation 5: It is recommended that the category of lecturer be abolished. [The report included the following discussion of the reasons for this recommendation.]

In April 1970, the faculty of Oberlin voted to abolish its 40-year-old anti-nepotism rule. The report of the Committee on Concurrent Employment of Family Members . . . concluded with a brief analysis of the connection between the status of lecturer and the discriminatory effects of the anti-nepotism rule on married women. The Committee asked that the College re-examine its policy with regard to lecturers.

The Committee on the Status of Women investigated the status of lecturers as well as the larger question of the status and definition of part-time teaching at Oberlin. Part-time teaching appointments in the past have provided only marginal or subprofessional status. At present regular faculty appointments are not usually made on a part-time basis. Nor is there, as the Colish report points out, any "provision in the lecturer rank as it is currently conceived for raises providing systematic rewards for experience and professional growth, for leaves of absence or for other fringe benefits. Lecturers do not have a vote in faculty meetings, although the matters decided . . . often have a direct bearing on their working conditions. . . .

The heritage of the anti-nepotism rule leaves us with some unfinished business. Because the rule strengthened associations between part-time teaching and marginal status, its effects are still felt in attitudes toward, and definitions of, part-time teaching positions. . . .

In the next decade, male as well as female academics may begin to feel the need for more flexible schedules and for new definitions of "regular" faculty status. Foreseeing that the opportunity for part-time full status teaching appointments will allow both men and women to create a greater variety of individual life and career patterns than is now possible, the Committee recommends the granting of full professional status to fully qualified women and men who wish, as the needs of departments allow, to teach part-time.

DELAY OF TENURE

Stanford:

In order to make Stanford University a more attractive institu
tion for women faculty, and to assure that untenured female fac
ulty have an appropriate opportunity to develop and prov
themselves as scholars, the following statement was appende
to the Statement of Policy on Appointment and Tenure. . . .

A faculty member who gives birth while serving under an appoin
ment which accrues time toward tenure by length of service may, sub
ject to any necessary reappointment, have the time after which tenu
would be conferred by length or service extended by one year. N
more than two such extensions shall be allowed.

University of the State of New York:

Colleges and universities should encourage adequate career op
portunities for women faculty members and administrators by
such arrangements as . . . authorizing maternity leaves, witł
guarantee of job reservation and the postponement of tenure
decisions by length of leave. . . .

ANTINEPOTISM POLICIES

Columbia:

Employment opportunities are offered to spouses and other relatives on a competitive basis. The University policy states a negative preference in cases where the job is under the immediate supervision of a spouse or close relative. Even in these cases, however, no prohibition is expressed, and a number of instances can be cited where close relatives work in the same University department.

Harvard:

The nepotism policy declares that members of the same immediate family "should not" work for each other in the same unit, with exceptions made at the discretion of the appropriate dean or vice-president.

Stanford:

It is the policy of Stanford University to seek for its faculty the best possible teachers and scholars, who are judged to be so in a national (or international) search preceding each appointment and promotion. There are no bars to the appointment of close relatives to the faculty, in the same or different departments, so long as each meets this standard. . . . No faculty member . . . shall vote, make recommendations, or in any way participate in the decision of any matter which may directly affect the appointment, tenure, promotion, salary, or other status or interest of a close relative.

University of the State of New York:

Colleges and universities should encourage adequate career opportunities for women faculty members and administrators by such arrangements as . . . eliminating nepotism rules.

University of California:

[Note: The issue of modifying the formerly strict antinepotism rules has been much debated at the University of California in recent years. The rules were liberalized somewhat in July 1971, and the policy then adopted is included here in full as it appears in the University personnel manual. We have been informed, however, that additional changes are under consideration.]

POLICY The employment of near relatives in the same department i
permitted when such employment has been authorized in ac
cordance with the following subsections. Such concurren
employment may arise under the following circumstances:

1 Two employees already holding positions in the same depart
ment subsequently become near relatives.

2 Simultaneous appointment of near relatives in the same depart
ment is recommended.

3 Appointment of one who is the near relative of an individual al
ready employed in the same department is recommended.

DEFINITION Near relatives include parents and children, husband, wife
brother, sister, brother-in-law, sister-in-law, mother-in-law
father-in-law, son-in-law, daughter-in-law; and step relative:
in the same relationship.

STANDARDS In searching for qualified candidates for a new or vacant position in a department, those persons responsible for recruitmen
shall not disqualify a candidate by reason of near relationship
to an appointee already in the department or by reason of neai
relationship when simultaneous appointment of near relatives
in the same department is recommended. When the recommended appointment involves such near relationship, this fact
shall be noted in the recommendation, and an analysis of the
possible conflict of interest or other disadvantage in the situation shall be forwarded through normal channels with the recommendation in sufficient time to permit complete review of
the case before the proposed effective date.

RESTRICTION A member of the University staff shall not participate in the
processes of review and decision-making on any matter concerning appointment, promotion, salary, retention, or termination of a near relative.

AUTHORITY Each Chancellor (or, for positions under his jurisdiction, a Vice
President) is authorized to approve an appointment in which a
near-relative relationship in a department is involved or when
simultaneous appointment of near relatives in the same department is recommended if, after review of the cases, he considers

the appointments to be justified and in the best interest of the University. Such review and approval by the Chancellor or Vice President is also required to authorize the continuance of the appointments of two members in the same department when a near-relative relationship is established between them.

This authority may not be redelegated.

MATERNITY LEAVE

Columbia:

Any employee with at least six month's service who is pregnant shall be eligible for unpaid maternity leave. . . . Such leave shall not exceed nine months in duration. . . . No employee shall be discharged by reason of pregnancy or direct medical results thereof while on maternity leave. Each employee, upon return to active status, shall be reemployed in the same position or in a position of equivalent rank and salary.

Harvard:

This latter policy [maternity leave] has been amended to grant a pregnant woman sick pay earned during her period of employment "for the period she is physically unable to work because of childbirth." Previously, maternity leaves of absence were taken without pay.

Oberlin:

Recommendation 16: The Committee recommends the establishment of a uniform maternity leave policy to apply to *all* females employees of the College. We support a policy which would grant women up to one month paid maternity leave and up to two additional months of unpaid child care leave, without penalty or loss of seniority.

Stanford:

The University has revised its operating policy on maternity leave to establish maternity leave as a right, and guarantees the same or comparable position to a person returning from maternity leave. . . . Stanford's health plans have been changed to extend existing maternity benefits to unwed mothers. . . . Stanford's health plans have been modified to include benefits for abortion.

University of the State of New York:

Colleges and universities should encourage adequate career opportunities for women faculty members and administrators by such arrangements as (1) authorizing maternity leaves, with guarantee of job reservation and the postponement of tenure decisions by length of leave. . . .

STUDENTS

Oberlin:

Recommendation 8: It is recommended that all faculty and other College personnel recognize the existence of differential treatment as experienced by students and examine their own attitudes and practices in this regard. Conscientious attempts must be made by all members of the College community to rectify existing attitudinal and functional inequities in the treatment of students. Students should be counseled according to their capabilities. This is particularly important as more students enter fields not in accordance with traditional sexual stereotypes and where few if any female role models exist.

Recommendation 9: It is recommended that the administrative units of the College responsible for the preparation and distribution of information to prospective students and to the outside community revise this literature in order to cease portraying students in traditional sex-based academic roles.

Recommendation 10: It is recommended that additional courses in Women's Studies be developed and offered within departments or programs or both.

Recommendation 11: It is recommended that the offices of the dean of students and associate dean of the College, together with a committee of women students, compile a roster of faculty and staff women, faculty wives, and women in the community who have specialties and careers which might be of interest to students, and that students and advisors be made aware of the existence of such a roster. . . .

University of the State of New York:

There must be no quota limitations on the admission of women in coeducational colleges, universities and professional schools. Admission standards must be the same for men and women, and individuals who meet the qualifications for admission must be accepted on the first come first served basis. . . . Loans, scholarships and fellowships must be available to all students without regard to sex.

References

Adams, B. N., and M. T. Meidam: "Economics, Family Structure, and College Attendance," *American Journal of Sociology,* vol. 74, pp. 230–239, November 1968.

Altman, L. K.: "Swedish Wife Awaits 3d Child, M.D. Degree," *New York Times,* June 7, 1973.

American Bar Association: *Annual Review of Legal Education, Fall 1972,* Chicago, 1973.

American Council on Education: *National Norms for Entering College Freshmen* (title varies slightly), Washington, D.C., annual, 1966 to 1971.

American Council on Education: *The American Freshman: National Norms for 1972,* ACE Research Reports, vol. 7, no. 5, Washington, D.C., 1972.

American Council on Education: *American Universities and Colleges,* 11th ed., Washington, D.C., 1973.

American Political Science Association: *Women in Political Science,* Studies and Reports of the APSA Committee on the Status of Women in the Profession, 1969–1971, Washington, D.C., 1971.

"Annual Report on Medical Education, 1972–73," *Journal of the American Medical Association,* vol. 222, pp., 961–1048, Nov. 20, 1972.

Armor, D. J.: *American School Counselor,* Russell Sage Foundation, New York, 1969.

Association of American Law Schools: *Directory of Law Teachers, 1970,* St. Paul, Minn., 1970.

Astin, A. W.: *College Dropouts: A National Profile,* ACE Research Reports, vol. 7, no. 1, American Council on Education, Washington, D.C., 1972.

Astin, A. W., and R. J. Panos: *The Educational and Vocational Development of College Students,* American Council on Education, Washington, D.C., 1969.

Astin, H. S.: *The Woman Doctorate in America,* Russell Sage Foundation, New York, 1969.

Astin, H. S., and A. E. Bayer: "Sex Discrimination in Academe," *Educational Record,* vol. 53, pp. 101–118, Spring 1972.

Australia: *Official Yearbook, 1968.*

Balderston, S. F., and Roy Radner: *Academic Demand for New Ph.D.'s, 1970–90: Its Sensitivity to Alternate Policies,* paper P-26 of the Ford Foundation Program for Research in University Administration, University of California, Berkeley, 1971. (Mimeographed.)

Bayer, A. E.: *College and University Faculty: A Statistical Description,* American Council on Education, Washington, D.C., 1970.

Bayer, A. E.: *The Black College Freshman: Characteristics and Recent Trends,* American Council on Education, Washington, D.C., 1972.

Bayer, A. E.: *Teaching Faculty in Academe: 1972–73,* ACE Research Reports, vol. 8, no. 2, American Council on Education, Washington, D.C., 1973.

Bayer, A. E., J. T. Royer, and R. M. Webb: *Four Years After College Entry,* ACE Research Reports, vol. 8, no. 1, American Council on Education, Washington, D.C., 1973.

Bazell, R. J.: "Sex Discrimination: Campuses Face Contract Loss Over HEW Demands," *Science,* vol. 170, pp. 834–835, Nov. 20, 1970.

Becker, G.: "A Theory of the Allocation of Time," *Economic Journal,* vol. 75, pp. 493–517, September 1965.

Bell, C. S.: "Report of the Committee on the Status of Women in the Economics Profession," *American Economic Review,* vol. 63, pp. 508–511, May 1973.

Bernard, J.: *Academic Women,* Pennsylvania State University Press, University Park, 1964.

Bird, C.: "Women's Colleges and Women's Lib," *Change,* pp. 60–65, April 1972.

Bird, C., with S. W. Briller: *Born Female: The High Cost of Keeping Women Down,* rev. ed., Pocket Books, New York, 1972.

Bock, E. W.: "Farmer's Daughter Effect: The Case of the Negro Female Professionals," in A. Theodore (ed.), *The Professional Woman,* Schenkman Publishing Company, Inc., Cambridge, Mass., 1971.

Bowers, J. J.: "Women in Medicine: An International Study," *New England Journal of Medicine,* vol. 275, pp. 362–365, Aug. 18, 1966.

British Council and The Association of Commonwealth Universities: *Higher Education in the United Kingdom, 1970–72: A Handbook for Students from Overseas and Their Advisers,* London, 1970.

"Budget Would Require Major Cutbacks by Medical Schools, Survey Shows," *Bulletin of the Association of American Medical Colleges,* May 1973.

California State Scholarship and Loan Commission: *Student Resources Survey,* Sacramento, Calif., 1972.

Carnegie Commission on Higher Education: *A Chance to Learn: An Action Agenda for Equal Opportunity in Higher Education,* McGraw-Hill Book Company, New York, 1970a.

Carnegie Commission on Higher Education: *Higher Education and the Nation's Health: Policies for Medical and Dental Education,* McGraw-Hill Book Company, New York, 1970b.

Carnegie Commission on Higher Education: *Less Time, More Options: Education Beyond the High School,* McGraw-Hill Book Company, New York, 1970c.

Carnegie Commission on Higher Education: *Quality and Equality: Revised Recommendations, New Levels of Federal Responsibility for Higher Education,* McGraw-Hill Book Company, New York, 1970d.

Carnegie Commission on Higher Education: *From Isolation to Mainstream: Problems of the Colleges Founded for Negroes,* McGraw-Hill Book Company, New York, 1971.

Carnegie Commission on Higher Education: *Reform on Campus: Changing Students, Changing Academic Programs,* McGraw-Hill Book Company, New York, 1972a.

Carnegie Commission on Higher Education: *The More Effective Use of Resources: An Imperative for Higher Education,* McGraw-Hill Book Company, New York, 1972b.

Carnegie Commission on Higher Education: *College Graduates and Jobs: Adjusting to a New Labor Market Situation,* McGraw-Hill Book Company, New York, 1973a.

Carnegie Commission on Higher Education: *Continuity and Discontinuity: Higher Education and the Schools,* McGraw-Hill Book Company, New York, 1973b.

Carnegie Commission on Higher Education: *Governance of Higher Education: Six Priority Problems,* McGraw-Hill Book Company, New York, 1973c.

Carnegie Commission on Higher Education: *The Purposes and the Performance of Higher Education in the United States,* McGraw-Hill Book Company, New York, 1973d.

Carnegie Commission on Higher Education: *Carnegie Commission Classification of Institutions of Higher Education,* Berkeley, Calif., forthcoming.

Carroll, M. A.: "Women in Administration in Higher Education," *Contemporary Education*, vol. 43, pp. 214–218, February 1972.

Cartter, A. M.: Unpublished revision of "Scientific Manpower for 1970–1985," *Science*, vol. 172, pp. 132–140, Ap. 9, 1971.

Chalmers, E. L., Jr.: "Achieving Equity for Women in Higher Education Graduate Enrollment and Faculty Status," *Journal of Higher Education*, vol. 43, pp. 517–524, October 1972.

Chancellor's Advisory Committee on the Establishment of a Center for Women's Education: *Report*, University of California, Berkeley, March 1972.

Coble, J. A.: "Who Goes to College," in S. B. Withey et al.: *A Degree and What Else? Correlates and Consequences of a College Education*, McGraw-Hill Book Company, New York, 1971.

Cole, N. S.: *On Measuring the Vocational Interests of Women*, ACT Research Report No. 49, American College Testing Program, Iowa City, Iowa, 1972.

"Columbia Contract Withheld," *Chronicle of Higher Education*, p. 2, Feb. 26, 1973.

"Columbia Passes U.S. Test on Jobs," *New York Times*, Sept. 2, 1972.

Columbia University: *Affirmative Action Program, Condensed Version* December 1972.

Conant, J. B.: *The American High School Today: A First Report to Interested Citizens*, McGraw-Hill Book Company, New York, 1959.

Creager, J. A.: *The American Graduate Student: A Normative Description*, American Council on Education, Washington, D. C., 1971.

Cross, K. P.: *Beyond the Open Door: New Students to Higher Education*, Jossey-Bass, Inc., San Francisco, 1971.

Cross, K. P.: "The Woman Student," in American Council on Education, *Women in Higher Education: Background Papers for Participants in the 55th Annual Meeting of the American Council on Education*, Washington, D.C., 1972.

Davis, K.: "Demographic Aspects of Poverty," in M. S. Gordon (ed.), *Poverty in America*, Chandler Publishing Company, San Francisco, 1965.

Economic Report of the President, U.S. Government Printing Office, Washington, D.C., 1973.

Educational Testing Service: *GRE: Guide to the Use of GRE Scores in Graduate Admissions, 1972–1973*, Princeton, N. J., 1972.

Employment Policies Regarding Pregnancy, Maternity, and Childbirth, Project on the Status and Education of Women, Association of American Colleges, Washington, D.C., February 1973.

Endicott, F. S.: *The Endicott Report: Trends in Employment of College and University Graduates in Business and Industry, 1973,* Northwestern University, Evanston, Ill., 1972.

Epstein, C. F.: *Woman's Place,* University of California Press, Berkeley and Los Angeles, 1971*a.*

Epstein, C. F.: "Women Lawyers and Their Profession: Inconsistency of Social Controls and Their Consequences for Professional Performance," in A. Theodore (ed.), *The Professional Woman,* Schenkman Publishing Company, Inc., Cambridge, Mass. 1971*b.*

Feldman, S. D.: *A Profile of Men and Women in Graduate Education,* unpublished manuscript, Carnegie Commission on Higher Education, Berkeley, California, 1972.

Fields, C. M.: "Congress Gives Women New Weapon in Effort to End Sex Bias," *Chronicle of Higher Education,* p. 2, March 27, 1972 a.

Fields, C. M.: "Government Intervention Laid to Failure of Colleges' Leadership," *Chronicle of Higher Education,* p. 3, Oct. 16, 1972*b.*

Flanagan, J. C., and W. W. Cooley: *Project Talent: One-Year Follow-Up Studies,* School of Education, University of Pittsburgh, 1966.

Fleming, R. W.: *The State of the University* (address to the faculty), University of Michigan, Ann Arbor, Sept. 25, 1972.

Fogarty, M. P., R. Rapoport, and R. N. Rapoport: *Sex, Career and Family,* George Allen & Unwin, Ltd., London, 1971.

Folger, J. K., H. S. Astin, and A. E. Bayer: *Human Resources and Higher Education: Staff Report of the Commission on Human Resources and Advanced Education,* Russell Sage Foundation, New York, 1970.

Freeman, R. B.: "The Implications of the Changing Labor Market for Members of Minority Groups," in M. S. Gordon (ed.), *Higher Education and the Labor Market,* McGraw-Hill Book Company, New York, forthcoming, 1973.

Friedersdorf, N. W.: *A Comparative Study of Counselor Attitudes Toward the Further Educational and Vocational Plans of High School Girls,* Purdue University Ph.D. thesis, 1969 (reproduced by University Microfilms, Inc., Ann Arbor, Michigan).

Froomkin, J.: *Aspirations, Enrollments, and Resources,* report prepared for the U.S. Office of Education, Washington, D.C., 1970.

Fulton, O.: *Rewards and Fairness: Academic Women in the United States,* unpublished manuscript, Carnegie Commission on Higher Education, Berkeley, Calif., 1973.

Galenson, M.: *Women and Work: An International Comparison,* New York State School of Industrial and Labor Relations, Cornell University, Ithaca, N.Y., 1973.

Gilman, R.: "The Fem Lib Case Against Sigmund Freud," *The New York Times Magazine,* Jan. 31, 1971.

Ginzberg, E., and associates: *Life Styles of Educated Women,* Columbia University Press, New York, 1966.

Gordon, R. A., and J. E. Howell: *Higher Education for Business,* Columbia University Press, New York, 1959.

Graham, P. A.: "Women in Academe," *Science,* vol. 169, pp. 1284–1290, Sept. 25, 1970.

Greenblatt, B., and L. Eberhard: *Children on Campus: A Survey of Pre Kindergarten Programs at Institutions of Higher Education in the United States,* State University of New York at Buffalo, January 1973.

Gurin, G., J. Veroff, and S. Feld: *Americans View Their Mental Health,* Basic Books, Inc., Publishers, New York, 1960.

Haggstrom, G. W.: *School and College Entrance and Graduation Rates, 1900–2000,* unpublished paper, Carnegie Commission on Higher Education, Berkeley, Calif., 1971*a*.

Haggstrom, G. W.: *The Growth of Higher Education in the United States,* unpublished paper, Carnegie Commission on Higher Education, Berkeley, Calif., 1971*b*.

Harmon, L. R., and H. Soldz: *Doctorate Production in United States Universities, 1920–1962,* National Academy of Sciences, National Research Council, Washington, D.C., 1963.

Heiss, A. M.: *Challenges to Graduate Schools,* Jossey-Bass, Inc., San Francisco, 1970.

"HEW Probing Alleged Employment Bias Against Women on at Least 18 Campuses," *Chronicle of Higher Education,* Nov. 9, 1970.

Hole, J., and E. Levine: *Rebirth of Feminism,* Quadrangle Books: A New York Times Company, New York, 1972.

Holmstrom, E. I., and R. W. Holmstrom: *The Plight of the Woman Doctoral Student,* Office of Research, American Council on Education, Washington, D.C., 1973.

Horner, M.: "Fail: Bright Women," in A. Theodore (ed.), *The Professional Woman,* Schenkman Publishing Company, Inc., Cambridge, Mass., 1971.

Keniston, E. and K. Keniston: "An American Anarchronism: The Image of Women and Work," *American Scholar,* vol. 33, pp. 355–375, Summer 1964.

Kovach, B.: "Wellesley Says It Won't Go Coed," *New York Times,* Mar. 9, 1973.

Kreps, J.: *Sex in the Marketplace: American Women at Work,* The Johns Hopkins Press, Baltimore, 1971.

Leibowitz, A.: "Education and the Allocation of Women's Time," in T. Juster (ed)., *Education, Income, and Human Behavior,* McGraw-Hill Book Company, New York, forthcoming.

Lerner, G.: "Black Liberation—Woman's Liberation: A Study in Ambivalence and Tension," in W. Furniss and P. Graham (eds.), *Women in Higher Education,* American Council on Education, Washington, D.C., 1973.

Lopate, C.: *Women in Medicine,* The Johns Hopkins Press, Baltimore, 1968.

Maeroff, G. I.: "Malcolm-King: A College Geared to Help Highly Motivated Adults," *New York Times,* June 18, 1973.

Michael, R.: "Education and Fertility," in T. Juster (ed.), *Education, Income, and Human Behavior,* McGraw-Hill Book Company, New York, forthcoming.

Mincer, J.: "Labor Force Participation of Married Women: A Study of Labor Supply," in National Bureau of Economic Research, *Aspects of Labor Economics: A Conference of Universities,* Princeton University Press, Princeton, N.J., 1962.

Mitchell, J.: *Woman's Estate,* Pantheon Books, Inc., New York, 1971.

National Education Association, Research: *Salaries Paid and Salary-Related Practices in Higher Education, 1970–71,* Washington, D.C., 1971.

National Education Association, Research: *Salaries Paid and Salary-Related Practices in Higher Education, 1971–72,* Washington, D.C., 1972.

National Research Council: *Summary Report, 1971 Doctorate Recipients from United States Universities,* OSP-MS-6, Washington, D.C., 1972.

New Zealand: *New Zealand Official Yearbook, 1972.*

Newcomer, M.: *A Century of Higher Education for American Women,* Harper & Brothers, New York, 1959.

"Number of Women's Colleges, 300 in 1960, Down to 146," *Chronicle of Higher Education,* May 7, 1973.

Oltman, R. M.: *Campus 1970: Where do Women Stand?,* American Association of University Women, Washington, D.C., 1970.

Pacific Training and Technical Assistance Corporation: *Care for Our Children: A Comprehensive Plan for Child Care Services,* Report prepared for the City of Berkeley and the Berkeley Unified School District, Berkeley, Calif., 1970.

Pearce, R. H., et al.: *Women in the Graduate Academic Sector of the University of California,* Report of an Ad Hoc Committee of the Coordinating Committee on Graduate Affairs, University of California, Los Angeles, June 1972.

Penn Women's Studies Planners: Summer Project Report, submitted to the University of Pennsylvania, Philadelphia, 1972.

Peterson, R. E.: *American College and University Enrollment Trends in 1971,* Carnegie Commission on Higher Education, Berkeley, Calif., 1972.

Pierson, F. C.: *The Education of American Businessmen,* McGraw-Hill Book Company, New York, 1959.

Pifer, A.: *Women in Higher Education,* paper presented at meeting of Southern Association of Colleges and Schools, Miami, Fla., Nov. 29, 1971.

Powers, L., R. D. Parmelle, and H. Wiesenfelder: "Practice Patterns of Women and Men Physicians," *Journal of Medical Education,* vol. 44, pp. 481–491, June 1969.

Price, D. N.: "Cash Benefits for Short-Term Sickness, 1948–71," *Social Security Bulletin,* vol. 36, pp. 20–29, January 1973.

Purdue University, Office of Manpower Studies: *Changing Trends in the Plans of High School Seniors,* Manpower Report 73–1, West Lafayette, Ind., 1973.

"Race, Sex Bias, Reported in Admissions," *Chronicle of Higher Education,* May 11, 1970.

Radcliffe Committee on Graduate Education for Women: *Graduate Education for Women: The Radcliffe Ph.D.,* Harvard University Press, Cambridge, Mass., 1956.

Rees, M.: "The Graduate Education of Women," in W. Furniss and P. Graham (eds.), *Women in Higher Education,* American Council on Education, Washington, D.C., 1973.

Riesman, D., with N. Glazer and R. Denney: *The Lonely Crowd,* abridged edition with a 1969 preface, Yale University Press, New Haven, Conn., 1969.

Robinson, L. H.: *Women's Studies: Courses and Programs in Higher Education,* ERIC/Higher Education Research Report No. 1, American Association for Higher Education, Washington, D.C., 1973.

Roose, K. D., and C. J. Andersen: *A Rating of Graduate Programs,* American Council on Education, Washington, D.C., 1970.

Rose, H. A., and C. F. Elton: "Sex and Occupational Choice," *Journal of Counseling Psychology,* vol. 18, pp. 456–461, September 1971.

Rossi, A. S.: "Status of Women in Graduate Departments of Sociology," *The American Sociologist,* vol. 5, pp. 1–12, February 1970.

Rothman, S. M.: "Other People's Children: the Day Care Experience in America," *The Public Interest,* no. 30, pp. 11–27, Winter 1973.

Sandler, B.: "The Day WEAL Opened Pandora's Box," *Chronicle of Higher Education,* p. 8, Jan. 22, 1973*a.*

Sandler, B.: "Employment Policies Regarding Pregnancy, Maternity and Childbirth," Project on the Status and Education of Women, Association of American Colleges, Washington, D.C., February 1973*b.*

Sandler, B., and S. E. Steinbach: "HEW Contract Compliance—Major Concerns of Institutions," Project on the Status and Education of Women, Association of American Colleges, Washington, D.C., 1972.

Schorr, A.: *Poor Kids,* Basic Books, Inc., Publishers, New York, 1966.

Schultz, T. W.: *New Economic Approaches to Fertility,* Proceedings of a Conference Sponsored by the National Bureau of Economic Research and the Population Council, *Journal of Political Economy,* vol. 81, pp. S1–S299, March–April 1973.

Sells, L. W.: *Preliminary Report on the Status of Graduate Women, University of California, Berkeley,* prepared for the Graduate Assembly's Committee on the Status of Women, Berkeley, Calif., 1973.

Semas, P. W.: "File an Acceptable Equal-Employment Plan or Lose U.S. Contracts, Columbia Told," *Chronicle of Higher Education,* p. 5, Nov. 15, 1971.

Shanahan, E.: "Nixon's Economists Say Job Bias Cuts Women's Pay 10 to 20%," *New York Times,* July 11, 1973.

Sicherman, B.: "The Invisible Woman: The Case for Women's Studies," in *Women in Higher Education: Background Papers for Participants in the 55th Annual Meeting of the American Council on Education,* Washington, D.C., 1972.

Simon, R. J., S. M. Clark, and K. Galway: "The Woman Ph.D.: A Needed Profile," *Social Problems,* vol. 13, pp. 221–236, 1967.

Solmon, L. C.: *Women in Graduate Education: Clues and Puzzles Regarding Discrimination,* unpublished paper, National Research Council and National Bureau of Economic Research, 1973.

Southern Methodist University: *Chemical Education at Southern Methodist University: Less Time—More Options: A Curriculum Proposal,* n.d.

Special Subcommittee on Education, Committee on Education an Labor, U.S. House of Representatives: *Discrimination Against Wome* Hearings, 91st Cong., 2d Sess., June 17, 26, 29, and 30, 1970, Wasl ington D.C., 1970.

Special Task Force to the Department of Health, Education and We fare: *Work in America,* Washington, D.C., 1973.

Spiegel, I.: "Paternity Leaves Offered in New City U. Contract," *Ne York Times,* Sept. 24, 1972.

Stanford University: *The Study of Graduate Education at Stanfor* Report of the Task Force on Women, Stanford, Calif., June 1972.

Stanford University, Committee on the Education of Women in tl University: *The Stanford Woman in 1972,* Stanford, Calif., 1972.

Task Force on Professional Utilization: *Report,* American Bar Associ tion, Chicago, 1973.

Taubman, P. J., and T. J. Wales: "Education as an Investment ar Screening Device," in T. Juster (ed.), *Education, Income, and Hum* *Behavior,* McGraw-Hill Book Company, New York, forthcoming.

Taubman, P. J., and T. J. Wales: "Higher Education, Mental Abilit and Screening," *Journal of Political Economy,* vol. 81, pp. 28–5 January–February 1973.

Teachers Insurance and Annuity Association of America, College R tirement Equities Fund: *Retirement Benefits for Men and Wome* Memorandum, New York, September 1972.

"Three-Year Degree Not Catching on as Anticipated," *Chronicle Higher Education,* May 14, 1973.

Tidball, M. E.: "Perspective on Academic Women and Affirmative A tion," *Educational Record,* vol. 54, no. 2, pp. 130–135, Spring 1973.

Trebilcock, A.: "An 'A' in Activism for Law School Women," *Juris Do tor,* pp. 12–13, March 1972.

"U. of Michigan, HEW Agree on Plan to End Sex Bias," *Chronicle Higher Education,* p. 4, Jan. 11, 1971.

U.S. Bureau of the Census: *U.S. Census of Population, 1940,* "Educatior Educational Attainment by Economic Characteristics and Marit Status," Washington, D.C., 1945.

U.S. Bureau of the Census: *Historical Statistics of the United States: Col nial Times to 1957,* Washington, D.C., 1960.

U.S. Bureau of the Census: "School Enrollment: October 1968 an 1967," *Current Population Reports,* ser. P-20, no. 190, Washingtor D.C., 1969.

U.S. Bureau of the Census: "School Enrollment: October 1969," *Current Population Reports,* ser. P-20, no. 206, Washington, D.C., 1970.

U.S. Bureau of the Census: "Educational Attainment: March 1971," *Current Population Reports,* ser. P-20, no. 229, Washington, D.C., 1971*a*.

U.S. Bureau of the Census: *Statistical Abstract of the United States: 1971,* Washington, D.C., 1971*b*.

U.S. Bureau of the Census: "Social and Economic Characteristics of Students: October 1971," *Current Population Reports,* ser. P-20, no. 241, Washington, D.C., 1972*a*.

U.S. Bureau of the Census: *1970 Census of Population,* Subject Report PC(2)-4C, "Marital Status," Washington, D.C., 1972*b*.

U.S. Bureau of the Census: *1970 Census of Population,* Subject Report PC(2)-7C, "Occupation by Industry," Washington, D.C., 1972*c*.

U.S. Bureau of the Census: "School Enrollment in the United States: 1972," *Current Population Reports,* ser. P-20, no. 247, Washington, D.C., 1973*a*.

U.S. Bureau of the Census: *1970 Census of Population,* Subject Report PC(2)-5B, "Educational Attainment," Washington, D.C., 1973*b*.

U.S. Bureau of Labor Statistics: "Educational Attainment of Workers," *Special Labor Force Report,* no. 148, Washington, D.C., 1972.

U.S. Manpower Administration, *Americans Volunteer,* Manpower / Automation Research Monograph No. 10, Washington, D.C., 1969.

U.S. Office of Education: *Digest of Educational Statistics, 1971,* Washington, D.C., 1972.

U.S. Office of Education: *Earned Degrees Conferred,* Washington, D.C., annual.

U.S. Office of Education: *Fall Enrollment in Higher Education: 1970, Supplementary Information, Institutional Data,* Washington, DC., 1971.

U.S. Public Health Service: *Monthly Vital Statistics Report,* March 1, 1973.

U.S. Social Security Administration: *Social Security Benefits Throughout the World, 1969,* Washington, D.C., 1970.

U.S. Women's Bureau: *Continuing Education Programs and Services for Women,* Washington, D.C., 1971.

University of California Retirement System: *The Retirement Plan,* Berkeley, Calif., 1972.

University of Michigan News, Mar. 29, 1973.

Van Dyne, L.: "Colleges' White Men Assail 'Preference' for Minc ties," *Chronicle of Higher Education,* Feb. 5, 1973.

Weinberg, E., and J. F. Rooney: "The Academic Performance Women Students in Medical School," *Journal of Medical Educati* vol. 48, pp. 240–247, March 1973.

White, J. J.: "Women in the Law," in A. Theodore (ed.), *The Prof sional Woman,* Schenkman Publishing Co., Inc., Cambridge, Mas 1971.

Withey, S., et al.: *A Degree and What Else? Correlates and Consequen of a College Education,* McGraw-Hill Book Company, New York, 19

"Women in Michigan: Academic Sexism under Siege," *Science,* v 178, pp. 841–843, Nov. 24, 1972.

"Women Ph.D.'s Hurt More Than Men by Job Shortage, Surv Shows," *Chronicle of Higher Education,* p. 4, Jan. 11, 1971.

"Women Physicists are Bucking the Tide at Harvard," *Boston Glo* Nov. 24, 1972.

"Women Sought by Engineering," *The Monday Paper,* University California, Berkeley, May 14, 1973.

"Women Students in U.S. Medical Schools: Past and Present Trend *Journal of Medical Education,* vol. 48, pp. 186–189, February 1973.

Carnegie Commission on Higher Education
Sponsored Research Studies

A DEGREE AND WHAT ELSE?
CORRELATES AND CONSEQUENCES OF A
COLLEGE EDUCATION
Stephen B. Withey, Jo Anne Coble, Gerald
Gurin, John P. Robinson, Burkhard Strumpel,
Elizabeth Keogh Taylor, and Arthur C. Wolfe

THE MULTICAMPUS UNIVERSITY:
A STUDY OF ACADEMIC GOVERNANCE
Eugene C. Lee and Frank M. Bowen

INSTITUTIONS IN TRANSITION:
A PROFILE OF CHANGE IN HIGHER
EDUCATION
(INCORPORATING THE 1970 STATISTICAL
REPORT)
Harold L. Hodgkinson

EFFICIENCY IN LIBERAL EDUCATION:
A STUDY OF COMPARATIVE INSTRUCTIONAL
COSTS FOR DIFFERENT WAYS OF ORGANIZ-
ING TEACHING-LEARNING IN A LIBERAL
ARTS COLLEGE
Howard R. Bowen and Gordon K. Douglass

CREDIT FOR COLLEGE:
PUBLIC POLICY FOR STUDENT LOANS
Robert W. Hartman

MODELS AND MAVERICKS:
A PROFILE OF PRIVATE LIBERAL ARTS
COLLEGES
Morris T. Keeton

BETWEEN TWO WORLDS:
A PROFILE OF NEGRO HIGHER EDUCATION
Frank Bowles and Frank A. DeCosta

BREAKING THE ACCESS BARRIERS:
A PROFILE OF TWO-YEAR COLLEGES
Leland L. Medsker and Dale Tillery

ANY PERSON, ANY STUDY:
AN ESSAY ON HIGHER EDUCATION IN THE
UNITED STATES
Eric Ashby

THE NEW DEPRESSION IN HIGHER
EDUCATION:
A STUDY OF FINANCIAL CONDITIONS AT 41
COLLEGES AND UNIVERSITIES
Earl F. Cheit

FINANCING MEDICAL EDUCATION:
AN ANALYSIS OF ALTERNATIVE POLICIES
AND MECHANISMS
Rashi Fein and Gerald I. Weber

HIGHER EDUCATION IN NINE COUNTRIES:
A COMPARATIVE STUDY OF COLLEGES AND
UNIVERSITIES ABROAD
Barbara B. Burn, Philip G. Altbach, Clark Kerr,
and James A. Perkins

BRIDGES TO UNDERSTANDING:
INTERNATIONAL PROGRAMS OF AMERICAN
COLLEGES AND UNIVERSITIES
Irwin T. Sanders and Jennifer C. Ward

GRADUATE AND PROFESSIONAL EDUCATION,
1980:
A SURVEY OF INSTITUTIONAL PLANS
Lewis B. Mayhew

THE AMERICAN COLLEGE AND AMERICAN
CULTURE:
SOCIALIZATION AS A FUNCTION OF HIGHER
EDUCATION
Oscar Handlin and Mary F. Handlin

RECENT ALUMNI AND HIGHER EDUCATION:
A SURVEY OF COLLEGE GRADUATES
Joe L. Spaeth and Andrew M. Greeley

CHANGE IN EDUCATIONAL POLICY:
SELF-STUDIES IN SELECTED COLLEGES AND
UNIVERSITIES
Dwight R. Ladd

STATE OFFICIALS AND HIGHER EDUCATION:
A SURVEY OF THE OPINIONS AND
EXPECTATIONS OF POLICY MAKERS IN NINE
STATES
Heinz Eulau and Harold Quinley

ACADEMIC DEGREE STRUCTURES:
INNOVATIVE APPROACHES
PRINCIPLES OF REFORM IN DEGREE
STRUCTURES IN THE UNITED STATES
Stephen H. Spurr

COLLEGES OF THE FORGOTTEN AMERICANS:
A PROFILE OF STATE COLLEGES AND
REGIONAL UNIVERSITIES
E. Alden Dunham

FROM BACKWATER TO MAINSTREAM:
A PROFILE OF CATHOLIC HIGHER
EDUCATION
Andrew M. Greeley

THE ECONOMICS OF THE MAJOR PRIVATE
UNIVERSITIES
William G. Bowen
(Out of print, but available from University Microfilms.)

THE FINANCE OF HIGHER EDUCATION
Howard R. Bowen
(Out of print, but available from University Microfilms.)

ALTERNATIVE METHODS OF FEDERAL
FUNDING FOR HIGHER EDUCATION
Ron Wolk
(Out of print, but available from University Microfilms.)

INVENTORY OF CURRENT RESEARCH ON
HIGHER EDUCATION 1968
Dale M. Heckman and Warren Bryan Martin
(Out of print, but available from University Microfilms.)

The following technical reports are available from the Carnegie Commission on Higher Education, 2150 Shattuck
Ave., Berkeley, California 94704.

RESOURCE USE IN HIGHER EDUCATION:
TRENDS IN OUTPUT AND INPUTS, 1930–1967
June O'Neill

TRENDS AND PROJECTIONS OF PHYSICIANS
IN THE UNITED STATES 1967–2002
Mark S. Blumberg

MAY 1970:
THE CAMPUS AFTERMATH OF CAMBODIA
AND KENT STATE
Richard E. Peterson and John A. Bilorusky

MENTAL ABILITY AND HIGHER EDUCATIONAL
ATTAINMENT IN THE 20TH CENTURY
Paul Taubman and Terence Wales

AMERICAN COLLEGE AND UNIVERSITY
ENROLLMENT TRENDS IN 1971
Richard E. Peterson

PAPERS ON EFFICIENCY IN THE
MANAGEMENT OF HIGHER EDUCATION
Alexander M. Mood, Colin Bell, Lawrence
Bogard, Helen Brownlee, and Joseph McCloskey

AN INVENTORY OF ACADEMIC INNOVATION
AND REFORM
Ann Heiss

ESTIMATING THE RETURNS TO EDUCATION:
A DISAGGREGATED APPROACH
Richard S. Eckaus

SOURCES OF FUNDS TO COLLEGES AND
UNIVERSITIES
June O'Neill

NEW DEPRESSION IN HIGHER
EDUCATION—TWO YEARS LATER
Earl F. Cheit

PROFESSORS, UNIONS, AND AMERICAN
HIGHER EDUCATION
Everett Carll Ladd, Jr. and Seymour
Martin Lipsett

The following reprints are available from the Carnegie Commission on Higher Education, 2150 Shattuck Av
Berkeley, California 94704.

ACCELERATED PROGRAMS OF MEDICAL EDUCATION, *by Mark S. Blumberg, reprinted fro*
JOURNAL OF MEDICAL EDUCATION, *vol. 46, no. 8, August 1971.**

NEW CHALLENGES TO THE COLLEGE AND UNIVERSITY, *by Clark Kerr, reprinted from Kerm*
Gordon (ed.), AGENDA FOR THE NATION, *The Brookings Institution, Washington, D.C*
*1968.**

PRESIDENTIAL DISCONTENT, *by Clark Kerr, reprinted from David C. Nichols (ed.),* PERSPEC
TIVES ON CAMPUS TENSIONS: PAPERS PREPARED FOR THE SPECIAL COMMITTEE ON CAMPU
TENSIONS, *American Council on Education, Washington, D.C., September 1970.**

STUDENT PROTEST—AN INSTITUTIONAL AND NATIONAL PROFILE, *by Harold Hodgkinso*
reprinted from THE RECORD, *vol. 71, no. 4, May 1970.**

WHAT'S BUGGING THE STUDENTS?, *by Kenneth Keniston, reprinted from* EDUCATIONA
RECORD, *American Council on Education, Washington, D.C., Spring 1970.**

THE POLITICS OF ACADEMIA, *by Seymour Martin Lipset, reprinted from David C. Nicho*
(ed.), PERSPECTIVES ON CAMPUS TENSIONS: PAPERS PREPARED FOR THE SPECIAL COMMIT
TEE ON CAMPUS TENSIONS, *American Council on Education, Washington, D.C., Septembe*
*1970.**

INTERNATIONAL PROGRAMS OF U.S. COLLEGES AND UNIVERSITIES: PRIORITIES FOR TH
SEVENTIES, *by James A. Perkins, reprinted by permission of the International Council fo*
Educational Development, Occasional Paper no. 1, July 1971.

FACULTY UNIONISM: FROM THEORY TO PRACTICE, *by Joseph W. Garbarino, reprinted fro*
INDUSTRIAL RELATIONS, *vol. 11, no. 1, pp. 1–17, February 1972.*

MORE FOR LESS: HIGHER EDUCATION'S NEW PRIORITY, *by Virginia B. Smith, reprinted fro*
UNIVERSAL HIGHER EDUCATION: COSTS AND BENEFITS, *American Council on Education*
Washington, D.C., 1971.

ACADEMIA AND POLITICS IN AMERICA, *by Seymour M. Lipset, reprinted from Thomas*
Nossiter (ed.), IMAGINATION AND PRECISION IN THE SOCIAL SCIENCES, *pp. 211–289, Fabe*
and Faber, London, 1972.

POLITICS OF ACADEMIC NATURAL SCIENTISTS AND ENGINEERS, *by Everett C. Ladd, Jr., an*
Seymour M. Lipset, reprinted from SCIENCE, *vol. 176, no. 4039, pp. 1091–1100, June 9*
1972.

The Commission's stock of this reprint has been exhausted.

THE INTELLECTUAL AS CRITIC AND REBEL, WITH SPECIAL REFERENCE TO THE UNITED STATES AND THE SOVIET UNION, by Seymour M. Lipset and Richard B. Dobson, reprinted from DAEDALUS, vol. 101, no. 3, pp. 137–198, Summer 1972.

THE POLITICS OF AMERICAN SOCIOLOGISTS, by Seymour M. Lipset and Everett C. Ladd, Jr., reprinted from THE AMERICAN JOURNAL OF SOCIOLOGY, vol. 78, no. 1, July 1972.

SCIENTIFIC MANPOWER FOR 1970–1985, by Allan M. Cartter, reprinted from SCIENCE, vol. 172, no. 3979, pp. 132–140, April 9, 1971.

A NEW METHOD OF MEASURING STATES' HIGHER EDUCATION BURDEN, by Neil Timm, reprinted from THE JOURNAL OF HIGHER EDUCATION, vol. 42, no. 1, pp. 27–33, January 1971.*

REGENT WATCHING, by Earl F. Cheit, reprinted from AGB REPORTS, vol. 13, no. 6, pp. 4–13, March 1971.*

COLLEGE GENERATIONS—FROM THE 1930S TO THE 1960S, by Seymour M. Lipset and Everett C. Ladd, Jr., reprinted from THE PUBLIC INTEREST, no. 25, Summer 1971.

AMERICAN SOCIAL SCIENTISTS AND THE GROWTH OF CAMPUS POLITICAL ACTIVISM IN THE 1960S, by Everett C. Ladd, Jr., and Seymour M. Lipset, reprinted from SOCIAL SCIENCES INFORMATION, vol. 10, no. 2, April 1971.

THE POLITICS OF AMERICAN POLITICAL SCIENTISTS, by Everett C. Ladd, Jr., and Seymour M. Lipset, reprinted from PS, vol. 4, no. 2, Spring 1971.*

THE DIVIDED PROFESSORIATE, by Seymour M. Lipset and Everett C. Ladd, Jr., reprinted from CHANGE, vol. 3, no. 3, pp. 54–60, May 1971.*

JEWISH ACADEMICS IN THE UNITED STATES: THEIR ACHIEVEMENTS, CULTURE AND POLITICS, by Seymour M. Lipset and Everett C. Ladd, Jr., reprinted from AMERICAN JEWISH YEAR BOOK, 1971.

THE UNHOLY ALLIANCE AGAINST THE CAMPUS, by Kenneth Keniston and Michael Lerner, reprinted from NEW YORK TIMES MAGAZINE, November 8, 1970.

PRECARIOUS PROFESSORS: NEW PATTERNS OF REPRESENTATION, by Joseph W. Garbarino, reprinted from INDUSTRIAL RELATIONS, vol. 10, no. 1, February 1971.*

. . . AND WHAT PROFESSORS THINK: ABOUT STUDENT PROTEST AND MANNERS, MORALS, POLITICS, AND CHAOS ON THE CAMPUS, by Seymour Martin Lipset and Everett C. Ladd, Jr., reprinted from PSYCHOLOGY TODAY, November 1970.*

DEMAND AND SUPPLY IN U.S. HIGHER EDUCATION: A PROGRESS REPORT, by Roy Radner and Leonard S. Miller, reprinted from AMERICAN ECONOMIC REVIEW, May 1970.*

*The Commission's stock of this reprint has been exhausted.

RESOURCES FOR HIGHER EDUCATION: AN ECONOMIST'S VIEW, by Theodore W. Schultz, reprinted from JOURNAL OF POLITICAL ECONOMY, vol. 76, no. 3, University of Chicago, May/June 1968.*

INDUSTRIAL RELATIONS AND UNIVERSITY RELATIONS, by Clark Kerr, reprinted from PROCEEDINGS OF THE 21ST ANNUAL WINTER MEETING OF THE INDUSTRIAL RELATIONS RESEARCH ASSOCIATION, pp. 15–25.*

THE DISTRIBUTION OF ACADEMIC TENURE IN AMERICAN HIGHER EDUCATION, by Martin Trow, reprinted from THE TENURE DEBATE, Bardwell Smith (ed.), Jossey-Bass, San Francisco, 1972.

THE NATURE AND ORIGINS OF THE CARNEGIE COMMISSION ON HIGHER EDUCATION, by Alan Pifer, based on a speech delivered to the Pennsylvania Association of Colleges and Universities, Oct. 16, 1972, reprinted by permission of the Carnegie Foundation for the Advancement of Teaching.

COMING OF MIDDLE AGE IN HIGHER EDUCATION, by Earl F. Cheit, address delivered to American Association of State Colleges and Universities and National Association of State Universities and Land-Grant Colleges, Nov. 13, 1972.